CHAITANA'S

LIFE AND TEACHINGS

CHAITANYA'S

LIFE AND TEACHINGS

From his contemporary Bengali biography

the Chaitanya-charit-amrita:

Translated into English

BY

JADUNATH SARKAR, M.A., I.E.S.

SECOND EDITION,

Revised and enlarged, with topographical notes.

GYAN

Published by

GYAN

Gyan Publishing House
5, Ansari Road
Daryaganj, New Delhi-110002
Phone: 011-47034999, 9811692060
E-mail: books@gyanbooks.com

Distribution Network
gyanbooks.com
India, USA, Canada, UK, Australia, France

ISBN : 978-81-212-9564-2 (PB)
First Published, 1922

2nd Impression 2023

Printed at: Gyan Press, Delhi.

CHAITANYA'S LIFE AND TEACHINGS
Author: JADUNATH SARKAR

CHAITANYA'S

LIFE AND TEACHINGS

From his contemporary Bengali biography
the *Chaitanya-charit-amrita*:

Translated into English

BY

JADUNATH SARKAR, M.A., I.E.S.

SECOND EDITION,
Revised and enlarged, with topographical notes.
1922

Published by S. C. Sarkar
M. C. Sarkar & Sons, 90/2A, Harrison Road, Calcutta.

Printer: S. C. Mazumdar
SRI GOURANGA PRESS
71/1, Mirzapur Street, Calcutta.

1481/21.

TO

Professor RAJA GOPALACHARIAR, M.A., B.L.,

WHO HAS DONE SO MUCH TO MAKE THE VAISHNAV SAINTS OF THE SOUTH KNOWN TO US,

I DEDICATE THIS ATTEMPT TO PLACE THE ORIGINAL LIFE OF CHAITANYA—THE GREATEST VAISHNAV TEACHER OF THE NORTH—WITHIN THE REACH OF ALL READERS OF ENGLISH WHO KNOW NOT THE BENGALI TONGUE.

PATNA COLLEGE,
10th April, 1913.

J. SARKAR

THE AUTHOR AND HIS BOOK

Krishna-das Kaviraj, the author of the *Chaitanya-charit-ámrita,* was born in the Vaidya caste, at Jhámatpur, a village of the Kátwá sub-division of the Burdwan district in Bengal, (1496 A.D.) Having lost his parents in early life, he was brought up by his late father's sister. He read Persian at the village school, and then began to study Sanskrit in order to qualify himself for practising Hindu medicine, the profession of his caste. Every part of his great poem bears evidence to his profound mastery of Sanskrit literature, particularly of the *Bhágabat Purán.* The young orphan, while still unmarried, was converted to Vaishnavism by Nityananda, and begged his way on foot to Brindaban, where he spent the remainder of his long life in religious study, meditation and worship. He was initiated as a Vaishnav monk by Raghunath-das, who along with Swarup Damodar had been body-servants to Chaitanya during that saint's stay at Jagannath. From his *guru,* Krishna-das learned the particulars of Chaitanya's life and teaching which he has embodied in the present biography.

His first efforts at authorship were in Sanskrit and dealt with the mysteries of *bhakti* and the service of Krishna. The great work of his life was the composition of his old age, and was undertaken at the request of the faithful. Every evening the Bengali Vaishnavs of Brindaban used to gather together and hear the acts of their Master read out from his poetical biography, the *Chaitanya Bhágbat* composed by Brindaban-das. But this book dealt with the saint's last years in too meagre and concise a fashion to satisfy the curiosity of his followers. They, therefore, led by Haridas Pandit, the chief servitor of the Govindaji temple, pressed Krishna-das to write a new and fuller life of the Master. The poet was old and infirm, but he regarded the request as a solemn charge which he was not free to decline. That very evening he prayed to the image of Madanmohan, and the god's approbation was shown by a sign,—a garland of flowers slipping down from his neck at the end of the prayer! On the bank of the Rádhá-kunda tank, the aged Krishna-das completed his *Chaitanya-charit-ámrita* in 1582 after nine years of unremitting toil. It is divided into three Books, the *Adi Lilá*, the *Madhya Lilá*, and the *Antya Lilá*, dealing respectively with the three stages of Chaitanya's life, *viz.*, (i) the 24 years from his birth to the time of his entering the monastic order, (ii) the six years of his pilgrimage, and (iii) the last eighteen years of his life, which were spent in residence at Puri. In spite of its epic length, prolixity, and repetitions, the *Chaitanya-charit-ámrita* is a masterpiece of early Bengali literature, and has the further merit of making the subtle doctrines of the Vaishnav faith intelligible to ordinary people. Indeed, the older school of Vaishnav Fathers, as represented by Jiv Goswami, had at first objected to its publication, lest the merits and completeness of this vernacular work should cause the learned Sanskrit treatises on *bhakti* exegetics to be neglected by the public! The author's manuscript is still preserved in the Radha-Damodar temple of Brindaban, and worshipped as a holy relic.

The Second Book (*Madhya Lilá*), which is the longest

and most detailed of the three and the foremost authority on Chaitanya's teachings, life and character, and contains the clearest and fullest exposition of Vaishnav philosophy,—has been here translated into English for the first time. In the second edition, many long extracts from the Third Book (*Antya Lílá*) have been added, to complete the story of Chaitanya's doings and sayings at Puri till his death. Readers to whom the Bengali tongue is unknown, will here find an unvarnished account of Chaitanya as his contemporaries knew him, without any modern gloss, interpolation or criticism. My version is literal; only, in certain places needless details have been curtailed, all repetitions have been avoided, and the texts so freely quoted by our author from the Sanskrit scriptures have been indicated by reference to chapter and verse, instead of being done into English. The word *Prabhu,* applied by the author to Chaitanya, has been rendered by me as *Master*.

There are three other contemporary lives of Chaitanya in old Bengali. The earliest of them is the *Chaitanya Bhágabat,* composed in 1535 A.D., by the Brahman Brindaban-das, a sister's son of Shribas Pandit of Navadwip. This author (*b.* 1507, *d.* 1589) was a votary of God as incarnate in Nityánanda; to him Chaitanya was almost a secondary object of adoration. His poem is encumbered with miracles and digressions, and far inferior to Krishna-das's work in wealth of philosophic exposition and description of men and events.

Trilochan-das (born 1523) wrote the *Chaitanya-Mangal* at the age of fourteen! It is full of marvellous incidents and should be classed with romances rather than with sober histories. Its text is still sung by wandering minstrels and is appreciated by the lower ranks of the Vaishnav community.

Jayananda Mishra (*b.* about 1511) wrote his *Chaitanya-Mangal* about 1568, and his poem gives us much new information about the saint and his family. He is our only authority for the narrative of Chaitanya's death, which I have translated at the end of this work.

* * * *

In the second edition parts of two chapters of the first edition, *viz.*, xviii. pp. 254-269 and xxii. pp. 290-303, have been omitted, as they can be understood only by very learned Sanskrit scholars, the remaining part of ch. xxii has been incorporated with ch. xxi, while ch. xxiii has been renumbered as xxii. In the present edition, all the chapters from xxiii to the end are taken from the *Antya Lilá.*

In preparing the second edition, the translation has been carefully compared with the text and minutely revised. Many mistakes have been detected and corrected ; some of them came no doubt from the manuscript from which the first edition was printed, but most of the others were due to the inefficiency and carelessness of the press. In going through the original a second time I have in a few places modified my interpretation of the text made twelve years ago.

A long and important appendix has now been added, giving the exact situation and some description of the various holy places visited by Chaitanya, (with references to the best and most modern sources of information, such as Gazetteers and maps).

A SHORT LIFE OF CHAITANYA

Navadwip, a town in the Nadia district of Bengal, situated on the river Ganges, 75 miles north of Calcutta, was a great trading centre and seat of Hindu learning in the 15th century. Sanskrit logic (*nyáy*) for which Bengal is most famous among all the provinces of India, was very highly developed and studied here, and the fame of its scholars was unsurpassed in the land. But, if we may believe the biographers of Chaitanya, the atmosphere of the town was sceptical and unspiritual. There was a lack of true religious fervour and sincere devotion. Proud of their intellectuality, proud of the vast wealth they acquired by gifts from rich Hindus, the local *pandits* despised *bhakti* or devotion as weak and vulgar, and engaged in idle ceremonies or idler amusements. Vedantism formed the topic of conversation of the cultured few; wine and goat's meat were taken to kindly by the majority of the people, and such *Shakta* rites as were accompanied by the offering of this drink and food to the goddess and their subsequent consumption by her votaries, were performed with zeal and enthusiasm.

Jagannáth Mishra, surnamed Purandar, a Brahman of the Vaidik sub-caste, had emigrated from his ancestral home in Sylhet and settled here in order to live on the bank of the holy Ganges. His wife was Shachi, a daughter of the scholar Nilámbar Chakravarti. One evening in February or March, 1485 A.D., when there was a lunar eclipse at the same time as full moon, a son was born to this couple. It was their tenth child; the first eight, all daughters, had died in infancy, and the ninth, a lad named Vishwarup, had abandoned the world at the age of sixteen when pressed to marry, and had entered a monastery in the Madras presidency.

The new-born child was named *Vishwambhar*. But the women, seeing that his mother had lost so many children before him, gave him the disparaging name of *Nimái* or 'short-lived,' in order to propitiate Nemesis. The neighbours called him *Gaur or Gauránga* ('fair complexioned') on account of his marvellous beauty. That the child was born amidst the chanting of Hari's name all over Navadwip on the occasion of the eclipse, was taken to be an omen that he would prove a teacher of *bhakti*. Passing over the lucky signs of his horoscope, and the miracles and Krishna-like antics with which pious imagination has invested his boyhood, we may note that he showed great keenness and precocity of intellect in mastering all branches of Sanskrit learning, especially grammar and logic.

On the death of his father, Vishwambhar, while still a student, married Lakshmi, the daughter of Vallabh Acharya, with whom he had fallen in love at first sight. He now became a householder, and began to take pupils, like many other Brahmans of Navadwip. As a *pandit* he surpassed the other scholars of the place and even defeated a renowned champion of another province, who was travelling all over India holding disputations.

On his return from a scholastic tour in East Bengal, in which he received many gifts from pious householders, he found that his wife had died of snake-bite during his absence. After a while the widower married Vishnu-priya. At this time his head was turned by the pride of scholarship, and his victories in argument made him slight other men. During a pilgrimage to Gayá, he met Ishwar Puri, a Vaishnav monk of the order of Mádhavácharya and a disciple of that Mádhavendra Puri who had first introduced the cult of *bhakti* for Krishna among the *sannyásis*. Vishwambhar took this Ishwar Puri as his *guru* or spiritual guide. A complete change now came over his spirit. His intellectual pride was gone; he became a *bhakta*; whatever subject he lectured on, the theme of his discourse was love of Krishna. Indeed, he developed religious ecstasy and for some time behaved like a mad man: he laughed, wept, incessantly shouted Krishna's name, climbed up trees, or raved in abstraction imagining himself to be Krishna. He now made the acquaintance of the elderly scholar and *bhakta* Adwaita Acharya, and was joined by a *sannyási* named Nityánanda, who became to him even more than what Paul was to Christ.

Many people of Navadwip now believed Chaitanya to be an incarnation of Krishna and did him worship, while Nityananda came to be regarded as Balaram, (the elder brother of Krishna). Religious processions were frequently got up, in which the devout, headed by the two, went dancing and singing through the streets or assembled in the courtyards of houses. This was the origin of the *nám-kirtan* ('chanting God's name') which has ever been the most distinctive feature of this creed. Chaitanya's greatest achievement at this time was the reclamation of two drunken ruffians, Jagái and Mádhái, who were a terror to the city. The apostles of *bhakti* had also to face mockery and persecution from scoffers and unbelievers (*páshandi*),—which were overcome by supernatural signs. We pass over the scenes of ecstasy, tireless exertion in *kirtan*, madness and miracles, which form the extant history of this period of Chaitanya's life. But the conversions among the learned were few, and Chaitanya at last in despair resolved to turn hermit for their salvation, arguing thus, "As I must deliver all these proud scholars, I have to take to an ascetic life. They will surely bow to me when they see me as a hermit, and thus their hearts will be purified and filled with *bhakti*. There is no other means." So, he induced Keshav Bhárati to initiate him as a *sannyási* (1509) under the name of Krishna-Chaitanya, usually shortened into CHAITANYA, which we have anticipated in this sketch. He was then 24 years of age. His mother, who had often before urged him not to desert her as his elder brother had done, was heart-broken at the loss of her sole surviving child, but Chaitanya consoled her in every possible way, and bowed to her wishes in many points in his after years as obediently as he had done before renouncing the life of a householder.

The next six years were passed by him in pilgrimages to Orissa, the Southern Land, and Brindaban, and in the preaching of *bhakti* in many parts of India, as described in detail in the present volume.

Thereafter, at the age of 30, he settled at Puri, and spent his remaining days in the constant adoration of Jagannáth. Disciples and admirers from many places, chiefly Bengal and Brindaban, visited him here ; and he edified them by his discourses, acts of humility, and penances. Towards the close of his life he hàd repeated fits of religious ecstasy in which he acted in utter disregard of his life,—once leaping into the blue ocean, at another time battering his face against the walls of his room.

At last in June-July, 1533, his physical frame broke down under such prolonged mental convulsion and self-inflicted torments, and he passed away under circumstances over which the piety of his biographers has drawn the veil of mystery.

In his lifetime his disciples had organized a mission. In Bengal the new creed was preached and spread far and wide by Nityananda, who afterwards came to be regarded as a god, co-ordinate with Chaitanya. Modern Brindaban, with its temples, Sanskrit seminaries and haunts for recluses, is the creation of the Bengali Vaishnavs, and it has eclipsed the older city of Mathura. Here the brothers Rup and Sanátan,—descended from a Prince of Karnat who had settled in Bengal and whose descendants had become completely Bengalized, joined Chaitanya's Church. These two and their nephew Jiv Goswámi were great Sanskrit scholars and their devotional works, commentaries, &c. encouraged a revival of Sanskrit studies in general in that Muslim age. These three, with Gopal Bhatta, nephew of the celebrated Vedantist Prakáshánanda who was latterly converted to *bhakti* by Chaitanya and changed his name into Prabodhánanda, and Raghunáth Bhatta, son of an up-country Brahman *bhakta,* and the last Raghunath-das, a Káyastha saint of the Saptagrám zamindar family of the Hugli district and the *guru* of our author, formed the six Fathers of Chaitanya's Church. Except Rup and Sanátan, most of the other disciples of Chaitanya adopted the Bengali tongue as their medium, and greatly enriched it with their songs, biographies, poems, travels, and translations of the *bhakti* literature from Sanskrit. The Vaishnav Goswámis, both at Brindaban and Navadwip, have kept up the study of Sanskrit to our own day. A classified list of Chaitanya's disciples is given in Book I. canto x and those of Nityananda and Adwaita's disciples in cantos xi and xii respectively.

GLOSSARY

Abadhut—an ascetic who has renounced the world.

Acharya—a family name or title of Brahmans, *lit.*, teacher.

Adwaita Acharya—an elderly scholar of Shantipur and associate in Chaitanya's devotions before he became a *sannyási*.

Arati—divine service performed to a god in the early morning or after dusk, with lamps, incense, and instrumental music, especially bells.

Balarám—the elder brother of Krishna; the images of the two with that of their sister Subhadrá between them, are worshipped in the temple of Jagannáth.

Banió—grocer, (also acts as banker).

Bhágabat—an adorer of Bhagabán or Vishnu as God; the *Bhágabat*, the name of a *Puran*, regarded by the Vaishnavs as their Scripture.

Bhakta—a devotee, who seeks salvation through faith.

Bhakti—faith, devotion.

Bhárati—the title of an order of monks.

Bhattácharya—a title of Brahmans.

Bhog—see *prasád*.

Dhoti—a sheet of cloth worn round the lower limbs by Hindu males.

Gandharva—a class of celestial musicians.

Garuda—a bird ridden by Vishnu, sacred to the Vaishnavs.

Gaur—(1) a city in the Malda district, the capital of Bengal during the Pathan period; also applied to the whole country of Bengal, (*Gaur*). (2) or *Gauránga*, a title of Chaitanya.

Gauriyá—a native of Bengal.

Ghághar—a musical instrument.

Ghát—bathing stairs in a river, usually sacred.

Ghee—melted butter.

Gopis—milk-maids of Brindaban with whom Krishna disported.

Goswámi—a title of respect, usually given to spiritual leaders among the Vaishnavs.

Govardhan—a sacred hill near Brindában.

Guru—spiritual preceptor, initiator into learning or a faith.

Haridás—a Muhammadan who had turned Vaishnav under Chaitanya's influence. There was another Haridás, a born Hindu, among Chaitanya's followers.

Jagannáth—or 'Lord of the Universe,' name of the idol of Krishna worshipped in the temple at Puri; also applied to the town of Puri.

Jhárikhand—'the jungle country,' Chota Nagpur and the Santhal parganas.

Kali yug—the present or iron age of the world.

Katak—the capital of Orissa and the seat of King Pratap Rudra of the Gajapati dynasty.

Khol—an instrument of music, being a long earthenware drum covered at both ends with leather; distinctive of the Bengali Vaishnavs.

Kirtan—or *sankirtan*, chanting God's name to the accompaniment of dance and song.

Kulin—(1) a man of blue blood (*kul*), descended from a mythical ancestor of high character or social position in a very far-off age.
(2) the name of a village in Bengal.

Kunda—a pool of water, sacred to some god or saint.

Lilá—the antic or sport of a god, particularly of Krishna.

Mádhav Puri—also Mádhavendra, a monk, the spiritual guide of that Ishwar Puri who was the *guru* of Chaitanya.

Mahá-pátra—minister of the Rajah of Orissa.

Mahá-prasád—food offered to Jagannáth and thereafter considered as holy.

Mangal-árati—early morning worship, see *árati*.

Mantra—spell, sacred verse (usually in Sanskrit).

Mahánta—the abbot of a Hindu monastery.

Niláchal—'the Blue Mountain,' name of the mound on which the temple of Jagannath at Puri is situated.

Nimái—a nick-name of Chaitanya.

Nupur—bells tied to the feet in dancing.

Odhra—Orissa.

Pándás—attendants at a temple (such as Jagannáth); they act as guides to pilgrims for a consideration.

Pandit—scholar, one versed in Sanskrit.

Parichhá—the highest servitor of the temple of Jagannath.

Prasád—food dedicated to a god at his worship, and thereafter eaten by the faithful as something holy.

Prayág—the town of Allahabad, at the junction of the Ganges and the Jamuna.

Prem—love, the highest form of *bhakti* or devotion.

Puri—(1) a town on the sea-coast in Orissa, containing the temple of Jagannáth. (2) the title of an order of monks.

Purushottam—a title of Vishnu; usually applied to the temple of Jagannath at Puri.

Rárh—the upland of Burdwan and Birbhum districts, west of the Ganges.

Sankirtan—see *kirtan*.

Sannyási—ascetic, monk, religious mendicant.

Sárvabhauma—*i.e.*, "universal doctor," a man of encyclopædic knowledge. In the book this title is applied to a great scholar and Vedántic philosopher of Navadwip, who had settled at Puri and was held in high honour by the local king. His father was the scholar Visharad, a fellow-student of Chaitanya's maternal grandfather. His sister's husband was Gopináth Acharya, who, too, lived at Puri. Also called 'the Bhattácharya', and *Bhatta*; not to be confounded with the Bhattácharya (*i.e.*, Balabhadra) of ch. xv-xxiii.

Shálgrám—a round dark pebble, worshipped as an emblem of Vishnu, (found in the Gandak river).

Shántipur—a town on the Ganges, some miles below Navadwip.

Shástra—Scripture.

Shikdár—the revenue collector of a district, local governor.

Shloka—a complete verse, couplet or quatrain.

Shripád—a title of respect, here applied to Nityánanda.

Shri-Vaishnav—one of the four main sects of the Vaishnavs; they adore Náráyan and Lakshmi (=*Shri*), instead of Krishna and Rádhá.

Shudra—the lowest caste among the Hindus.

Subhadrá—the sister of Krishna.

Thug—a class of professional robbers who used to strangle or poison their victims, after mixing with them on the way, disguised as travellers.

2

Tirtha—sacred place, usually containing a bathing place.

Tulsi—(1) the Indian Basil plant, sacred to Vishnu, and venerated by the Vaishnavs as almost divine. "She is the Indian Daphne" *(Birdwood)*. (2) the name of a minister of the king of Orissa.

Vaikuntha—the heaven of Vishnu.

Vaishnav—worshipper of Vishnu, the preserver, one incarnation of whom is Krishna. The *Shaivas* are the worshippers of Shiva the destroyer, while the *Shaktas* are the worshippers of Shakti or energy, the wife of Shiva.

Varáha—the "Boar," the 3rd incarnation of Vishnu.

Vidyá-nagar—Rajmahendri, in the Madras presidency.

Vrihaspati—the teacher of the gods; hence, a man versed in all the branches of learning.

Vishwarup—Chaitanya's elder brother, who turned a *sannyási* under the title of Shankaráyana and died in the monastery of Pandharpur in Southern India.

Yug—era or cycle of time.

KING PRATAP RUDRA BOWING TO CHAITANYA

(From an old painting in the possession of the Zamindar of Kunjaghata).

CHAITANYA-CHARIT-AMRITA

CHAPTER I

At the House of Adwaita

Glory to Shri Chaitanya! Glory to Nityananda, to Adwaita, and to all followers of Gaur! In the month of Mágh when the Master completed His twenty-fourth year, in the bright fortnight, He turned hermit. Then led by devotion He set off for Brindaban, and wandered for three days in the *Rárh* country, hallowing it with His footsteps and chanting the following verse in rapture:

*"I too shall cross the terrible and dark ocean of the world by means of devotion to the Supreme Being, as the sages did of yore,—by service at the lotus-like feet of Mukunda."**

The Master said, "True are the words of this Brahman, who chose the service of Mukunda as his life's task. The highest robe [in which a man can clothe himself] is devotion to the Supreme Soul,—the service of Mukunda which brings salvation. That robe he put on. Now shall I go to Brindaban and serve Krishna in solitude."

So saying the Master moved day and night, the picture of religious ecstasy, heedless which way He walked. Nityananda, Acharya Ratna, and Mukunda, all three followed Him. All who saw Him, cried "Hari!

* From the Brahman mendicant's speech reported in the *Shrimad Bhagabat,* XI. xxiii. verse 53.

Hari!" in devotion, and forgot sorrow and loss. The cow-boys shouted Hari's name, at the sight of the Master, who stroked their heads saying, "Go on with your chant," and thanked them saying, "Blessed are ye! ye have gratified me by pouring Hari's name into my ears!" Nityananda took the boys apart and thus tutored them, "When the Master asks you about the road to Brindaban, show Him the path leading to the Ganges." This they did and He took that path. Nityananda spoke to Acharya Ratna, "Hasten to Adwaita and tell him that I shall lead the Master to his house. He should keep a boat ready at the riverside. Thence go to Navadwip and fetch Shachi and all the disciples."

Sending him off, Nityananda came before the Master and showed himself. "Whither are you going, Shripád?" the Master asked. "With thee to Brindaban" was the reply. "How far is Brindaban?" "Behold, yonder is the Jamuna!" So saying Nityananda led the Master to the Ganges. This river He mistook for the Jamuna. He thanked His stars that He had beheld the Jamuna, sang its praise, and after bowing bathed in it. He had no second clothing except His loin-cloth with Him. Just then Adwaita arrived in a boat, with a fresh loin-cloth and upper garment, and appeared bowing before the Master, who was puzzled to see him and asked, "You are the Acharya Goswami. Why have you come here? How did you know that I was at Brindaban?" The Acharya replied "It is Brindaban wherever you are. It is my good luck that you have come to the Ganges bank." The Master said, "So, Nityananda has played me a trick: he has led me to the Ganges and called it the Jamuna!" The Acharya replied, "False are not the words of Shripad.

You have now indeed bathed in the Jamuna, for the Ganges and the Jamuna flow in one channel, the eastern waters being called Gangá and the western (in which you have bathed) Jamuna. Change your wet cloth for a dry one. Four days have you fasted in fervour of love. Come to my house to-day, I invite thee. I have cooked a handful of rice, with dry coarse curry, broth and green herbs." Saying this he took the Master on board to his house, and joyfully washed His feet. His wife had already done the cooking. The Acharya himself dedicated the food to Vishnu, and served it in three equal portions. [Description of the dinner omitted.]

The Master said, "Long have you made me dance, now leave it off. Dine with Mukunda and Haridas." Then the Acharya broke his fast with those two, to his heart's content. The people of Shantipur, hearing of the Master's arrival, flocked to gaze on His feet. In joy they cried "Hari! Hari!" and wondered at His beauty. His fair complexion, which eclipsed the Sun in splendour, was set off by his red robe. Endless streams of people came and went throughout the day. At dusk the Acharya began a *sankirtan;* he danced, while the Master gazed on. Goswami Nityananda danced hand in hand with the Acharya, and Haridas behind them. This song accompanied their dance:

"How shall I speak of my bliss to-day?
The Beloved (Krishna) *has entered my temple for ever!"*

With perspiration, thrill, tears of joy, shout, and roar, they turned and turned, touching the Master's feet now and then. The Acharya embraced Him and said "Long did you wander after escaping from me. Now that I have got you in my house, I shall hold you fast!" So the

Acharya continued dancing and singing for three hours after nightfall. The Master was in an attitude of longing as He had not yet gained union with Krishna, and this separation made His love burn the more fiercely. Impatiently He fell down on the ground, at which the Acharya stopped his dance. Mukunda, who knew the Master's heart well, began to sing verses apt for His passion. The Acharya raised Him to make Him dance. At the verses, the Master could no longer be held back. He was all tears, tremour, thrill, sweat, and broken accents,—now rising up, now falling down, now weeping.

The song: [Rádhá speaks]

Woe is me, dear sister, for my present state!
The love of Krishna has caught my body and soul like a poison.
My heart burns day and night; I know no peace.
O that I could fly where Kanu (Krishna) *is to be found!*

Sweetly did Mukunda sing the above ditty, which made the Master's heart burst, as the emotions of penitence, melancholy, rapture, frolicsomeness, pride, and humility struggled with it. He was stricken down by the force of His passion, and lay down breathless on the ground. The faithful grew alarmed, when lo! He sprang up with a shout, overcome with ecstasy and saying "Chant, chant, [the name of Hari]." None could understand the strong tides of His emotion.

Nityananda moved on holding Him, while the Acharya and Haridas danced behind them. Three hours did He pass thus, now joy now sadness surging in His heart. The dinner had come after five days of fasting; so the wild dance greatly fatigued Him, but He felt it not to His ecstasy. Nityananda held Him back by main force; the Acharya ended the *kirtan*, and laid the Master in His bed with every care.

In the same way ten days were passed in dinners and singing. In the morning the Acharya brought mother Shachi in a litter followed by the faithful. All the people of Navadwip came,—old and young, men and women,—forming a vast crowd. The Master was dancing and singing the Name, when Shachi arrived at Adwaita's house, and He fell prone at her feet. She took Him up into her bosom and wept, both of them being rapt at seeing each other. Shachi was distracted at seeing His shaven crown: she wiped His body, kissed His mouth, and gazed at Him intently; but could not see anything as tears filled her eyes. She mourned saying, "My darling Nimái! be not cruel to me as Vishwarup was, whom I never saw after he had turned hermit. If *you* too do so, it will be the death of me." The Master replied amidst tears, "Listen, mother! This body is your gift and not my own. My birth is from you, my body has been nursed by you. In ten million births I cannot repay my debt to you. True, I have become a *sannyasi* with or without your consent, but I shall never slight your wishes. I shall live wherever you bid me, I shall do whatever you command." So saying He bowed to her again and again, while she joyfully clasped Him repeatedly.

Then the Acharya led her in, and the Master made haste to receive the faithful, welcoming them, looking into their faces and embracing them, one after another. They grieved at the sight of His bare head, and yet delighted at His beauty. How can I name all the devotees—Shrivas, Ramai, Vidyanidhi, Gadadhar, Gangadas, Vakreshwar, Murari, Shuklambar, Buddhimanta Khan, Nandan,

Shridhar, Vijay, Vasudev, Damodar, Mukunda and Sanjay? Graciously He smiled on meeting the people of Navadwip. They danced in delight singing "Hari, Hari." The Acharya's house was turned into Vishnu's Heaven. From Navadwip and many villages men flocked to see the Master. For many days the Acharya supplied them all with food, drink and quarters; his store was inexhaustible, the more he spent the more was it filled again. From that day forward Shachi herself did the cooking, and the Master dined in the company of the faithful. In the day they had the Acharya's love and the sight of the Master, at night His dance and song. While He was singing all passions swept over Him, now He stood still, now trembled, now shed tears of joy or uttered broken words, now He fainted. At times He fell down on the ground, at which mother Shachi wept, saying "Methinks Nimai's body has been shattered." Then she piteously prayed to Vishnu, "Grant me this reward for my worship of thee since my infancy, that when Nimai falls on the ground, it may not hurt Him!" The loving mother Shachi was out of herself with transports of delight and meekness.

Shrinivas and other Brahmans wanted to feast the Master. But Shachi entreated them saying, "Where again shall I see Nimai? You will meet Him elsewhere, but for me, miserable one, this is His only visit. Therefore, so long as He lives with the Acharya, I shall feed Him. I beg this favour of you all."

The faithful bowed in assent to the mother's wish. The Master too, caught His mother's love-longing and said to His assembled followers: "I had started for Brindaban without your consent. So my journey was cut short by a hindrance. True, I have embraced the monastic life all of a sudden, yet I shall not be dead to you all. I shall not leave you in life, nor shall I leave my mother. It does not, however, become a hermit to live with his kindred in his birth-place. Let me not lay myself open to this charge. Devise a means by which I can be true to both my duties."

At these sweet words, the Acharya and others went to Shachi and told her of His wish. Shachi, the Mother of the World, answered, "I shall be happy if He stays here, but if He is blamed it will grieve me. This plan strikes me as a happy solution: let Him live on the Niláchal (Puri), which is as it were a next door house from Navadwip; men pass frequently between the two places, and I shall always get news of Him. You all may come and go, and He too may sometimes visit Navadwip at the Ganges bath. I count not my own joy or sorrow. What makes Him happy is happiness to me."

The faithful praised her, "Mother, thy words are like an oracle of the gods!" At their report the Master rejoiced, did reverence to the people of Navadwip and other adorers, and said, "You are my greatest friends. Grant this my prayer, all of you, that you may ever in your homes sing Krishna's *sankirtan*,—Krishna's name, Krishna's deeds, Krishna's worship. Now give me leave to go to the Niláchal; I shall visit you between whiles." Smiling He bade them farewell with due respect. But when He wished to start, Haridas cried piteously "You are going to the Nilachal, but what will be my salvation? I have not strength enough to go there. How can this lowly one hold to his sinful life without getting sight of you?" The Master answered, "Have done with thy self-abasement. It agitates my mind. For thy sake I shall pray to Jagannáth ; I shall take thee to Purushottam." Then the Acharya meekly begged Him to stay for a few days more, and the Master listened to him and did not go away. So, the Acharya, Shachi, and the faithful rejoiced. Daily did the Acharya hold the grand celebration—the sweet discourse on Krishna in the company of the devout in the day-time, and the revelry of *sankirtan* at night. Joyfully did Shachi cook, and merrily did the Master dine with the faithful. The service of the Master brought fulfilment to Acharya's reverence, devotion, home, and wealth, while Shachi delighted in gazing on her son, and feasting Him to her heart's content.

Thus did the faithful beguile some days in the Acharya's house in great bliss. At last the Master told them, "Go you all to your own homes; there make Krishna's *sankirtan*. We shall meet again ; sometimes you will go to Puri, at others I shall come to you at the Bathing in the Ganges." Goswami Nityananda, Pandit Jagadananda, Pandit Damodar, and Mukunda Datta,—these four* were sent by the Acharya to bear the Master company. Comforting His mother, He bowed at her feet, walked round her, and then set off. The cry of lamentation rose in the Acharya's house, but the Master quickened His pace, heedless of it. Adwaita followed Him some distance weeping, when He turned back with clasped hands, solaced him, and spoke these gentle words, "You should comfort my mother and look after the congregation, for if you give way to grief they will all die!" Embracing He turned Adwaita back, and passed

---

* The *Chaitanya Bhágabat* mentions two others, Govinda and Gadadhar. (III. 2).

on freely. To the bank of the Ganges He went with the four, and then to Puri by way of Chhatrabhog.* [*Madhya Lila,* text, canto 3.]

---

* *Chhatrabhog.*—A village where the Ganges divides into innumerable branches before falling into the sea. It is famous for its submerged Shiva styled *Ambu-linga.*

CHAPTER II

The Miracles of Madhav Puri

So the Master went to the Nilachal, with His four companions, absorbed in the *kirtan* (singing) of Krishna. One day He entered a village and brought back a large quantity of rice by personally begging for alms. On the way the ferrymen did not refuse Him a crossing. He blessed them and came to Remuna,* where He devoutly visited the charming image of Gopinath. As He bowed down at the feet of the image, the bunch of flowers on its crown dropped upon His head. At this Master rejoiced and danced and sang long with the faithful. The attendants of Gopinath marvelled at His power, ardour, beauty, and accomplishments, and served Him in many ways. There He passed the night, in desire of the *kshir prasád* (condensed milk) of which He had heard from Ishwar Puri before. The god was known as the *Gopinath who stole the kshir,* because, as the devotees told the tale, he had once stolen *kshir* for Madhav Puri.

In days gone by Madhav Puri had wandered on to Govardhan, near Brindaban, in his ecstasy heeding not whether it was day or night, and falling down to the ground without caring what sort of place it was. After making a circuit of the rock, he came to the Govinda-*kunda* (pool), bathed, and sat down under a tree in the evening. A Cow-boy came and held a pail of milk before

---

Remuna, 10 miles north-west of Baleshwar in Orissa.

him, saying with a smile, "Puri! drink this milk. Why don't you take what you have longed for? What are you musing on?" The Child's beauty charmed the heart of the Puri, and his sweet words took away his hunger and thirst. The Puri asked, "Who are you and where do you live? How did you know that I was fasting?" The Boy answered, "I am a milk-man of this village. In *my* village none can remain fasting. Some beg for rice, some for milk. I convey food to those who do not beg. The women who had come to draw water saw you, and sent me with this milk for you. I must be off now to milk my cows, but I shall come again for my pail." Then the Boy went away and was not seen again. Madhav Puri wondered, laid the emptied pail down, and began to pray without sleeping. Towards the end of the night he dozed off into unconsciousness, and dreamt that the Boy came and led him by the hand to a bower saying "Here I dwell, suffering much from cold and rain, wind and sun. Bring the villagers together, remove me from the bower to the hill-top and there lodge me properly in a monastery. Bathe me profusely in cold water. Long have I looked forward to the day when Madhav would come to serve me. Moved by thy love I have accepted thy service, and I shall appear in the flesh to save the world by my sight. I am Gopal, the Uplifter of Govardhan Hill. My image was installed by King Bajra,* and is the guardian deity of this place. My attendant, in fear of the misbelievers, removed me from the hill to this grove for concealment and then fled. Since then I have been here.

* The great-grandson of Krishna and his successor on the throne of Mathura.

It is well that you have come. Now bring me out carefully." So saying the Boy disappeared. Madhav Puri awoke, and judging that he had seen Shri Krishna without recognizing him, he rolled on the ground in a transport of devotion. After some weeping he calmed his mind and set about to carry out the Lord's bidding. After his morning bath he went into the village, called the people together, and said, "The Lord of your village, the Uplifter of Govardhan, is in a grove. Let us seek him out. The grove is dense and hard to enter. Take hatchets and spades with yourselves to make a door." The villagers joyfully accompanied him, and cut an entrance into the grove, where they found to their joy and wonder the image lying hidden under earth and grass. Removing the covering they knew (the image). But it was very heavy, so the strongest men joined together to take it up the hill. There the idol was placed on a stone seat, with another big stone at its back as a support. The Brahmans of the village fetched water from the Govinda-*kunda* in fresh pots. Nine hundred pots of water were brought; many musical instruments were played; the women sang. It was a great festival with dancing and singing. All the curd milk and *ghee* in the village were brought there with sweets, and all other articles of offering. The image was bathed by Madhav Puri himself, worshipped and installed there. All the food available in the village was brought to the hill, offered to the god and an *anna-kut* (pyramid of consecrated food) was formed. In one day's preparation this grand feast was accomplished. The image was laid on a bedstead, a straw thatch built over it, with walls of straw.

The Goswami Puri ordered the Brahmans to feast all

the villagers, old and young. They dined, the Brahmans and Brahmanis first, then the others in due order. The people who came from other villages looked at Gopal and got his *prasád*. Men wondered at the power of the Puri who had produced the pyramid of rice. He brought all the Brahmans to Vaishnavism and employed them in the various services (of the god). Again, at close of day he roused the god, offered some light refreshments as *bhog*. It was noised abroad that Gopal had appeared there, and people flocked from neighbouring villages to see the god. The villagers joyfully gave feasts in honour of him on different days, each building up a pyramid of rice. At night the image was laid to rest; the Puri drank a little milk.

Next morning the same kind of service began. The people of a village came with all their milk, curd, *ghee* and rice, and offered them to Gopal. The Brahmans cooked as before and Gopal tasted of the heap of rice. The people of Brindaban love Gopal of themselves, and he too loves them. They all came, partook of the holy *prasád* and forgot their sorrow and loss at the sight of him. From other provinces men arrived with presents when they heard that Gopal had appeared there. The rich men of Mathura sent costly offerings out of devotion. Gold, silver, cloth, incense and food stuffs were daily presented in vast quantities and swelled the store (of the temple). One very rich Kshatriya built the temple (at his own cost), some one else the kitchen, another the walls. The citizen of Brindaban presented a cow each, and thus Gopal got a thousand cows. Two Brahman hermits came from Bengal, and the Puri received them with attention, made them his disciples, and entrusted to them the service of the god. So he waited on the god for some two years, glad to see him served right royally.

One night the Puri had a dream, in which Gopal spoke to him, "I burn, I burn! Rub me with sandal wood from the Blue Mountain, and from nowhere else, and then shall I be cooled. Go there quickly." The Puri, inspired by devotion, travelled to the eastern country to do the Lord's behest, appointing others to carry on the service. At Shantipur he visited Adwaita Acharya, who was moved by his devotion to get himself initiated by him and became his disciple. Thence the Puri proceeded south [*i.e.*, to Orissa], and at Remuna saw the Gopinath, whose beauty threw him into ecstasy. After singing and dancing he sat down in the vestibule and asked the (attendant) Brahman about the different dishes served to the god. The splendour of the service made him infer that the *bhog* was excellent. So he resolved to inquire into the character of the *bhog* and appoint it for his Gopal too. The Brahman described to him how twelve earthen pots full of *kshir*, called *amrita-keli* (the cream of nectar) famous and unmatched in the world, were offered to the god every evening. Just then that *bhog* was presented. The Puri inly thought, "If I can get a little of the *kshir prasad* unasked, I may learn its taste for the purpose of establishing it as my Gopal's *bhog.*" But the longing shamed him and he prayed to Vishnu.

Then the *bhog* was removed and the *ârati* was celebrated. The Puri bowed and went out without saying a word. He was passionless, indifferent to the world, vowed not to ask for anything. If he got anything unasked he ate it, otherwise he fasted; the nectar of love was enough for him, he felt not hunger or thirst. That he had coveted the *kshir* struck him as a sin. So he sat down in the deserted square of the village-market singing hymns.

In the meantime the priest laid the image to sleep, finished his duties, and went to bed, where he had a dream. The god came and told him, "Up, priest, and open my door. I have kept a pot of *kshir* for the hermit. You will find it concealed under the skirt of my lower garment. You all did not notice it under my illusion. Take the *kshir* quickly to Madhav Puri who is sitting in the market place." The priest arose, bathed, opened the shrine, and found the *kshir* under the lappet of the god's *dhoti.* He washed the spot and went into the village with the pot of *kshir* and walked through the market crying, "Take this *kshir,* whosoever is named Madhav Puri! For your sake Gopinath had concealed this *kshir.* Take it and eat it, Puri, thou luckiest man in the three worlds."

At this the Puri disclosed himself. The priest gave him the *kshir,* bowed, and told the whole story, to the rapture of the Puri. The attendant priest marvelled at his devotion and said, "It is only fitting that Krishna should be obedient to him."

Lovingly did the Puri drink the *kshir,* then he washed the pot, broke it, and tied the sherds in a corner of his sheet, eating one of the broken pieces every day, at which he grew wonderfully enraptured. At the close of the night he set off for Puri (Jagannath), bowing to Gopinath then and there, in fear that a crowd would gather round him next morning, when they heard that the Lord had sent him *kshir.*

So he fared on, till he came to Puri in the Blue Mountain; the sight of Jagannath threw him into an ecstasy, he rose up and fell down, he laughed, danced, and sang, in intense delight. It was noised abroad that Madhav Puri had come to the holy place: men flocked to do him reverence. Such is the nature of fame, it comes God-sent to those who seek it not. In fear of public notice the Puri had fled thither, but fame clung to this devotee of Krishna all the way. Eager as he was to escape from the place, the need of sandal for his god held him back. He told the story of Gopal to the attendants of Jagannath and the *mohants,* and begged sandal wood for him. The faithful exerted themselves for it. Those who knew the Rajah's minister (*pátra*) begged him and thus collected the camphor and sandal. A Brahman and a servant for carrying the sandal were sent with the Puri, and given their travelling expenses. Royal passports were given to the Puri by the minister, addressed to the officers of the frontier outposts and the ferries.

So he returned to Remuna after some time, made many bows to Gopinath, and danced and sang long in rapture. The servitors of the temple did him reverence and fed him on the *kshir prasád.* While sleeping in the temple, he had a dream at the close of night: Gopal came and told him, "Hark thee, Madhav! I have got all the camphor and sandal. Rub this sandal with camphor and anoint Gopinath with it daily. Gopinath's body is one with mine! Lay the sandal on him and I shall feel the cooling effect. Doubt not, hesitate not, believe and give up the sandal as I bid you." So saying, Gopal vanished; the Goswami awoke, called together the servitors of Gopinath, and told them, "The Lord bids you rub all this sandal and camphor on Gopinath's person; for thus will Gopal be cooled. He is the Supreme Lord and his order is mighty. In summer Gopinath should be anointed with sandal paste." The servitors rejoiced at it. The Puri set the two men to rub the sandal into paste and hired two other men also [for the work]. So he daily rubbed the sandal and the attending priests laid it on gleefully. He stayed there doing this till the sandal was all gone. At the end of summer he again went to the Nilachal and passed there four months.

The Master told His disciples of the sweet life of Madhav Puri and remarked, "Think of it, Nityananda; happiest of men is the Puri. Krishna appeared to him on the pretext of giving him milk. Thrice did he appear to him in dream to lay his commands. His love so influenced the god that he revealed himself, accepted the Puri's service, and saved the world. For his sake Gopinath stole the *kshir* and got the surname of "*kshir*-stealer." On the god's body did he lay camphor and sandal, and his love overflowed at it. Hard it is to carry camphor and sandal through a Muslim country (Bengal and Upper India). Gopal knew that the Puri would be put in distress in doing this task. So, the gracious god, ever tender to his devotees, himself took the sandal (at Remuna) in order that the Puri's task might be done. Think of the Puri's extreme devotion! It transcends nature, it amazes the mind! He is silent, passionless, indifferent to every earthly thing. He keeps with himself no companion, lest he should have to speak on any ungodly material subject. That such a man, on receiving Gopal's command, travelled two thousand miles to beg for sandal! He lay fasting and yet did not ask for food! Such a man carried the sandal—one *maund* of sandal and 20 *tolas* of camphor, rejoicing that he would lay them on Gopal! The frontier custom-officer of Orissa stopped him but he showed the royal pass and was set free. He never reflected how he would carry the sandal through the Muslim land, long distance, and countless hindrances. He had not a shell (*kowri*) with him to pay duty at the custom barrier, and yet in his enthusiasm he set forth to carry the sandal. Such is the natural effect of true love, —not to think of one's own sufferings and troubles! Gopal had bidden him bring the sandal, only to show to the world the Puri's deep devotion. And he brought it joyfully through all hardships to Remuna. Gopal had meant by it only to try him, and when the trial was over the god grew gracious. We are powerless to understand the depth of his love for Krishna and Krishna's graciousness to his devotee."

So saying the Master recited a stanza of the Puri's composition, which has lighted the world like the moon. Discourse on the stanza only revealed its full beauty, just as the odour of sandal wood spreads with rubbing. I deem this stanza the rarest gem in poetry. Radha speaks it through the mouth of Madhavendra. How did Chaitanya relish it! None besides these three can know its full flavour. The Puri finally attained to the supreme realization [*i.e.*, death], reciting this stanza:

The stanza [Radhika speaks]:—

"O Lord! Gracious to the lowly! thou art now in Mathura. When wilt thou come to me? Darling mine! my heart runs about in pain of longing to see thee. What shall I do?"

On reciting the stanza the Master fell down on the ground in a trance, senseless with the intensity of love. Nityananda hurriedly took Him up in his arms.

Chaitanya rose weeping, and ran hither and thither in a transport of devotion, shouting, laughing, dancing, and singing. Oft did He repeat the first word of the stanza, His voice choked with emotion and tears running down His cheeks. He trembled, perspired, wept with joy, stood still, changed colour,—now showing remorse, now grief, now stupor, now pride or meekness. The stanza opened the gate of His love. The servitors of Gopinath gazed on the Master's outpouring of love. But He came back to Himself on seeing a crowd gathering. The *bhog* was performed, then the *árati*. The priest laid the god to rest, came out of the shrine and placed the twelve pots of *kshir* before the Master, who joyfully took five pots for Himself and His disciples and returned the other seven to the priest. True, the sight of Gopinath had been food enough for Him; but He now drank the *kshir* as a mark of reverence. The night was passed in singing the Name. In the morning He attended the *mangal árati* and then departed. [Text, canto 4.]

CHAPTER III

The Legend of 'Gopal the Witness'

Glory to Chaitanya! Glory to Nityananda! Glory to Adwaita! and Glory to the followers of Chaitanya!

On His way the Master came to the village of Jajpur, where He bowed to the image of Varáha. He danced and sang in love and prayed long, passing the night in that village. To Katak* He went to see the Sákshi-Gopál, whose beauty threw Him into a rapture. After dance and song He prayed to the Gopal with abstraction. That night during His halt there with His disciples He heard the legend of Gopal. Nityananda in his former pilgrimage had come to Katak, seen the Sakshi-Gopal, and heard the legends of the god, which he now narrated to the Master.

Once on a time two Brahmans of Vidya-nagar [Rajmahendri] set out on a pilgrimage, and after visiting Gayá, Benares, Allahabad, &c., reached Mathura. They made a tour of the [Mahá-] ban, and beheld Govardhan and the Twelve Woods, known as *Dwádash ban,* finally going to Brindaban. In the great temple Gopal was worshipped with great pomp. They bathed at the Keshi ghat, the pool of Káliya, and other places, and rested in the temple of Gopal, whose beauty ravished their hearts. There they blissfully passed a few days. One of the Brahmans being old had been tended carefully by the

* The image of Sakshi-Gopal is now installed at a village of the same name 48 miles south of Katak town.

younger one. The old man, pleased with his attendance, said, "Long have you served me, and through your help have I performed my pilgrimage. Even a son does not serve his father so lovingly. Through your kindness I have been saved every trouble. It will be rank ingratitude if I do not honour you. So I shall wed my daughter to you." The youth replied, "Listen, sir! Why talk of that which cannot be? You are a high *kulin*, great in learning and wealth, while I am a non-*kulin* lacking in scholarship and riches. I am no worthy match for your daughter. Through love of Krishna have I served you, as he is pleased with attention to Brahmans. What pleases the Lord increases the store of faith." The elder answered, "Doubt not. What wonder is there in it that I should give you my daughter?" The younger Brahman rejoined, "You have a large circle of kindred, friends and sons, without whose consent you cannot possibly wed your daughter to me. Witness the case of Bhishmak, the father of Rukmini, who was opposed by his son in giving his daughter, as he wished, to Krishna." The old man answered, "My daughter is my property. Who can oppose me in giving away what is mine? I shall give you my daughter in despite of all. Don't doubt it, but give your consent." The youth said, "If you have really decided to give me your daughter, make a vow before Gopal." The old Brahman addressed Gopal and said, "Know that I shall give my daughter to this man." The youth added, 'Lord, be thou my witness, and I shall summon thee to give thy testimony if he breaks his promise."

So saying the two returned to their homes, the young man serving the other like an elder. The old man now reflected, "I pledged my word to this Brahman in a holy place, but how can I keep it? I must consult my wife, sons, kindred and friends." So, one day he gathered his own folk and told them the whole story, at which they lamented and cried "Never utter such words again! You will lose your *kul* if you wed your daughter to a low-born man. You will be a laughing stock to all!" The Brahman urged, "How can I retract a promise made in a holy place? Come what may, I will give him my daughter." His kinsfolk threatened to boycott him, and his wife and children to take poison. The Brahman pleaded, "He will make a case of it by calling his witness. When he wins my daughter by a decree, my faith will be proved worthless!" His son answered, "Oh! the witness is an idol in a far-off land. Who will bear testimony against you? Do not be alarmed. You need not tell the lie that you had never made him such a promise; you will only have to pretend forgetfulness. If you do that I shall beat the Brahman in court." At this the Brahman, full of anxiety, prayed intently to Gopal, "Gopal, to thee I appeal: save my faith and save my kindred,—save both sides!"

One day the younger Brahman visited him, bowed reverently, and said with folded hands, "You promised me your daughter, but are now silent on the point! Is this your sense of justice?" The old man remained silent; but his son ran with a stick to beat the visitor, crying, "Wretch! you want to wed my sister! Dwarf, you wish to catch the moon!" The youth fled, but another day he called all the villagers together, who summoned the old man. Then the younger Brahman spoke, "This man promised his daughter to me. Ask him why he does not give her up now." On being questioned by the people, the elder Brahman replied, "Listen, friends, I do not remember what I said so long ago." At this his son got the chance to put in his words boldly, "My father had much money with him during his pilgrimage. This villain, his only companion, coveted the money, intoxicated him with *dhuturá*, robbed him and said that thieves had taken away his money, and then spread the tale that he had promised his daughter to him. Judge ye all, whether he is a worthy match for my sister." The assembled people were filled with suspicion, as greed often makes men commit sin. The younger Brahman pleaded, "Hear, my masters, he is lying to win the case. His father, pleased with my attendance, promised me his daughter voluntarily, and when I declined alleging my unworthiness and our disparity in wealth, learning and *kul*, he repeatedly pressed me to accept her,...and at my suggestion called Gopal to witness his promise. I conjured the god to bear testimony for me, should this Brahman break his word. He is my witness, whose word is held true in the three worlds." The old man replied, "This is good. If Gopal appears here and bears testimony, I shall certainly give you my daughter." His son agreed to it. The old man inly thought, "Kind is Krishna. Surely he will bear my word out." His son was confident that the image would not come to act as a witness. So thinking diversely they agreed. At the younger Brahman's request both parties signed a written deed of agreement to abide by this test, to prevent future disputes. It was left with an umpire. The young man continued, "Listen, all ye here! This Brahman is pious and true of speech, never wishing to retract his word. It is only his fear of the suicide of his kinsfolk that has made him tell a lie. Thanks to his piety, I will bring Krishna as a witness and enable him to keep his word." At this the sceptics laughed; some said, "God is good, He may come."

Then the younger Brahman went to Brindaban, prostrated himself and prayed to the image, "God of the Brahmans! thou art ever kind. Have pity and save the honour of two Brahmans. I mind not whether I get the girl or not, but it would be a great pity if a Brahman's promise is broken. For this reason, do thou bear witness, for he who will not bear testimony to the truth that he knows, commits a sin." Krishna replied, "Brahman! return home, assemble the public, and meditate on me. I shall appear and give my evidence. But my image cannot be taken there." The Brahman protested, "Even if you appear in your four-armed form, none will believe you. But if this very image goes there and speaks out of its mouth, then all will deem it true." Krishna said, "Nobody ever heard of an idol travelling!" The Brahman replied "Why do you speak of being an idol? You are not a mere image but the Darling of Brindaban. Do an unprecedented act for the sake of a Brahman." Laughingly Gopal said, "Hear, Brahman, I shall travel after you; but do not look behind, or else I shall stop there. You will hear (on the way) only the jingling of my *nupur,* and thus know that I am going on. Give me one *seer* of rice [daily], which I shall eat when accompanying you." Next day, after taking the Lord's leave, the Brahman set out on his return, delighted to hear the jingle of the *nupur* behind him, and offering excellent rice to the image. So he arrived near his village and then thought, "Now have I come to my village and shall go home and tell the people of the arrival of my witness. But I cannot believe if I do not see him with my own eyes. It will be no harm if he stays here. So he looked behind him ; and Gopal stopped there, saying with a smile, "Go home; here will I stay without going any further."

When the Brahman reported the tale, the people marvelled at it, and came to see the witness. They bowed to Gopal, delighted with his beauty and amazed to hear that the image had travelled thither. Then the old Brahman in joy prostrated himself before Gopal, who gave his evidence before the people, and the younger Brahman got his betrothed bride. The Lord spoke to the two Brahmans, "You will be my servants birth after birth. I am pleased with you ; beg a boon." They prayed together, "Grant us this that you remain here, so that all may know your favour to your servants." Gopal remained there, and the two served him. The people of the country flocked to see him. The king of the land heard the wonderful legend and beheld the Gopal with supreme delight. He built a temple and endowed the service of the god, who became famous under the name of GOPAL THE WITNESS. Thus has *Sakshi-Gopal* accepted worship and stayed at Vidyá-nagar for long. Purushottam, the Rajah of Orissa, conquered the country in battle and seized the many-jewelled throne named *mánik-sinhásan*. Purushottam Dev was a great devotee and entreated Gopal to go to his capital. Gopal, pleased with his piety, consented and was taken to Katak, where his worship was installed. The Rajah gave the *mánik-sinhásan* to Jagannath. His queen, when visiting Gopal, gave him many ornaments in devotion. A costly pearl hung from her nose, and wishing to give it too she reflected, "Ah, if there had been a hole in the Lord's nose, I, his handmaid, could have made him put this pearl on!" With this thought she bowed and returned home. At the end of the night Gopal appeared to her in a dream and said, "In my infancy my mother had bored my nose and very tenderly hung there a pearl. The hole is there still. Make me wear the pearl you wished to give." The queen spoke to her husband, and the two went to the temple with the pearl, hung it from the hole in the nose which was found out, and a great festival of joy was held. From that day on has Gopal stayed at Katak and been known as *Sakshi-Gopal.*

The master with all His disciples heard the legend of Gopal from Nityananda and was delighted. While He stood before Gopal, the faithful seemed to see them both as of one body, of one complexion, large-limbed, red-robed, grave of mien, beaming with glory, lotus-eyed, moon-faced, both of them in rapture for each other.

At the sight of both, Nityananda in great joy winked at the faithful and they all smiled. So the night was passed in great entertainment, and next morning, after witnessing the matin service, they set off. Brindaban-das has described fully how He visited Bhubaneshwar on the way (to the Blue Mountain). At Kamalpur He bathed in the Bhagi* river, and gave His mendicant's stick to Nityananda to carry. With his disciples He went to see Kapoteshwar [Shiva]. Here Nityananda broke the Master's stick into three and threw it (into the river). From that Shiva shrine the Master returned, and was

* *Indian Atlas* (sheet 116) names the river here as *Bargovee.*

thrown into ecstasy by the sight of the spire* of the temple of Jagannath. He prostrated Himself and danced in love; the disciples too, in love, danced and sang, following the Master on the highway. He laughed, wept, danced, roared and shouted, and made a thousand leagues of those six miles. On reaching Athárá-nálá (Eighteen Water-courses) the Master came to His senses a little and asked Nityananda for His stick. But Nityananda answered, "It was broken into three bits. You fell down in a swoon of devotion, and as I caught you, we two tumbled on the stick which was broken by our weight. I know not where it was dropped. Through my fault was your stick broken. Punish me as you think fit." The Master was sad and spoke a little bitterly, "You have all done me great good, forsooth, by coming to the Blue Mountain! You could not even preserve the stick, my only property. You go before me to see Jagannath or let me go there before you. But we will not go together." Mukunda Datta said, "Master, go thou before us; we shall arrive after and not in thy company." The Master hastened there. None could understand the cause why one Master broke the other's stick and why the latter suffered it to be done, or was angry at the result. The deep mystery of the breaking of the stick can be understood only by him who has constant faith in the two Masters. [Text, canto 5.]

---

* The place meant is evidently Jagannath Vallabh, six miles north of Puri; from this place the spire of the temple of Jagannath can be seen. *Athara-nala* is two miles north of Puri.

CHAPTER IV

The Conversion of Sarvabhauma

The Master went in an ecstatic mood to the temple of Jagannath, and was beside Himself with love at the sight of the god. He rushed to embrace the image, but fell down on the temple floor, senseless with devotion. Happily Sárvabhauma noticed Him, and stopped the door-keeper (*Parichhá*, mace-bearer) who was about to beat the Master. Sárvabhauma marvelled exceedingly as he gazed on the beauty of the Master and His transport of love. The hour of *bhog* arrived, yet the Master did not come to His senses. Sárvabhauma then thought of a plan, and had Him conveyed by his disciple the door-keeper to his house and laid Him down on a clean spot. But the Master showed no respiration, no heaving of the chest. The Bhattácharya grew alarmed. He held a fine piece of cotton to the Master's nose ; it stirred, and he was reassured. The Bhattacharya sat musing thus, "This is the *sáttvika* form of the passion for Krishna. It is named the "bright-pure" (*sudipta sáttvika*), and is displayed only by a devotee who has attained to constant realization (*nitya-siddhi*). This ecstasy is possible only in one whose devotion is extreme. I wonder to see it manifested in an [ordinary] man's person."

While he was pondering thus, Nityananda and the others arrived at the main gate, and overheard the people talking among themselves, "A *sannyasi* came here and swooned away at the sight of Jagannath ; he is still in a trance. Sarvabhauma has conveyed him to his own house." They knew from this that it was the Great Master. Just then came there Gopinath Acharya, the son-in-law of Vishárad of Nadia, and a devotee and acquaintance of the Master. He knew Mukunda from before, and was surprised to see him there. Mukunda bowed, the Acharya embraced him and asked him news of the Master. Mukunda replied, "The Master has come here, and we with Him." The Acharya bowed to Nityananda Goswami, and again asked them all about the Master. Mukunda said, "After taking the monastic vow, the Master came to the Blue Mountain taking us with Him. Leaving us behind He came to visit this temple, and we have arrived now to seek Him. From what we have heard from others, we conclude that He is in Sarvabhauma's house, whither He was removed on fainting at the sight of the god. I have met you luckily, just as I was wishing for your sight. Let us go to Sarvabhauma's house, and after seeing the Master we shall visit the temple."

Gopinath in delight conducted them to Sarvabhauma's house, where he beheld the Master and felt mingled joy and grief. He introduced them all to Sarvabhauma, and took them inside. Sarvabhauma bowed to Nityananda Goswami and saluted the others in the proper mode. Then he sent them all in charge of his son Chandaneshwar, to the temple. They joyed to behold the god. Nityananda went out of himself in devotion, but the others quieted him. The servitor of the shrine presented them with the garland and *prasád* of the god, to their great delight. Then they returned to the Master, and chanted the divine name loud and long. In the third quarter [of the day],

Chaitanya awoke, and rose up shouting, *Hari! Hari!* Reverently Sarvabhauma took the dust of His feet [to place it on his own head], and entreated Him, "Take your midday meal soon. I shall feed you to-day with Jagannath's *mahá-prasád.*" The Master quickly came back from His bath in the sea, and feasted with His followers on the rice, broth and other kinds of *prasád,* which Sarvabhauma served to them from golden dishes. The Master said, "Help me with the hash of gourd (*lau*) and other vegetables, and serve these others with cakes and sweets." But the Bhattacharya entreated Him with folded palms, "How has Jagannath himself fed? Do you too taste all of these," and so made Him eat the cakes and sweets too. After the dinner, he helped the Master to wash, then took leave to retire with Gopinath Acharya and eat their own meals. When they returned, [the Acharya] bowed saying "I salute Narayan," and the Master responded with "Be thy mind constant in Krishna!" At these words Sarvabhauma knew Him to be a Vaishnav hermit. He then asked Gopinath Acharya about the worldly life of the Master. The Acharya replied, "His home was at Navadwip; his father Jagannath Mishra, surnamed Purandar Mishra, gave him the name of Vishwambhar. His maternal grandfather was Nilambar Chakravarti." Sarvabhauma added "Nilambar Chakravarti! why, he was a fellow-student of my father Vishárad, who, I know, had a high regard for Purandar Mishra, too. I honour both for their connection with my father."

Delighted to hear that Chaitanya was a man of Nadia, Sarvabhauma thus addressed Him, "You are of honourable birth, and a *sannyasi* in addition. Make me, therefore, your personal disciple." At this the Master cried out, "O

Vishnu! O Vishnu!" and then spoke humbly to the Bhattacharya, "You are the teacher of the world and the benefactor of mankind. You teach *Vedánta* and [thereby] benefit men of monastic life. I am a young monk, ignorant of good and evil. I have sought refuge with you, regarding you as my teacher. For your society have I come here, hoping that you will train me in all ways. You saved me in my great danger to-day." The Bhattacharya said, "Never go to the temple alone, but always with me or one of my men." The Master replied, "I shall not enter the shrine, but gaze from the Garuda [pillar in the quadrangle]." Then Sarvabhauma addressed Gopinath Acharya, "You will be guide to this Goswami in visiting the temple. Lodge him in the house of my mother's sister, which is a quiet place, and look to all his needs." So he did. Next day Gopinath took the Master to the temple to show Him Jagannath as he rose from his bed. Mukunda Datta led Him back to Sarvabhauma's house, who spoke thus, "This *sannyasi* is meek in disposition, lovely in form. I daily love Him the more. Tell me what order He has joined and what name He has chosen." Gopinath replied, "He has been named Shri Krishna-Chaitanya; His spiritual guide is Keshav Bharati, blessed man!" Sarvabhauma remarked, "His name is well-chosen, but the Bharati order is not ranked high [among the ten classes of *sannyasis*]."

Gopinath answered, "He does not care for outward [dignity]. Hence His indifference to the more famous orders of monks." The Bhattacharya joined in, "Ah, He is in the full bloom of youth. How can He keep the monastic rules? However, I shall ceaselessly teach Him Vedanta, and lead Him on to the rank of a recluse of the Monist school (*adwaita*). If He then wishes it, I shall robe Him anew with the yellow robe of a *yogi*, purify Him, and enter Him into one of the higher orders."

Gopinath and Mukunda grieved to hear it; and the former expostulated, "Bhattacharya! You know not His greatness. The signs of divinity have reached their extreme limit in Him! Hence He is famed as the Great God. But in a place of ignorance even the wise know nothing."

The [Sarvabhauma's] disciples asked, "What proof is there of His divinity?" The Acharya replied, "The belief of the wise is proof of divinity." The disciples objected, saying, "It is by inference that God is recognized." But the Acharya answered, "No, God is not known by inference, but only by those on whom He bestows His grace,—even a particle of it. Witness Brahma's praise of Vishnu in the *Shrimad Bhagabat*, Book X. canto xiv. verse 28:

'Lord! true it is that knowledge can gain salvation, but Thy glories can be known only by him who has been blessed even with a particle of favour from Thy lotus-like feet. O Perfect Being! A man lacking Thy grace, may be free from earthly lusts, may have studied the scriptures for ages, but still he cannot know Thee fully!'

O Sarvabhauma, you may be the World's Teacher, a master of theology, unrivalled in the world in scholarship. But you have not gained God's grace, hence you cannot know God. I do not blame you, but the scripture says clearly that the knowledge of God cannot come from mere scholarship."

Sarvabhauma replied, "Weigh thy words well, Acharya! How do you prove that you have gained God's grace?" The Acharya replied, "We know a material thing by observing it. Our knowledge of the nature of a thing is proved by grace. On this sannyasi's person are all the marks of divinity. You yourself witnessed his ecstasy of spiritual love. And yet you know not God! Such are the ways of God's illusion,—materialists see Him and yet recognize Him not!"

Smilingly spoke Sarvabhauma, "We are arguing in a friendly spirit. Don't get warm. Blame me not, I am only arguing from the strict standpoint of view of *Shastra.* Chaitanya Goswami is [I admit] a great saint. But there is no incarnation of Vishnu in the Kali era. Hence Vishnu's epithet *Tri-yug* or the Lord of Three Æons. But scripture tells us that the Kali era is without an incarnation."

Sadly did the Acharya answer, "You pride yourself on your knowledge of scripture, but you do not mind the *Bhágabat* and the *Mahábhárat,* which are the chief of scriptures. Both of them assert that God will appear in the human form in the Kali era, and yet you maintain the contrary! As God will not appear in Kali for mere earthly exploits [but only for purifying faith], we call him *Tri-yug.* In every era Krishna appears for the spiritual needs of the age. You are a logician, and yet you do not perceive this!

Texts quoted in support ;—*Bhagabat,* X viii. 9, XI. v. 28, 29 ; *Mahabharat,* Anushasan Parva, Dan-dharma, canto 149, v. 75-92.

I need not waste these many words on you. They will bear no more fruit than seed sown on sterile soil. When His grace is on you, you will be convinced. Your disciple, who is plying me with all sorts of sophistic arguments, I blame him not ; he is under illusion (*máyá*). As the *Bhagabat*, Book VI. canto iv. verse 26, puts it:—

[The words of Daksha to God] *I bow to the Omnipotent Supreme God, whose power of illusion raises endless controversies among logicians fond of dispute, and keeps their souls ever wrapt in delusion!*

Again, the *Bhagabat*, XI. xxii. 3, [Krishna's words to Uddhava]."

Then Sarvabhauma said, "Go to the monk [Chaitanya] and invite him and his followers to my house. First feed them with *prasád*, and then give me lessons [in theology]!" The Acharya, being Sarvabhauma's sister's husband, could [boldly] blame, praise, laugh at or school him.

Mukunda was greatly pleased with the Acharya's reasoning, as he was inly grieved and angry at the speech of Sarvabhauma.

The Acharya came to Chaitanya's house and invited Him on behalf of the Bhattacharya. As he talked with Mukunda he spoke ill of Sarvabhauma in a pained spirit. But the Master broke in with, "Say not so. The Bhattacharya has really favoured me; he wants to safeguard my monastic life, and has taken pity on me out of tenderness. Why blame him for it?"

Next day, the Master visited the temple of Jagannath in the company of the Bhattacharya, and then accompanied him to his house. The Bhattacharya seated the Master first and began to teach Him *Vedánta*. With mingled tenderness and reverence he said, "It is a *sannyasi's* duty to hear the Vedanta read. You should constantly attend to it." The Master answered, "Show me thy favour. Whatever you bid me is indeed my duty."

For seven days did the Master thus listen to the expounding of the Vedanta, without making any comment of His own. On the eighth day, Sarvabhauma asked Him, "For seven days have you heard me in unbroken silence. I know not whether you follow me or not." The Master replied, "I am ignorant, and have not studied [the subject]. I merelv listen at your bidding. I listen only because such is a *sannyasi's* duty. But I cannot follow your interpretation." The Bhattacharya retorted, "He who is conscious of his own ignorance asks for a second explanation. But you remain ever silent as you listen. I know not your mind's workings." The Master replied, "I understand the verses clearly enough. But it is your commentary that puzzles me. A commentary should elucidate the text, whereas your exposition conceals the text! You do not expound the plain meaning of the aphorisms, but cover them up with your fanciful interpretation. The primary meaning is the plain sense of the terms of the *Upanishad*, and Vyas says it in his aphorisms. You [on the other hand] let the primary sense go, and give a conjectural secondary sense. You reject the meanings of words as given in lexicons, and attribute to them meanings evolved from your imagination. *Shruti* is the chief of proofs. The primary meaning as given by *Shruti* can alone carry conviction.

What are conchshells and cowdung but naturally unclean things, *viz.*, the bone and ordure of animals? And yet they are taken as very pure, because *Shruti* says so. Of the spiritual truth that is held forth [in Vedanta] the meaning is plain and self-evident. Fanciful interpretation only spoils the clear sense. The sense of Vyas's aphorisms is clear like the sun; you are only enveloping it with the cloud of your conjectural commentary. The *Vedas* and the *Puráns* tell us how to discern Brahma. That Brahma is [only another name for] God in His totality. The Supreme Being is full of all powers, and yet you describe Him as formless? The *Shrutis* that speak of Him as abstract (*nir-bishesha*), exclude the natural and set up the unnatural.

From Brahma originates the Universe, it lives in Brahma, and it is merged again in the same Brahma. The three attributes of God are that He is the three cases,—Ablative, Instrumental and Locative [in relation to the Universe]. These three qualities particularize God. When He desired to be many, He looked at [=employed] His 'natural powers'. The physical mind and eye could not have then existed. Therefore, the Immaterial Brahma *had* an eye to see and a mind to will with. The terms 'Brahma' means the 'Perfect Supreme Being' (*Bhagabán*), and the scriptures affirm that Krishna is the Supreme Being. The meaning of the Vedas is too deep for human understanding, the Purans make their senses clear. Witness Brahma's address to God in the *Bhagabat*, X. xiv. 31:—

'Blessed, blessed are Nanda the cowherd and other citizens of Mathura, whose friend is the Beatific Perfect Eternal Brahma'.

Shruti itself denies to Brahma material hands and feet, and yet it says that God 'moves swiftly' and 'receives everything'! Therefore, *Shruti* asserts Brahma to be particular (*sa-bishesha*). It is only a fanciful interpretation—as opposed to a direct one,—that speaks of

Brahma as abstract (*nir-bishesha*). How do you call that God formless who has the six qualities and is supremely blissful? You conclude Him to be powerless, who has the three natural powers, as is evident from the *Vishnu Puran,* VI. vii. 60 and 61, and I. xii. 41.

God's nature consists of *sat, chit* and *ánanda.* The *chit* power assumes three different forms in three aspects; it becomes *hládini* from the *ánanda* aspect; it becomes *sandhini* in the *sat* aspect, and *sambita* (known as 'knowledge of Krishna') in the *chit* aspect. The *chit* power is God's very essence [or inner nature]; the life power (*jiba-shakti*) appertains to Him only occasionally; *máyá* is entirely outside Him [*i.e.*, affects creation only]. But all these three offer devotion in the form of love. The Lord's six powers are only manifestations of the *chit* power. And yet you have the presumption to deny such a power? God and creation differ as the master and the slave of illusion respectively, and yet you affirm that creation is identical with the Creator! In the *Gita* creation is recognized as a force exerted by God, and yet you make such creation one with God! See the *Gitá,* vii. 4, the words of Shri Krishna to Arjun:—

Earth, water, fire, air, ether, mind, sense, and self-consciousness—these eight powers (or *natures*) *have emanated from me.*

Again, the next verse in the *Gitá:*—

'Valiant hero! the eight 'natures' (prakriti) *about which I have already spoken to you, are inferior. Beyond them I have a higher or living 'nature' which upholds this Universe.'*

God's form is composed of *sat, chit* and *ánanda;* and yet you assert that form to be a corruption of the *satwa* quality! He is a wretch who denies form to God; touch not, behold not that slave of Death. The Buddhists are atheists from not respecting the Vedas. Atheism in a believer of the Vedas is a worse heresy than Buddhism. Vyas composed his aphorisms for the salvation of men, but the interpretation of these aphorisms by the 'school of illusion' (*máyá-vádi*) is the cause of perdition.

Vyas's aphorisms accept the 'theory of effect' (*parinám*). God is an incomprehensible power, but He is manifested as creation. The philosopher's stone produces gold without undergoing any change in itself, similarly God takes the form of creation without suffering any corruption. Objecting to this aphorism as an error of Vyas, you have set up the theory of *bivarta* by a fanciful interpretation [of it]. Error consists in a creature imagining 'I am one with the Creator'. But creation is not unreal, it is only perishable. The great word *Pranaba* is the image of God; from that *Pranaba* all the Vedas have sprung in this world. The words 'Thou art That' (*tat-twam asi*) when applied to creation are only fractional (*prádeshika*), but you, without minding the *Pranaba,* call these words the supreme truth."

Thus did the Master find a hundred faults with the fanciful interpretation [of the Vedantists]. The Bhattacharya supported his own position, using refutation, feint, pressure, and other logical devices. But the Master answered them all and established His own view. The Vedas [he maintained] assert only three things about God, *viz.*, our relation to Him, devotional exercises, and love (our need) as the fruit of devotion. All the rest [attributed to Him] is mere conjecture. The words of the Veda are self-evident, and should not be interpreted with the help of conjecture. But Sarvabhauma was not to blame for it ; he was merely carrying out God's will, in expounding atheistical philosophy based on fancy. *Vide* the *Padma Purán,* Part II. canto 62, verse 31.

The Bhattacharya was speechless and motionless with wonder as he heard these words. The Master addressed him, "Marvel not, O Bhattacharya! The supreme manhood consists in faith in God. Even those who directly commune with God (*átmárám*) adore Him, the Supreme Being's attributes are so incomprehensible! Witness the *Bhagabat,* I. vii. 10, Suta's words to Saunaka and others :—

'Such are the attributes of Hari that even mystical and passionless recluses feel for Him unreasoning devotion.'

The Bhattacharya said, "Sir, I long to hear this verse interpreted." The Master replied, "Do *you* first explain it, and then I shall say what I think of it." The Bhattacharya expounded the verse, like a logician, in nine different ways in accordance with the scriptures. But the Master smiled as He said, "I know, Bhattacharya, that you are a veritable Vrihaspati, and surpass all other men in interpreting the scriptures. But your interpretation shows mere scholarship. The verse has yet another sense!" Then at the Bhattacharya's request the Master gave His own interpretation ; passing by the nine interpretations given by the Bhattacharya, He gave 18 other explanations of His own. First He determined the meaning of each of the eleven words contained in the verse, as taken separately ; then He gave different explanations in connection with *átmárám,* laying emphasis on each of the eleven words in succession. The Lord, His powers, and His attributes,—all three are incomprehensibly, unspeakably great! These three steal the heart of the devotee, to the neglect of all other forms of devotion. Sanak, Shukadev and others bear witness to this. His diverse expositions filled the Bhattacharya with wonder, and the self-abasing belief that the Master was Krishna indeed. "Alas!" thought he, "He is Krishna incarnate, but I in my ignorance have grievously sinned by showing pride to Him." Penitently he sought refuge with the Master, who graciously appeared to him in His divine form,—first as four-armed (Vishnu), then as Krishna playing on the flute. At this vision Sarvabhauma fell prostrate on the ground, then rose again and prayed to Him with clasped hands. The Master's grace made spiritual knowledge illumine his heart,—he now knew the glory of God's name, faith, gift, the esoteric meanings of the letters of the alphabet, &c. In a moment he composed a hundred verses, such as even Vrihaspati would have failed to frame. The delighted Master embraced him, and the Bhattacharya fainted in an ecstasy of joy,—weeping, standing still, tumbling down at the Master's feet.

The sight delighted Gopinath Acharya. The Master's disciples smiled at the dance of Sarvabhauma. Gopinath spoke to the Master, "You have so transformed that Bhattacharya!" The Master replied, "You are a devotee, your society has so wrought on him through the great grace of Jagannath." Then He composed Bhattacharya, who thereafter praised Him long, saying, "It was a light work to Thee to save the world, in comparison with the wonderful power Thou hast manifested in converting me. Logic had made me hard like an ingot of iron. Thou hast melted me. Oh Thy wondrous might!"

The Master returned to His quarters; Sarvabhauma

feasted Him by means of Gopinath Acharya. Next day He went to Jagannath's temple, and beheld the god rise from his bed. The attending priest presented to the Master the garland and offered rice of the god. The Master rejoiced at it, tied the gifts to the hem of his garment, and hastened to Bhattacharya's house. It was dawn; Bhattacharya awoke just then and cried out "O Krishna! O Krishna!" to the delight of the Master. Coming out Bhattacharya met the Master, bowed at His feet in a tumult of reverence, and seated Him. The Master untied the knot in His skirt and presented the *prasád* to Sarvabhauma, who joyously ate it after reciting the following verse, though he had not yet bathed, nor said his matin prayer, nor even cleaned his teeth,—because Chaitanya's grace removed all stupor from his mind.

From the *Padma Purán*,—*Taste the mahá-prasád as soon as you get it, though it may be dry, stale or brought from a distance. Wait not for a more proper time in this case.*

Then, again, Hari has said, '*In tasting the maha-prasad no rule of time or place should be observed; a good man should eat it as soon as he gets it.*'

At this the Master was delighted and embraced Sarvabhauma in a transport. They both danced, Master and pupil, clasping each other, perspiring, trembling, shedding tears in ecstasy. The Master said, "To-day have I conquered the three worlds lightly! To-day have I ascended Baikuntha! To-day all my wishes are realized! Because Sarvabhauma has shown faith in the *mahá-prasád*. To-day you have taken refuge in Krishna with all your heart. Krishna has taken pity on you without any reserve. To-day he has removed your bondage to flesh;

to-day you have torn off the meshes of illusion. To-day your heart has been made worthy to gain Krishna, because you have eaten the *prasád* in violation of Vedic ceremonies. As the *Bhágabat*, II. vii. 41, puts it:—

Those whom the Lord favours and who take refuge at His feet with all their heart and without reserve, can conquer illusion. Then they no longer look upon this fleshly body—the food of dogs and jackals—as 'I' or 'mine.' "

So saying the Master returned home. Thenceforth Bhattacharya lost his pride (of learning). Thenceforth he knew of nothing except Chaitanya's feet, and expounded no scripture except that of *bhakti*. At his deep Vaishnavism, Gopinath Acharya danced, clapping his hands and crying *Hari! Hari!* Next day Bhattacharya came to visit the Master, without having first gone to Jagannath. He lay prostrate, and thanked the Master much, penitently recounting his own former follies. As he wished to hear of the chief means of cultivating faith, the Master instructed him by chanting Hari's name.

"Hari's name, Hari's name, Hari's name alone; in the Kali era there is no other means of salvation, no other, indeed no other!" [*Vrihad Narad Puran.*]

In full detail did the Master hold forth on the meaning of the above verse. Bhattacharya was filled with wonder. Gopinath Acharya said, "Bhattacharya! I told you before that you would come to this!" Bhattacharya bowed to him thankfully and replied, "The Master has blessed me by reason of my being related to you. You are a great devotee, and I a blind logician. For your sake has the Master favoured me." Pleased with his meekness, Chaitanya embraced him and then said, "Now go and see the god." Bhattacharya, after visiting Jagannath, came home with Jagadánanda and Damodar [two disciples of Chaitanya], and sent to Chaitanya many kinds of choice *prasád* with his own cook in their company, and also put two verses of his own written on a palm leaf into the hands of Jagadánanda for Chaitanya. When they arrived at the Master's house, Mukunda Datta took the letter from his hand, and wrote the two verses on the outer wall. Then Jagadánanda took the letter inside to Chaitanya, who read and tore it up, but the followers learnt the verses by rote from the wall. The verses are given in *Chaitanya-chandrodaya,* Act VI. Sc. 32:—

I seek refuge with that unequalled supreme Man, who has become incarnate as Shri Krishna Chaitanya, in order to teach passionlessness (bairágya) and devotion through faith (bhakti-yog). May my mind, like a bee, settle firmly on the lotus-feet of the Lord Shri Krishna Chaitanya, who has appeared in order to revive his own bhakti-yog, which had perished through the wickedness of ages.

Sarvabhauma became a disciple of the Master, attending to nothing but His service. Ever did he meditate, pray, and recite the name 'Shri Krishna-Chaitanya, the son of Shachi, the abode of virtues!' One day he came to the Master, bowed, and recited Brahma's hymn to God from the *Bhagabat,* changing two letters near its end. The *Bhágabat,* X. xiv. 8:—

'Lord! That man alone enters into the inheritance of Thy salvation like a true heir, who in eager longing for the day of Thy grace passes his life worshipping Thee with all his mind body and speech and enjoying the fruits of his actions without being attached to them.

The Master interrupted him saying, "The text has 'Thy salvation' (*muktipada*). Why do you read it as 'Thy faith' (*bhaktipada*)?" Bhattacharya answered, "Salvation is not the fruit at which the faithful fix their gaze; as for those who lack faith in the Lord, salvation becomes a sort of punishment to them [as they are annihilated in the Lord without being able to serve and love Him]. He who does not admit the incarnate Krishna, and he who blames and fights against that incarnation,—both of them are punished by being merged in the Lord (*Brahma sáyujya mukti*). The devotee does not long for emancipation. There are five kinds of salvation, *viz.*, *sálokya* (living in the same plane with God), *sámipya* (nearness to God), *sárupya* (assuming the same form as God), *sárshti* (equalling the glory of God) and *sáyujya* (absorption in the Deity). Though the first four afford means of serving the Lord, yet true devotees seldom elect them, but they dread and despise the *sayujya* emancipation, preferring hell to it. 'Absorption in the abstract God (*Brahma*)' and 'Absorption in the God clad in attributes (*saguna ishwar*)' are two forms of the same thing, indeed the latter is worse still. *Vide* the *Bhagabat* III. xxix. 11, Kapil's speech to Devahuti."

The Master objected, "The term *muktipada* has other senses too; it means God Himself, *i.e.*, 'He whose feet are the means of salvation.' It may also mean 'The abode of salvation,' which is the 9th object [mentioned in the *Bhágabat*, II. x. 1]. Both etymologies yield the sense of Krishna. Why need you change the text to *Bhaktipada*?" Bhattacharya replied, "No, I cannot adopt the reading. Though you interpret the term *muktipada* in the same sense of *bhaktipada*, yet the former is objectionable as ambiguous. Though *mukti* has five connotations, yet its principal meaning is 'absorption in God.' So, the word *mukti* fills me with fear and contempt, while *bhakti* kindles delight in the heart.'' At this the delighted Master smiled and clasped Bhattacharya firmly to His bosom. It was a pure act of grace on Chaitanya's part that Bhattacharya, who had been a student and teacher of the doctrine of illusion, spoke thus. We recognize the philosopher's stone only when it touches a piece of iron. So all men knew the Master for the veritable Darling of Braja (Krishna) when they saw the deep the Vaishnav spirit of [His disciple] Bhattacharya. Then did Kashi Mishra and others of the Blue Mountain come and seek asylum at the Master's feet. I shall first describe how Sarvabhauma served the Master, and how carefully he fed Him. [Text, canto 6.]

CHAPTER V

Healing the leper Vasudev

The Master renounced the world in the bright fortnight of Mágh, and came to reside at Puri in Fálgun. At the end of the latter month He witnessed the swinging ceremony of Jagannath and danced and sang long in ecstasy. In Chaitra He liberated Sarvabhauma. Early in Baishakh He wished to travel to the South. He assembled His followers, embraced them, held them by the hand, and spoke humbly, "I know you to be dearer than life. Life I can part with, but not with you. You my friends have done me a good turn by bringing me here to see Jagannath. Now I beg one favour from you all,—give me leave to go to the South. I must set out to seek Vishwarup [my elder brother], and I will travel alone, taking none with me. Do you all stay at Puri till I return from Setubandha."

They all knew that Vishwarup had attained to liberation, and that the quest of him was only a ruse of the Master for carrying salvation to Southern India. Greatly did they grieve on hearing His words, and sat silent with woe-begone faces. Nityananda said, "How can that be? We cannot let you go alone. One or two of us must bear you company, lest mishap should befall you. Choose any two that you like. I know the roads to the holy places of the South. Bid me, Master, go with you." The Master replied, "I am as a dancer and you are like the manager (*sutradhár*) of the play. I dance as you make me. On turning hermit I set out for Brindaban, but you brought me to Adwaita's house. On the way to the Nilachal you broke my staff. Your deep love is marring my [life's] work. Jagadánanda wants me to turn a worldling. In fear of him I have to do whatever he bids, me. If ever I disobey him he in anger speaks not to me for three days! Mukunda grieves at the rigours of my monastic life: the three baths daily even in winter, the sleep on the bare ground. He grieves inly, though he speaks not of it; but his sorrow makes me doubly unhappy. I am a *sannyasi*, Damodar is a Brahmachari, and yet he constantly holds the pedagogue's rod over me. I did not know his character before. My conduct must be quite different from his. Having gained the favour of Krishna, he cares not for the opinions of other men; but I cannot be so regardless of the public. Do you all, therefore, stay behind at Puri, while I make my pilgrimage alone for some time."

Under the pretext of picking their faults the Master really pointed out the merits which had made them win His heart. Words cannot describe Chaitanya's love for His devotees. He himself bore the hardship of an ascetic's life, but when one of His devotees grieved at the sight of these hardships, the Master could not bear the sight of his grief! He set forth on His pilgrimage as a solitary hermit. Four of them entreated Him hard for permission to accompany Him, but He followed His own will and did not listen to them. At last Nityananda urged, "As you please. It is my duty [to obey you], be the result my happiness or sorrow. But one further request I must make: consider whether you can accept it. Your loin-band wrapper and gourd of water,—these are the only articles that you will take with you. But your two hands are ever busy in counting your recitation of Hari's name [on the notches of your fingers]. How, then, will you carry your wrapper and gourd? Who will take care of these when you fall down on the road in a trance? Keep my word: take this honest Brahman Krishna-dás with you. He will only carry your wrapper and gourd, and never say a word, whatever you may do." The Master consented. They took him to Sarvabhauma's house, who seated them all after salutation. After a varied discourse on Krishna, the Master said, "I have come to beg your permission. I must search for Vishwarup who retired as a hermit to the South. Give me leave to go South. Your permission will enable me to return in safety." At these words Sarvabhauma was much grieved at heart; clasping the Master's feet he said piteously, "Through the accumulated merit of many previous births have I gained your society. But Fate has now parted our company. I can bear the death of a son through a stroke of lightning, but not the pang of separation from you! You are your own master and shall go; but stay some days more and let me gaze on your feet." His humility relaxed the Master's resolution and He lingered for some time longer. Eagerly did the Bhattacharya invite and feast Him with dishes cooked in his own house. His wife, called 'Sháthi's mother,' cooked the meal: her history is marvellous, and I shall narrate it in detail later on.

After a halt of five days at the Bhattacharya's place, the Master asked leave to start. His eagerness forced the Bhattacharya to consent. He went with him to the temple and sought the permission of Jagannath. The serving priest presented the Master with the god's garland, which He joyously took as a symbol of permission.

The Lord Gaur started for the South in joy, after walking round Jagannath in the company of His disciples and the Bhattacharya. He took the road of Alálnáth, along the shore. Sarvabhauma sent Gopinath Acharya to bring from his house four loin-bands and wrappers and some *prasad*, to the Vipradwár gate. Then he begged the Master, "You must keep my request. On the bank of the Godavari dwells Rámánanda Ráy, governor of Vidyánagar.* Despise him not as a Shudra and worldling. See him for my sake. He is worthy of your society. The world has not another appreciative devotee like him. In him scholarship and faith have reached their extreme points. When you talk with him you will know his worth. I used to laugh at him as a Vaishnav, because I failed to understand his superhuman words. But Thy grace has now made me know his true merit. Conversation with him will disclose his greatness." The Master agreed, embraced him and bade him farewell saying, "Worship Krishna at home and bless me, so that through your favour I may return to Puri."

---

* *Vidya-nagar.*—Evidently *Rajmahendri*, now on the left bank of the Godavari. It was an important strategic point, being on the natural frontier between Kalinga and the kingdoms of the Madras coast.........In 1469 a minister of the Gajapati king was ruling in this town; in 1470 it was captured by the Muhammadan Sultan of the Bahmani dynasty. Soon after 1480 it was taken by the king of Orissa; about 1515 it was captured by Krishna Dev, the king of Vijayanagar, but restored. In 1543 we find it ruled by Vidyádri, a Prince of the Gajapati line, who lost it finally to the Muhammadans in 1571. (*Godavari Gazetteer*, 244-245.)

When the Master turned to go, Sarvabhauma fell down there in a faint, but the Master moved on quickly, without heeding him. Who can understand the heart and mind of the Master? The hearts of the great are at once tender as flowers and hard as the thunderbolt. Nityananda raised Bhattacharya and sent him home with his men. The faithful quickly overtook the Master, and Gopinath also arrived with the clothes and *prasád*. The Master went with them to Alálnáth, where He sang hymns for a long time, dancing and singing in rapture. The persons present flocked to gaze on the scene: they shouted *Hari! Hari!* while the Master danced in ecstasy in their midst. The people marvelled as they gazed at His golden hue, His crimson robe, and His tears of delight, His tremour and perspiration, which set off His beauty. All who came to see it forgot their homes and stayed to join in the dance and song of Shri Krishna Gopal; men and women, old and young, all were swept away by the tide of spiritual love. Seeing it Nityananda said to the faithful, "He will dance thus at every village [on the way]." It was high time, but the people did not leave Him; so Nityananda contrived a plan: He took the Master away for His noonday bath, the people rushing on all sides to look on. After the bath he led the Master to the temple, and as soon as his own men had entered he shut the door. He fed the Master, and they all ate His leavings. The crowd gathered outside the gate, shouting '*Hari! Hari!* Then he opened the door and the people entered joyfully to gaze on the Master.

The stream of people thus passed and repassed till the evening. They all became Vaishnavs and danced and sang [with the Master]. He passed the night there with the faithful, in delightful discourses on Krishna. Next morning after the morning bath, He bade farewell to the faithful. They fainted, but He looked not at them. The Master wended His way grieving at separation from them, Krishna-das following Him with the gourd. The faithful passed the day there in a fast, and returned sorrowing to Puri the next day. Like a raging lion the Master walked forth, chanting God's name in a transport of love. His words were :

Krishna! Krishna! Krishna! Krishna! Krishna!
Krishna! Krishna! O!
Krishna! Krishna! Krishna! Krishna! Krishna!
Krishna! Krishna! O!
Krishna! Krishna! Krishna! Krishna!
Krishna! Krishna! Save me!
Krishna! Krishna! Krishna! Krishna!
Krishna! Krishna! Deliver me!
Ram Raghav! Ram Raghav! Ram Raghav! Save me!
Krishna Keshav! Krishna Keshav! Krishna Keshav!
Deliver me!

As the Lord Gaur walked on reciting the above verses He met a wayfarer and asked him to chant Hari's name. Mad with love that man cried 'Hari! Krishna!' and followed the Master out of longing to gaze at Him. After a long embrace the Master dismissed him, filled with spiritual power.

The man on returning home made all his village Vaishnav, talking of Krishna, laughing, weeping, dancing incessantly, and urging all to take Krishna's name. Chance visitors from other villages became like Him from the sight of Him, and spread Vaishnavism in their own villages. In this way was the whole Southern country converted to

Vaishnavism. In this way did the Master make hundreds Vaishnav by embracing them in His travels. If He lodged and dined in anybody's house in a village, all the villagers flocked to see Him. Through the Master's grace they became great *bhaktas*, and acted as apostles for the deliverance of mankind. All the way to Setubandha, He did this; connection with Him made all the land Vaishnav. The power He had not manifested at Navadwip, He now put forth for the salvation of the South. He who worships the Master gains His favour and realizes the truth of these miracles. He who believes not in supernatural miracles loses both this world and the next.

In this way the Master travelled to the shrine of the Tortoise* [the Second Incarnation], saluted and praised the god, dancing, singing, smiling and weeping in rapture, to the wonder of by-standers. Crowds gathered to see Him; the very sight of His marvellous beauty and devotion made them Vaishnavs. They danced with uplifted arms chanting Krishna's name in deep emotion. These very men converted other villages. Thus did the nectar of Krishna's name overflow the country, Vaishnavism spreading from man to man.

After a time the Master came back to His senses. The priest of the Tortoise did Him great reverence. This happened everywhere that He went. In that village a Vaidik Brahman named Kurma, very reverently invited the Master, brought Him home, washed His feet, and with his whole family drank the washing of His feet; then he lovingly fed the Master with many kinds of dishes, and

---

* *Sri Kurmam*, 8 m.e. of Chicacole and the greatest place of pilgrimage to the Telegus. (*Ganjam Manual* 62).

they all partook of the leavings. He praised the Master thus: "Thy lotus-like feet, which Brahma himself adores, have come to my house. O my boundless good fortune! To-day my birth, race, and faith have been glorified. Lord, have mercy on me and take me with Thee! I cannot bear the sorrows of this worldly life." But the Master replied, "Say not so! Stay at home and recite Krishna's name ceaselessly. Teach Krishna's lore to whomsoever you meet with. At my bidding be thou an apostle and save this land! The world will never entangle you, but you will see me here again."

Every one at whose house He dined, made this request, and received this charge from the Master. Everywhere in His pilgrimage, till the return to Puri, it was exactly what He did at the Tortoise temple.

The night spent there, next morning, the Master bathed and resumed His journey; the Brahman Kurma followed Him long, but at last the Master persuaded him to return home. A high-minded Brahman named Vásudev, was covered with leprosy, but as the maggots dropped from his rotting limbs he used to pick them up and restore them to their places.* At night he heard of Chaitanya's arrival, and next morning went to Kurma's house to see Him; on hearing that the Master was gone, he fell down in a faint, and lamented in many ways. Just then the Master returned, embraced him, and lo! his leprosy as well as grief was gone at the touch and his body became sound and beautiful! He marvelled at the Master's grace and clasped His feet and praised Him by repeating the verse in the

* In Christian hagiology the same story is told about a saint of Europe, who addressed the maggots, "Eat, brothers, eat!"

Bhágabat X. lxxxi. 14, (Rukmini's message sent to Krishna by the mouth of a Brahman).

Long did he thank the Master, saying, "Listen, Gracious One! No man has your virtue. Even wretches fled from me at the stench of my body. But thou, Supreme Lord, hast touched me! Better for me my former state of misery, because henceforth my heart will swell with pride." The Master soothed him saying, "No, you will not be puffed up. Ever take Krishna's name, and save men by teaching them about Krishna. Soon will Krishna accept you."

So saying the Master vanished. The two Brahmans wept with joy at His grace, clasping each other by the neck. [Text, canto 7.]

CHAPTER VI

The Meeting with Ramananda Ray

Thus did the Master wend His way. On reaching the temple of the Nrisingha (Man-lion) Incarnation at Jiyad,* He made His bow and rapturously sang and danced long in honour of the god, saying, "Glory to Nrisingha! Glory to Nrisingha! Prahlád's Lord! Glory to you, O Lotus-lipped, O Bee on the Lotus!" [The *Bhágabat,* VII. ix. 1. verse quoted in Shridhar Goswami's commentary].

Many such verses did the Master recite as He prayed to the god. The serving priest presented Him with the god's garland. As before, a Brahman invited and fed the Master, who passed the night there. Next morning He took up His journey again, His emotion of faith making Him heedless of outer things day and night. As before, He made the people turn Vaishnav, and after a long time reached the bank of the Godavari, which reminded Him of the Jamuna, while the wood on the bank suggested Brindaban. After dancing in the wood, He crossed the river and bathed there. Sitting at the water's edge away from the *ghát,* the Master chanted Krishna's name. Just then arrived Rámánanda Ráy in a litter, attended by

---

* *Jiyad.*—Evidently *Simhachalam,* a hill five miles north of Vizagapatam, containing a temple to Narasimha. This is the most famous, richest and best sculptured shrine in Vizagapatam.......An inscription shows that a queen of Gonka III. covered the image with gold.... Architecturally the temple apparently deserves high praise. (*Vizagapatam Gazetteer,* 323-325, 28-29.)

musicians and many Vaidik Brahmans, to bathe. He bathed and performed the rites duly. The Master at first sight knew him for Ramananda Ráy, and longed to meet him, but sat checking His eagerness. Ramananda Ray came up to Him on seeing a *sannyási,* and wondered as he gazed on His person beaming like a hundred suns, His robe of the hue of the morning sun, His large vigorous frame, His eyes like the lotus. As he prostrated himself before the Master, the latter stood up and said, "Rise, and chant Krishna's name", and though thirsting with desire to embrace him, He asked, "Art thou Ramananda Ray?" The man answered, "Yes, I am that slave,—a vile Shudra." Passionately did the Master embrace him, and both tumbled down on the ground in excess of devotion, senseless with love, inert or perspiring, weeping, trembling, with hair standing on end, pale of hue, and lisping 'Krishna ! Krishna !'

The Vaidik Brahmans marvelled as they beheld it, and inly thought, "This *sannyasi,* we see, is powerful like Brahmá. Why does he weep after embracing a Shudra? This noble is a grave and learned man ; why then has he been maddened by the touch of the *sannyasi?*" The Master checked Himself on seeing strangers. The two composed themselves and sat down there. Smilingly the Master began, "Sarvabhauma Bhattacharya has spoken to me of your merits, and pressed me to see you. For that purpose have I come here. It is well that I have met you so easily." The Ray replied, "Sarvabhauma knows me for his servant, and is ever on the watch to do me good even indirectly. Through his grace have I met you, and to-day my life has become a success. That you have graciously touched this untouchable Shudra is the proof of your mercy and that of Sarvabhauma. Thou art the God Nárâyan himself, and I—a royal servant, a worldling, a wretch! In touching me thou didst not feel repulsion or fear of the Vedas! The Vedas forbid you even to look at me. Thy mercy leads thee to perform a forbidden act. Thou art God indeed; who can know thy ways? For delivering me hast thou come here, O Fountain of Mercy! O Saviour of the Fallen! Such is the habit of the great, —to save a wretch he goes out of his way to pay him a visit! *Vide* the *Bhágabat*, X. viii. 2, Nanda's words to Garga:—

'Master, that saints travel from their own hermitages is only for doing [spiritual] good to those householders who cannot leave their houses; there is no other purpose in it.'

The thousand men, Brahmans and others, in my train, have had their hearts melted by Thy sight. All of them are shouting *Krishna*! *Hari*! All are tremulous, all are weeping in joy. Verily you have every characteristic, internal and external, of God. No mortal can possess such supernatural power!"

The Master replied, "You are the greatest of devotees. It is *your* sight that has softened the hearts of all. Why impute it to another? I am only a *sannyasi* holding the theory of illusion (*máyá-vád*), but even I have been steeped in the love of Krishna by your touch. Knowing that my heart is hard to reform, Sarvabhauma had asked me to meet you."

Thus did the two praise each other, each delighted to see the other. Then a Vaishnav Vaidik Brahman bowed and invited the Master, who accepted the invitation knowing him to be a Vaishnav. Smiling, the Master said to Ramananda, "I wish to hear the discourse of Krishna from your lips. I hope I shall see you again." The Ray replied, "You have come here to save this sinner. But my wicked heart has not been cleansed by the mere sight of you. Stay for 5 or 7 days to purge my hard heart of its sins." Ramananda Ray bowed and went away, though loth to part, while the Master went to the Brahman's house to dine. Eagerly did the two look for their meeting in the evening. As the Master was sitting after his sunset bath, the Rây arrived with a servant. He bowed to the Master, who embraced him. The two conversed in a retired spot. The Master bade him recite the verses indicating the means of gaining devotion (*sádhya*). The Ray replied, "We acquire faith in Vishnu by doing the duties of our rank. As the *Vishnu Puran*, III. viii. 8, says, '*Worship the Supreme Being Vishnu by doing the prescribed duties of your caste. There is no other means of pleasing Him.*'" The Master objected, "This is only an external means. Mention one more advanced." The Ray replied, "The highest means of acquiring devotion is to resign to Krishna the fruits of our acts, as the *Gitá*, IX. 27, puts it:

'*O Son of Kunti, consign to me whatever you do, be it eating, performing the hom ceremony, alms-giving, or austerity.*'"

The Master again objected, "This too is external. Go deeper into the subject." The Ray answered, "The highest means of devotion is abandoning one's caste-duties [out of love for Krishna], as the Lord says to Uddhav in the *Bhágabat*, XI. xi. 32:

'*He too is the highest of holy men, who knowing well the gain and loss of such a course, worships me by renouncing the Vedic rites and ceremonies of his caste, though these too were ordained by me.'*

Also, as the *Gitá*, xviii. 66, has it:—

'Take refuge in ME alone, giving up all religions. Grieve not; I will deliver thee from all sins.'"

But to this the Master objected, "This too is external. Tell me of a still higher means." The Ray answered, "Faith based on knowledge is the highest means of devotion. As Shri Krishna says to Arjun in the *Gitá*, xviii. 54:

'The peaceful soul that dwells on Brahma, and feels not sorrow or desire, but is the same in all states, gains my supreme bhakti.'"

Again the Master objected as before. The Ray answered, "Faith independent of knowledge is the highest instrument of devotion. Witness Brahmá's words to God in the *Bhagábat*, X. xiv. 3:

'Lord, hard as Thou art to be won in the Universe, yet they realize Thee who reject the quest of theological knowledge but stay at home, listening to Thy story as told by holy men and accepting it with all their mind, body and soul.'"

The Master remarked, "It is so; but mention a higher still." The Ray said, "The highest devotion is *love* (*prem-bhakti*)." Witness the following verses of Ramananda Ray quoted in the *Padyávali*, cantos xi and xii respectively:

'We relish food and drink only so long as we have hunger and thirst. Similarly, the devotee delights not in worshipping his heart's darling with elaborate preparations, but in love alone.'

'Get a heart inspired with love of Krishna, if ever you

can get it. Its only price is greed,—a price which we cannot acquire even by the accumulated merits of ten millions of births.' "

The Master remarked as before. The Ray replied, "The love of a *servant* is the highest devotion. Witness the speech of Durváshá in the *Bhágabat,* IX. v. 11:—

'What is too hard for the Lord's servants to gain, as the very listening to His name purifies all creatures?' "

The Master remarked, "It is so, but give a still deeper cause." The Ray replied, "Love as for a *comrade* is the highest form of devotion. Witness Shukdev's words to Parikshit, in the *Bhágabat,* X. xii. 10:—

'God is known to the good as the consciousness of divine pleasure (brahma-sukhánubhuti), and to His servants as the Supreme Object of Adoration. That such a God played with the deluded cow-boys in the garb of a human child, was due to their excessive merit.' "

The Master said, "This too is good. Mention a higher one still." The Ray went on, "The highest devotion is love as for a *child.* Witness the following verses of the *Bhagabat*:

'O Shukdev! what high-class meritorious deeds did Nanda perform, and what did the blessed Yashoda do that she suckled the Divine Being?" (X. viii. 36).

'The bliss that the cowherd's wife Yashodá derived from her Saviour-son was never gained by Brahmá, or Shiva, or even by Lakshmi though clasped to His person.' (X. ix. 15.)"

The Master said, "This is good, no doubt. But mention a higher still." The Ray replied, "Passion as for a *lover* is the highest form of devotion. Witness the following verses of the *Bhagabat*:

'Verily the favour shown by the Supreme Being to the fair ones of Brindaban, when in the rása sport He clasped them round the neck with His arms,—was not enjoyed even by Lakshmi, who is held to His heart, nor by the heavenly nymphs though blooming and odorous like the lotus; not to speak of other women.' (X. xlvii. 53.)"'

The Ray continued, "Many are the means of attaining to Krishna, and there are degrees of such attainment. By whichever of these means a man is inspired, it appears as the highest to him. It is only when we judge from a position of detachment that we can discriminate them as good, better, and best.

The preceding five passions are arranged in the order of their upward development. With the increase of quality there is an increase of deliciousness at each step. The *shánta* passion attains its maturity in the *dásya*, the *dásya* in the *sakhya*, the *sakhya* in the *bátsalya*, and all of these four are concentrated in the *madhura*,—just as the properties of the four elements, *viz.*, sky, air, &c. increase in an advancing order and are all united in the fifth element, the Earth. The full attainment of Krishna results from this last passion of conjugal love (*premá*). The *Bhagabat* asserts that Krishna is a slave to devotion in the form of *premá*.

Krishna's purpose remains constant in all ages: He makes a return to our adoration in exactly the same form in which we offer it. But He cannot reciprocate this *prem* adoration to the full, and so remains our debtor, as the *Bhagabat* affirms. (X. xxxii. 21, Krishna's words to the milk-maids).

True, Krishna is the highest type of beauty and grace,

but even His charm increases when He is in the company of the Lady of Braja. Witness the *Bhagabat*, X. xxxiii. 6:

'As the beauty of the emerald is set off when it is placed amidst golden-coloured gems, so shines Krishna when girt round by the beaming girls of Brindaban.' "

The Master remarked, "This is indeed the extreme point among the means of devotion. Kindly tell me if there is anything beyond it!" The Ray said, "I did not know before that the earth contained any man who would inquire beyond this point! Of all kinds of conjugal passion Radha's love is celebrated in all our Scriptures as the highest.

The Master said, "Speak on! I delight to hear. A wondrous stream of nectar is flowing out of your lips. Show how Krishna abducted Rádhá for fear of interruption by the other cow-herd girls; because a love that extends to others than the beloved is not deep enough. If you can show that for Radha's sake Krishna openly forsook the other Gopis, then I shall know that he passionately loved her." The Ray replied, "Hear, then, of this glorious power of love. The three worlds cannot match Radha's love. Krishna broke away from the circle of the *rása* dance of the Gopis and wandered through the woods mourning for Radha. Witness the *Git-Govinda*, canto III. verses 2 and 1, and the *Ujjwala-Nilmani*, verse 43.

Radha left the dance in anger and wounded pride. Krishna grew restless as he lost her. His whole heart was set on the *rása* dance, and Radha was the chain that bound his heart to it. In her absence, the *rása* dance palled on his taste. So he left the circle of dancers to seek her out. As he roamed hither and thither, without finding her, he grieved, stricken with Cupid's dart. A thousand million Gopis could not satiate his passion. From this you may infer Radha's merit!"

The Master said, "I have now learnt those spiritual mysteries for which I came to you. Now have I learnt how to ascertain the various methods of adoration. But I long to hear more: tell me of Krishna's form, of Radha's form,—what mystery is *rása,* what is the essence of love (*prem*). Be kind and tell me these mysteries; none but you can expound them." The Ray answered, "I know nothing of these things, but only utter what you inspire me with, as the parrot repeats what it has learnt by rote. You are God incarnate; who can comprehend your artifice? You send your message to my heart, and make my tongue deliver it, without my knowing whether I am speaking well or ill!"

The Master answered, "I am merely a *sannyasi,* a slave to the theory of illusion and ignorant of the mysteries of faith (*bhakti*). The society of Sarvabhauma has purified my mind, and I asked him to speak on devotion to Krishna. But he replied that he knew not Krishna's lore, and referred me to you as a master of it. So I came to you, on hearing of your reputation, and yet you praise me because I am a *sannyasi!* Be he a Brahman, be he a hermit, be he even a Shudra,—if he knows Krishna's mysteries, he is a *guru.* Cheat me not [of such knowledge] for my being a *sannyasi.* Fill my mind by holding forth on the mysteries of Radha and Krishna."

The Ray was a great devotee and adorer of Vishnu, and his mind was proof against Krishna's illusion. But he yielded to the Master's pressing, and his will was shaken. So he said, "I am a dancer and you are the manager of the theatre; I dance as you make me. My tongue is merely a harp, and you the musician who plays on it. I utter whatever you think of in your mind.

Krishna is the Highest God, the Perfect Being Himself, the source of all Incarnations, the chief of all causes. He is the source of the eternal Heaven, the eternal Incarnation, the eternal Universe. His body is composed of *sat, chit* and *ánanda;* He is the Son of Mathura's lord,—full of all wealth, all power, all *ras. Vide* the *Brahma Samhita* V. i.

At Brindaban He appeared as the supernatural youthful Cupid, at whose adoration the formula recited is Love, the offering presented is the seed of Love. There He drew all hearts—of men and women, of the animate and the inanimate. He was Cupid's self, the conqueror of hearts. Witness the *Bhagabat,* X. xxxii. 2.

He ravished the hearts of Incarnations like Lakshmi's husband, [*Vide,* the *Bhagabat,* X. lxxxix. 32]; He drew to Himself women like Lakshmi [*Vide* the *Bhagabat,* X. xvi. 32.]

His own beauty charmed His own heart, and He wished to embrace Himself [*Vide* the *Lalita-Mádhav,* Act viii. verse 28.]

Such in brief is Krishna's form. Now let me tell you a little of Radha's self. Krishna's powers are infinite, but three of them are the chief, *viz.,* the *chit* power, the illusion power (*máyá*), and the preservation power (*jiba*). These three I call the internal, the external, and the marginal (or adjacent). The highest is the internal *swarup* power. Witness the *Vishnu Puran,* VI. vii. 60.

Krishna's self is composed of *sat, chit* and *ánanda.* Therefore His *swarup* power must be of three kinds:

in the *ánanda* portion it is *hládini,* in the *sat* portion it is *sandhini,* in the *chit* portion it is *sambita.* Witness the *Vishnu Puran,* I. xii. 48:

What delights Krishna is named the *Ahladini* power, by which He enjoys delight. Krishna is Himself delight, and yet He tastes delight. *Hladini* has been created to give enjoyment to the faithful. The essence of *hladini* is named *prem* (love). The story of *prem* is filled with the emotions of *ánanda* and *chit. The* supreme emotion (*mahábhába*), is the quintessence of *prem.* The lady Radha is the personation of that supreme emotion. [*Vide* the *Brahma Samhita,* V. 33]." *** ***

The Master spoke, "This is the limit of the thing adored. Through your grace I have learnt it of a verity. None can gain the Adorable without adoration. Tell me kindly the way to gain Him."

The Ray answered, "I speak as you make me, without my knowing what I say. Where in all the three worlds can we find the constant man who cannot be shaken by your illusive play? You are speaking through my mouth; yet you are my listener! Hear, then, the deep mystery of adoration. The play of Radha with Krishna is extremely deep, and cannot be learnt from the *dásya, bátsalya* and other moods. The *sakhis* (female associates) alone are qualified for it; from them has this play (*lilá*) spread. This play cannot be kept up without *sakhis*; they alone relish this *lila* in full. *Sakhis* alone have a right to this *lila, i.e.,* those who adore Krishna in the spirit of His *sakhis.* Such votaries can practise devotion in the form of attending on Krishna and Radha in their secret bower. There is no other means of mastering this form of devotion. Witness the *Git-Govinda,* x. 17:

'What man versed in the deepest mystery (ras) will not take refuge at the feet of the sakhis,—the personations of the chief power, without whose help Radha and Krishna's pleasure-force and ' pleasure-manifestation, though self-expressive, cannot for a moment attain to fulness of development?''

The character of the *sakhis* baffles description. A *sakhi* does not long to play with Krishna all by herself; but she feels a keener delight in contriving Krishna's dalliance with Radha. Radha is verily the Wishing creeper (*Kalpalatá*) of the love of Krishna, and the *sakhis* are the leaves, flowers, and shoots of this creeper! If the nectar of dalliance with Krishna waters the creeper, the leaves, &c. delight in it ten million times more than if they themselves had been watered! *Vide* the *Git-Govinda,* x. 16.

The *sakhis* do not wish for Krishna's embrace, but they exert themselves to make Krishna embrace Radha. For this purpose they send Krishna to her under a thousand pretexts. Thereby they gain a pleasure ten million times sweeter than that of selfish enjoyment. The unselfish devotion of these towards each other strengthens the deliciousness (*ras*), and the sight of such unselfish love delights Krishna. The love felt by the Gopis is not truly earthly lust; for the sake of analogy we call it lust (*kám*).

Earthly lust seeks sensual gratification for one's own self. The passion of the Gopis, on the other hand, seeks Krishna's enjoyment, abandoning all idea of self. They hanker not for their own pleasure, but if they embrace Krishna it is only to please *Him.*

He whose heart is lured by the nectar of the Gopi's

passion, adores Krishna abandoning Vedic worship. That man wins in Brindaban the Darling of Braja's lord, who adores Him by following the path of passionate love (*rág*). He who adores Krishna in the spirit of any of the people of Braja [contemporaneous with Krishna], is born at Braja in his next birth in the form of that person whose passion he imitated, and thus gains Krishna. This is proved by the *Upanishads* and the *Shrutis*. Witness the *Bhagabat*, X. lxxxvii. 19.

In that verse the term *samadrisha* indicates adoration in that spirit, the term *samáh* speaks of the acquisition by the gods of the persons of the Gopis, *anghri padma sudhá* means the delight of Krishna's society. At Braja you will not gain Krishna by following the path of prescribed ceremonies. *Vide* the *Bhagabat*, X. ix. 16:

'Ascetics proud of their conquest of the flesh, and scholars centred in themselves, cannot gain the Supreme Lord so easily as His devotees (bhaktas) can.'

Therefore, having taken on ourselves the attitude of the Gopis, we daily meditate on Krishna's dalliance with Radhá. In the *siddhi* body we meditate and serve it, and in the next birth we gain Radha-Krishna's feet by being born as *sakhis*. You cannot gain Krishna, however much you adore Him, if you only meditate on Him as a divinity and not serve Him as a Gopi. See, how Lakshmi adored Him, but could not gain Him in Braja. *Vide* the *Bhagabat*, X. xlvii. 53."

On hearing all this the Master embraced him, and the two wept holding each other by the neck. Thus did they pass the night in transports of devotion, and at dawn parted, each to his own work. When taking leave, Ramananda Ray clasped the Master's feet and begged him,

"You have come here out of pity for me. Stay here therefore for some ten days to reform my sinful heart. None but you can deliver mankind ; none else can impart love for Krishna."

The Master answered, "I came here on hearing of your merits, to purify my own mind by listening to your discourses on Krishna. You are indeed worthy of your reputation. You are the limit of human knowledge as regards the mystery of the love of Krishna and Radha. What of ten days? So long as I live, I cannot part with you. Let us two dwell together at Puri, passing our days happily in talk about Krishna." So they parted. In the evening the Ray came again. The two sat together in seclusion and held a delightful dialogue, the Master asking and Ramananda answering throughout the night.

The Master asked, "Which science is the chief of sciences?" The Ray answered, "There is no [true] science except devotion to Krishna." "What is the greatest glory in a creature?" "The fame of being a devotee of Krishna's love." "What wealth is estimable among human possessions?" "He is wealthy indeed who loves Radha and Krishna." "What is the heaviest of sorrows?" "There is no sorrow other than lack of devotion to Krishna." "Whom should we consider as truly liberated?" "He is the foremost of the emancipated who loves Krishna." "What song among all songs is peculiarly own to creatures?" "That ditty which speaks of the amorous sports of Krishna and Radha." "What is the best of right courses?" "There is no right course except the society of Krishna's devotees." "Whom does creation ceaselessly remember?" "The name, virtues, and exploits of Krishna are the chief things to be remembered." "What is the proper subject of meditation for mankind?" "The lotus-feet of Radha and Krishna are the chief object of meditation." "Where ought a man to live abandoning all else?" "Brindaban, the land of Braja, where the *rása* play was performed." "What is the best thing for a creature to hear?" "The love-dalliance of Radhá and Krishna is a potent medicine to the ear." "What is the chief object of worship?" "The highest objects of adoration are the coupled names Radha-Krishna." "What are the respective destinations of those who desire liberation and devotion?" "One gets an immovable body, the other a celestial person. The foolish crow pecks at the ash-fruit (*nimba*), while the connoisseur cuckoo feeds on the mango-blossom of love. The luckless scholar tastes arid theological knowledge, while the lucky [devotee] drinks the nectar of Krishna's love."

Thus did the two while away the night in talking of Krishna, dancing, singing, and weeping. At dawn they returned, each to his own duties.

Next evening the Ray came again, and after discoursing on Krishna in a loving communion for some time, he clasped the Master's feet and implored Him, "The mysteries of Krishna, Radha, love, *rása*, and *lilá*, are diverse. But you have made them all clear to my heart. It has been as if Narayan taught the Vedas to Brahmá. Such are the ways of the Searcher of Hearts; He does not outwardly tell us of a thing, but reveals it to our hearts. *Vide* the *Bhágabat*, I. i. 1.

There is one doubt still in my heart. Be good enough to resolve it. When I first saw you, you looked like a *sannyasi*; but now I behold in you Krishna, the cowherd!

Lo, there stands before you a golden idol, the golden hue of which envelopes all your body. That reveals the flute held to your lips and your lotus-eyes glancing with many emotions! I marvel as I behold you in this form. Tell me truly the cause of it." The Master replied, "Deep is your love for Krishna. Know this to be the effect of love that when the true devotee gazes on any object, animate or inanimate, Krishna is manifested to him in that object. The object gazed at may be inanimate or animate, but he sees not its natural form; his adored deity appears in everything. *Vide* the *Bhagabat*, XI. ii. 43, Hari's words to Janak:—

He is the highest of devotees who beholds in every creature the God of his adoration, and all creation in the spirit of God.

Also, the *Bhagabat*, X. xxxv. 5, the speech of the Gopis to Krishna:—

Then the fruit and flower laden branches of plants and creepers felt as it were within themselves the God who was manifesting Himself, and with their limbs thrilling with delight began to shed drops of honey.

Deep is your love for Radha and Krishna; hence you behold Them in everything." The Ray objected, "Master, leave thou thy tricks. Conceal not thy true form from me. Having taken on thyself the emotion and beauty of Radhiká, thou hast become incarnate in order to taste thy own delight. Thy secret object is the enjoyment of love; incidentally thou hast filled the universe with love. Thou hast come of thy own accord to deliver me. And now thou deludest me! What sort of conduct is this?"

Then the Master smiled and manifested His true form in which were blended Krishna, the Prince of delight (*ras*) and God, the Supreme Emotion. In rapture Ramananda fainted and rolled on the ground. The Master touched his arm and brought him back to his senses. Then the Ráy beheld the Master looking like a *sannyasi*; but the latter embraced him and soothed him thus, "Who else than you can behold this form? You know fully my essence and mysterious exploits (*lilá*); hence have I shown you this form. My body is not of a fair complexion, but this complexion is due to contact with Radha's body. She touches none except the Prince of the Cowherds. I make my own heart imagine her emotions, and thus I taste the delicious sweetness of Krishna. My acts are not hidden from you. Even if I were to conceal any, you would know it by the compelling force of your love. Keep this matter a secret from the public, lest people should laugh at my endeavours as those of a mad man. I am a mad man, and so are you; we two are a match!"

Thus did the Master spend ten days happily in sweet discourse about Krishna with Ramananda Ray. Much did He discuss the secret pleasure-sport of Brindaban, but could not come to the end of the subject. If a man discovers a mine with copper, bronze, silver, gold, gem, and the wishing stone deposited in successive layers, he comes upon richer and richer things as he goes on digging. Similarly did the Master question Rámá Ráy and get his answer.

Next day He took leave of the Ray and ordered him, "Give up your earthly concerns and go to Puri, where I shall soon return after finishing my pilgrimage. There we shall live together passing our days happily in talking about Krishna."

So saying He sent Ramananda home with an embrace,

and then lay down to sleep. At dawn the Master saw a Hanumán (monkey), bowed to it, and set out. All classes of people at Vidyá-pur, on meeting with the Master, quitted their own faiths and turned Vaishnav. Ramananda was distracted by the absence of the Master and ever meditated on Him, utterly disregarding all his own affairs...... Chaitanya's character is by nature like thickened milk, Ramananda's character is sugar added to it, and the dalliance of Radha and Krishna is like camphor thrown into this compound, which only the fortunate can taste. He who once drinks it in through his ears, can never leave it for its deliciousness. All spiritual truths are learnt if you hear it ; it creates faith and love in Radha-Krishna's feet.

Know the hidden truth of Chaitanya from this episode. Attend to it with faith ; do not reason. This supernatural deed is deeply mysterious. You can realize it if you believe, but reasoning will only set it afar off. This precious thing is for them only whose sole riches are the feet of Shri Chaitanya, Nityananda, and Adwaita...I have celebrated the Meeting with Ramananda on the basis of Damodar Swarup's Diary (*Karchá*). [Text, canto 8.]

CHAPTER VII

The Pilgrimage to the South

The Master travelled very extensively in the South, visiting thousands of holy places. At His touch they became the holiest of holy places. Under the pretext of a pilgrimage He delivered the people of that country. I shall only give a list of the places without arranging them in the order in which they were visited.

As before, whoever met Him on the way and all the people of every village that He lodged in, were turned into Vaishnavs and made to chant Hari's name. *They* in their turn converted other villages. Diverse were the people of the South,—some scholars, some ritualists, some extreme sceptics. Lo! the marvellous effect of the sight of the Master! all such men gave up their own creeds and turned Vaishnav. Even among the Vaishnavs [of the South] some were worshippers of Vishnu in the incarnation of Ram, some the followers of Madhwacharya, some of Ramanuj's sect of Shri Vaishnavs. All of them, on meeting with the Master, became worshippers of Vishṇu in the incarnation of Krishna, and began to chant Krishna's name.

The Master journeyed on, reciting the verse:

O Ram Raghav! O Ram Raghav! O Ram Raghav!
Deliver me!
O Krishna Keshav! O Krishna Keshav! O Krishna Keshav!
Save me!

He bathed in the Ganga Gotami (Godavari). At

Mallikárjun He visited the shrine of Mahesha, where He made all the people recite Krishna's name. He beheld the Rámdás Mahádev, and also the Man-Lion at Ahobal, bowing to and glorifying the latter. At Siddha-bat is the image of Sitá's lord ; the Master bowed to the image of Ram and sang hymns to it. There He was invited by a Brahman of the place, who incessantly took Ram's name and no other. After passing the day in his house as his guest, the Master proceeded on. At Skanda-kshetra He visited Kártik, and at Tri-matha the god Tri-vikrama, whence He returned to that Brahman's house at Siddha-bat, but found him chanting Krishna's name! After dinner the Master asked him, "Why, Brahman! has this change come over you? Formerly you used to cry 'Ram, Ram' and now you chant Krishna's name!" The Brahman replied, "This is the effect of your visit. The sight of you changed my life-long habit. From childhood have I been chanting Ram's name ; but when I met you I once uttered the word 'Krishna,' and since then Krishna's name has settled on my tongue. It is Krishna's name that comes out of my mouth, while the name of Ram has disappeared. It had been my practice since my boyhood to collect the texts bearing on the glory of God's names. In the *Pádma Purán*, we read :

'Yogis sport (rama) in the eternal God, whose self is composed of sat, chit, *and* ananda. *Hence the term Rám means the Supreme God.'*

Again, the *Mahábhárat,* Udyog Parba, canto lxxi. 4, says *'The term "Krishna", meaning the Supreme God, has been derived from the verb* krish *meaning existence and the inflexion* na *meaning cessation.*

So, the two names *Ram* and *Krishna* appeared equal,

but I next found texts making a discrimination between them. The *Padma Purán* has this:

'O perfect-featured Darling! O my heart's Delight! reciting the word Rám thrice earns as much merit as taking [God's] name a thousand times!'

The *Brahmánda Purán* asserts,—

'A single utterance of the name of Krishna is as efficacious as reciting God's thousand sacred epithets three times in succession.

The last text proves the immeasurable excellence of Krishna's name. And yet I could not repeat it, only because I found delight in the name of *Ram*, the god of my vows (*ishtadev*), and took the latter incessantly. When at your visit the word *Krishna* rose [to my lips], my heart recognized its glory. And I truly inferred that you are Krishna himself." So saying the Brahman fell at the Master's feet, who after bestowing His grace left him the next day.

At Vriddha Kashi the Master visited Shiva, and thence went on to another village, where He lodged with the Brahmans. So great was His power that countless people, —hundreds of thousand, millions even,— came to see [Him]. Beholding the beauty and religious ecstasy of the Master they all chanted Krishna's name, and the whole region was converted to Vaishnavism. He refuted and proved faulty all the doctrines of the logicians, *mimánsakas*, illusionists, and the followers of Sánkhya, Patanjal, Smriti, Purán, and Veda,—though they were strong in defending their tenets. Everywhere the Master established the dogmas of Vaishnavism, which none could refute. His vanquished antagonists accepted His creed, and so He made the South Vaishnav. On hearing of His scholarship the sceptics (*páshandi*) came to Him, boastfully bringing their pupils with them. A very learned Buddhist professor held forth on the nine doctrines of his church before the Master. Though the Buddhists are unfit to be talked to or even to be looked at, yet the Master argued with him to lower his pride. The very Buddhist philosophy of nine tenets, though rich in logical reasoning, was torn to pieces by the Master's argumentation. The Buddhist professor raised all his nine questions, but only to be refuted by the Master's vigorous logic. The great philosophers were all vanquished ; the audience tittered ; the Buddhist felt shame and alarm. Knowing that the Master was a Vaishnav, the Buddhists retired and hatched a wicked plan : They placed before the Master a plate of unclean rice, describing it as Vishnu's *prasád*. But just then a huge bird swooped down and carried off the plate in its beak ! The rice falling on the bodies of the Buddhists was [openly] rendered impure ; the plate fell down slanting on the Buddhist professor's head, cutting it open, and throwing him down in a fit. His disciples lifted up their voices in lamentation, and sought the Master's feet imploring Him, "Thou art God incarnate ! O forgive us ! Out of thy grace restore our teacher." The Master replied, "Cry out, all of you, Krishna's name. Pour the word loudly into your teacher's ears, and he will recover." They did it, the professor rose up and began to chant *Hari! Hari!* He did reverence to the Master saluting Him as Krishna, to the wonder of all. After this playful act the Son of Shachi vanished ; none could see Him.

He arrived at Tirupati Tirumal, where He beheld the four-armed idol, and then advanced to Venkátár. At Tirupati He beheld the image of Ram, to which He bowed and sang hymns. The people marvelled at His powers. Then He came to the Man-Lion of Páná, which He saluted and extolled in a transport of love. At Shiva Kánchi he visited Shiva ; His power turned the worshippers of Shakti and Shiva into Vaishnavs. At Vishnu Kanchi he beheld Lakshmi and Narayan, to whom He bowed and prayed long, danced and sang in fervour. His stay of two days bowed the hearts of men to Krishna. Thence by way of Tirumal He went to Tri-kál-hasti, and bowed to the image of Mahadev there. And so on to the Paksha-tirtha, the Shiva, the Vriddhakál-tirtha (the shrine of the White Boar), Pitámbar [probably Chidambaram] (the shrine of Shiva), the Shiyáli Bhairabi Devi, the bank of the Kaveri, Gosamáj (Shaiva holy place) and Bedáwan, (where He adored the Amrita-linga Shiva). Everywhere the worshippers at Shiva's shrines were turned into Vaishnavs. Thence He reached Devasthan, a Vaishnav shrine, and there kept constant company with the Shri-Vaishnavs. Proceeding further He visited the lake formed by Kumbhakarna's skull, the Shiva-kshetra, Pápa-náshan (a shrine of Vishnu), and Shri-rangam, where He bathed in the Kaveri and then adored Ranganath, bowing and hymning to the god to His heart's satisfaction, and dancing and singing in rapture, to the marvel of all beholders.

Here a Shri-Vaishnav named Venkata Bhatta invited the Master to his house, reverently washed His feet and with his whole family drank off the water. After feeding he besought the Master thus:—"Master, the four months of asceticism (*cháturmásya*) are at hand. I pray thee pass them in my house, and of thy grace save me by discoursing on Krishna." At his house the Master stayed for four months, passing the time happily in talking about Krishna with the Bhatta. Daily He bathed in the Kaveri, visited Shri Ranga, and danced in ecstasy. All men flocked to gaze on His beauty and rapture of devotion, and at the sight they forgot sorrow and misery. From all quarters flocked hundreds of thousands, and as they beheld the Master they chanted Krishna's name and no other term. All became worshippers of Krishna, to the marvel of mankind. The Brahmans resident at Shri Ranga invited Him on successive days; but when the four months were over there were some Brahmans left who had had no opportunity to entertain Him.

In that holy place dwelt a Brahman devoted to Vishnu, who recited the *Gitá* in the temple. In the fervour of delight he read the 18 cantos, making mistakes, at which some scoffed, some laughed, some chid him, but he heeded them not and went on with his readings in a rapt mood. The Master delighted as He beheld the reader's tears of delight, tremour, and perspiration at his task, and asked him, "Hark you, Sir! what [deep] meaning inspires you with such rapture?" The Brahman replied, "I am an ignorant man, not knowing the meanings of words. The *Gitá* I read at my *guru's* bidding, correctly or incorrectly as it may be. My heart is rapt when I behold [before my mind's eye] the dark beauty of Krishna as he sits as driver in Arjun's chariot giving moral lessons. I can never bring myself to give up reading the *Gitá*, because I ever behold HIM so long as I read the book." To him the Master spoke thus, "Thou alone art truly worthy to read the *Gitá*, as thou knowest the essence of its meaning." So saying He embraced the Brahman, who, however, clasped His feet and prayed, "The sight of you gives me double the joy. Verily I think you are that Krishna." He could recognize the true nature of the Master, as the love of Krishna had purged his mind [of its grossness]. But the Master cautioned him not to tell it to any one else. The Brahman became a devout admirer of the Master and never parted from Him in those four months, which He spent at the Bhatta's house in blissful discourse about Krishna. The Bhatta's household gods were Lakshmi and Narayan. The Master, pleased with his devotion, ever treated the Bhatta like a friend, constantly joking with him, as is the manner of friendship. One day He asked, "Bhatta! your Lakshmi is the type of devoted and chaste wives. My god is Krishna, a cow-herd. How could such a chaste lady seek this other man's society? Why did she for this object discard pleasure and perform endless austerities? Witness the following verse of the *Bhagabat*, X. xvi. 32:—

"Lord! Out of a longing to be worthy to touch the dust of Thy feet, Lakshmi, though a [weak] woman, abstained from enjoyment and went through long penances, etc."

The Bhatta answered, "Krishna and Narayan are essentially one; only Krishna showed more of sportiveness and charm. Hence Lakshmi's chastity was not marred when she, for the sake of delight, sought Krishna's company [Quotation from the *Bhakti-rasámrita-sindhu*]. Playful Lakshmi desired Krishna for the sake of the greater gain and *rása* delight afforded by His society. What harm is there in it? Why are you joking?" The Master rejoined, "I know there is nothing to blame in it. The *Shastra* asserts that Lakshmi never enjoyed the *rása* dance with Krishna [*Vide Bhagabat*, X. xlvii. 53]. But the Shrutis attained to Krishna's society by their austerities. [*Ibid*, X. lxxxvii. 19]. What was the reason of this difference?" "My mind fails to explain the reason, as I am a petty creature with a weak understanding, while God's acts are infinite like the deep ocean. You are Krishna's self and know your own exploits. Their inner meaning is known only to those on whom you have bestowed such knowledge." The Master said, "Such is the natural characteristic of Krishna that by His sweetness He wins all hearts. The men of Brindaban knew Him not as God, because He came to them as one of themselves. One tied Him to the wooden pestle (*udukhal*), fancying Him to be her son. Some mounted on His back, taking Him to be a play-fellow. The people of Brindaban knew Him as the son of Braja's chief, and not as the Godhead. He who adores Krishna in the manner of the people of Brindaban, can alone attain to Him there. *Vide Bhagabat,* X. ix. 16. The Shrutis imitated the milk-maids [*Gopis*] and by taking the form of the Gopis they obtained the Son of the Queen of Mathura. They were incarnated in the bodies of the Gopis of Braja, and so disported with Krishna in the *rása* play. Krishna was of the milkman caste; the Gopis were his dear ones; so Krishna refused goddesses and other women. Lakshmi wanted to unite with Krishna in His form of a milkman, and yet she did not seek Him by assuming the shape of a Gopi. But in no other form than that of a Gopi can the *rása* pleasure be consummated, as Vyás has said in his verses, *viz., Bhagabat,* X. xlvii. 53."

Before this the Bhatta used to think in his pride, "Narayan is God Himself, and the worship of Him is the highest stage. And therefore the worship offered by the Shri-Vaishnavs is the highest form of adoration." But the Master, to dash his folly down, opened all this controversy by means of a jest. He addressed him thus, "Bhatta, doubt not, know of a verity that Krishna is God Himself. Narayan is only the manifestation of the power (*vilás*) of Krishna. Therefore could Krishna steal the hearts of Lakshmi and others. (*Vide Bhagabat* I. iii 28). Krishna surpassed Narayan in power. Hence did Lakshmi ever long for Krishna. The verse you have read proves that Krishna is God incarnate. (*Vide Bhakti-rasámrita-sindhu*, pt. 1. ii. 32). Krishna stole the heart of Lakshmi but Narayan could not (conversely) win the love of the Gopis. What to speak of Narayan? Even Krishna himself, when He assumed the form of the four-armed Narayan to amuse the Gopis, failed to win their love in that shape! (*Vide Lalita-Madhav*, vi. 13)." Thus did the Master humble his pride, but then He gave a new turn to the conclusion to soothe the Bhatta's feelings, saying, "Grieve not, Bhatta, I have only jested. Listen to the teaching of the *Shastra* in which Vaishnavs believe: Just as Narayan and Krishna are one essence, so are Lakshmi and the Gopis identical and not diverse. Lakshmi in the garb of the Gopis tasted Krishna's company. In theology it is a sin to recognize a plurality of gods. The devotee meditates on one and the same God [diversely according to his fancy]; he gives different images to the same deity."

The Bhatta spoke, "I am a miserable creature, while thou art that Krishna, the Incarnate God. I know nothing of the unfathomable ways of God, but I hold as truth whatever you tell me. Fully have I been blessed by Lakshmi-Narayan, as His grace has enabled me to see thy feet. Thou hast graciously spoken to me of the glory of Krishna, whose beauty, qualities and powers are beyond human calculation. Now have I learnt that devotion to

Krishna passes all else. You have blest me by unfolding this truth." So saying the Bhatta clasped the Master's feet, who graciously hugged him to His bosom.

The four months came to an end. The Master took leave of the Bhatta and from Shri-rangam set out for the South. The Bhatta wanted to leave his home and follow Him, but with great effort the Master turned him back. When He left, the Bhatta fainted away (in grief). Thus did Shachi's Son disport Himself.

To the Rishava peak He went and there prayed to the deity Narayan, and visited Paramananda Puri, who was spending his "four months" there. The Master bowed at the feet of the Puri, who embraced Him. For three days they lived together in that Brahman's house, lovingly talking on Krishna's delightful lore. The Puri said, "I am going to Jagannath, whence I shall proceed to Bengal to bathe in the Ganges." The Master answered, "Go to the Niláchal, where I shall shortly join you on my return from Setubandha. I long to keep company with you. Do kindly visit the Nilachal." So He parted from the Puri and joyfully proceeded further south. The Puri went to the Nilachal, while the Master visited Shri-Shaila, where lived a Brahman named Shiva-Durga. Rejoicing to see the Master, he feasted Him for three days, and the two discoursed of mysteries in secret. After friendly association with him, the Master left him and went to the city of Kámakoshti, and thence to the Southern Mathura [Madura], where He was invited by a Brahman, noble-minded, detached from the world, and a worshipper of Ram. After bathing in the Kritamálá, the Master went to his house ; but as the Brahman never cooked, he could place no food before the guest. The Master asked, "Hark you, Sir, it is noon and yet you are not cooking? Why is it?" The Brahman replied, "Master, I live in the forest, where at present nothing can be had for cooking. But Lakshman will bring some wild herbs, fruits, and roots, and then will Sita cook them." The Master was pleased with the Brahman's devotion. The host now hurriedly began cooking and the Master was fed in the third quarter of the day. But the Brahman himself fasted, at which the Master asked, "Why do you fast? What grieves you? Why mourn you?" The Brahman replied, "I have no need to live; I shall destroy myself by jumping into fire or water. The divine Sita, the mother of the world and the emblem of Supreme Goodness, was (rudely) touched by a demon, as I hear. So I ought not to live. This sorrow consumes me, though my spirit does not leave the body." To him the Master thus: "Think not so any longer. You are learned and yet you do not judge the matter in your mind! Sita, the beloved of God, is the embodiment of spirituality and bliss (*chit ánanda*). Physical senses cannot see her, not to speak of touching her. Ravan abducted only an illusive image of Sita, while the true Sita had disappeared.* The Vedas and the Purans constantly teach this truth that the Material cannot take cognisance of what is non-Material. Believe my words, and never harbour such sad thoughts again." Reassured by the Master's words the Brahman dined and took delight in life.

After bathing in the Kritamálá, the Master went to Durbesan, where he saw the image of Raghunath. Thence

---

* This is exactly like the version of the legend of the abduction of Helen given by Stesichorus and accepted by Euripides in his *Helena*.

to Mahendra hill, where He adored Parashu Ram. At Setubandha He bathed in the Dhanu-tirtha (Bow shrine). Visiting Rameshwar, He rested there. An assembly of Brahmans was listening to the reading of the *Kurma Puran*, in the course of which the episode of chaste women was reached. The narrative declared that Ravan stole only a false phantom of Sita. At the sight of Ravan the true Sita sought refuge with Fire, who lodged her with Parvati, while he deluded Ravan by giving up to him a false image of Sita. After Ram had slain Ravan, and Sita submitted to the ordeal of fire, the false Sita vanished, while the real Sita was delivered to Ram by Fire. The Master was delighted to hear this theory. So He borrowed from the Brahman the leaf (containing the passage), and made a copy for being placed in the book, while He took the old leaf for creating conviction and returned to the Southern Mathura, where He gave the leaf to the Brahman Rámdas.

At this the Brahman was overjoyed and clasped the Master's feet weeping and saying, "Thou art Rám incarnate, visiting me in the disguise of a *sannyasi*, and raising me from deep sorrow. Do consent to dine at my house to-day, because on that day I was too melancholy to entertain thee worthily. It is my good fortune that thou hast come again!"

So saying the Brahman cooked deliciously and feasted the Master nicely. After passing the night under his roof, the Master went to the Támraparni in the Pandya land, where He bathed in the river and wandered on the bank gazing at the Nine Tirupadis in wonder.

Thence He visited Chiyartálá (the shrine of Ram Lakshman), Til Kánchi (the shrine of Shiva), Gajendra-Mokshan (where there was an image of Vishnu), Pána-garhi (shrine of Rám), Chámtápur (Rám Lakshman), Shri Vaikuntha (Vishnu), the Malay Mountain (Agastya), Kanyá Kumári [Cape Comorin], Amlitalá (Rám), the Mallar land (where the Bhattamáris dwelt), and then after seeing Tamal Kártik, He reached Betápáni (Raghunath's shrine), where He passed the night.

The Master's companion, the Brahman Krishna-das, met a Bhattamari, who tempted the simple Brahman by offering him a woman and money. In the morning Krishna-das went away to the Bhattamari. Soon the Master came in quest of him and addressed the Bhattamari tribe thus, "Why have you detained my Brahman (follower)? I am, as you see, a *sannyasi*; and so are you too. It is unfair of you to put me in trouble."

At this the Bhattamaris took up arms and flocked round the Master to thrash Him. But the weapons dropped from their hands and struck their own limbs, so that they fled awav on all sides. Lamentation rose in their houses. The Master dragged Krishna-das away by the hair, and that day reached the Payaswini river, in which He bathed and visited the temple of Adi Keshav, where He bowed, prayed, danced and sang for a long while in rapture, to the amazement of the beholders. All the people treated Him very respectfully and He joined the assembly of the very devout there. Here He got a manuscript of the book *Brahma-samhitádhyáya* to His boundless delight, tremour, weeping, thrill, perspiration, stupor, and frenzy (of joy),—because the *Brahma Samhita* is unrivalled among works of exegetics (*siddhanta shastra*) and it is the chief instrument for teaching the glory of Govinda, as it expresses vast dogmas in a few words. It is the very cream of Vaishnav sacred writings.

Very carefully did He get the book copied. Thence He went to Ananta Padmanáv, where He spent two days, to Shri Janárdan, where also He hymned and danced for some two days, to Payoshni, where Shankar Narayan is worshipped, to the monastery of Shringeri, the seat of Sankaráchárya, to *Matsya-tirṭha* (Fish shrine), to the river Tungabhadrá, and to [Upidi], the seat of Madhwáchárya, the spokesman of spiritual truth. Here He gazed devotedly on the Udupa-Krishna. The image of Krishna in the form of the dancing young cowherd (*Gopál*) was very charming. Madhwacharya was moved by a dream to rescue this image from a cargo of consecrated earth (*Gobi-chandan*) in a sunken ship, and to instal it [at Udipi], where it is worshipped to this day.

The Master was overjoyed to see the image of Krishna, and in fervour of devotion danced and sang (before it) for many a day. The *tattwavádis*, taking the Master for a *máyávadi*, at first slighted Him, but afterwards they marvelled at His religious ecstasy, and venerated Him greatly as a (true) Vaishnav. Aware of their pride in Vaishnavism, the Master began a discourse with them. The high priest of the *tattwavádis* was an expert in all the holy books. The Master, assuming the tone of a humble inquirer, put questions to him: "I do not clearly comprehend *sádhya* (end) and *sádhan* (means). Do please enlighten me on the subject." The high priest replied, "To the worshipper of Krishna the highest *sádhan* is to resign to Krishna the religious system centring round caste and *áshram*. Translation to Vishnu's heaven, after attaining to the fivefold salvation, is the supreme *sádhya*. Thus speak the *Shastras*." The Master objected, "The *Shastras* assert that the supreme *sadhan* of the love and service of Krishna is listening to and singing His praise. *Vide Bhágabat*, VII. v. 18.

From listening to and singing hymns, one comes to love Krishna. That is the fifth human end, the limit of human attainment. *Vide Bhagabat*, XI. ii. 38. All kinds of scripture condemn (devotion to) work and teach us to abstain from the fruit of our works. Therefore from work cannot spring love and devotion to Krishna. *Vide Bhágabat*, XI. xi. 32 ; also *Gitá*, xviii. 66 ; *Bhágabat*, XI. xx. 9. Truly devoted men renounce the fivefold salvation ; in their eyes salvation is worthless, no better than hell ! *Vide Bhagabat*, III. xxix. 11 ; V. xiv. 43 ; VI. xvii. 23.

The devout abjure salvation and work alike. And you establish these two things as the end and means ! Ah ! you are only befooling me as I am a [mere] *sannyasi*. You have not told me of the true characteristics of end and means."

At this the high priest of the *tattwa* School was inly ashamed, while he marvelled at the Vaishnav spirit of the Master. So he replied, "Your exposition is the true one. All *Shastras* declare this to be the Vaishnav dogma. Yet our order holds the views laid down by Madhwacharya." The Master rejoined, "The votary of work and the votary of knowledge are alike lacking in faith. In your order I see signs of these two. I see only one merit in your order : you have fixed upon the true God."

After thus humbling the pride of that sect the Master went to the Falgu shrine, then to Tritakup (the shrine of Vishálá), Panchápsará, Gokarna (where Shiva is worshipped), Dwaipáyani, Supárak, Kolhápur (where He beheld Lakshmi and Kshir Bhagavati), Nánga-Ganesh,

Chor Párvati, and Pándupur [=Pandharpur]. Here before Vithal's image He sang and danced long.

A Brahman of the place invited and reverently fed the Master. Learning the good news that Shri Ranga Puri, a disciple of Madhav Puri, was residing in another Brahman's house in that village the Master went to see him. As He prostrated Himself before the Puri in devotion, He wept, trembled and was thrilled and covered all over with sweat. Shri Ranga Puri wondered at the sight and cried out, "Rise, blessed one. Surely you are connected with my *guru*, or you could not have displayed such fervour of devotion." So, he raised and embraced the Master, and the two wept clasping each other's neck. After a spell of rapture, the two came round, and the Master said how He was related to Ishwar Puri. (At this) their love welled out wondrously and each honoured the other. Day and night they held forth on Krishna for a week or so.

The Puri asked about His birth-place. The Master replied 'Navadwip'. Shri Ranga Puri had once visited that town in the train of Madhav Puri. He spoke how he had been feasted in the house of Jagannath Mishra, how delicious the hash of green banana-flower (*mochá*) had tasted, what a chaste woman and tender to the world like a mother was Jagannath's wife, how she was matchless in the universe for her skill in cookery, and how she had feasted the *sannyasis* as lovingly as if they were her own sons, how one of her sons had turned monk in youth with the title of Shankaráranya and had attained to death in that very place (*viz.*, Pandupur). The Master broke in, "In his earthly life Shankar was my brother. Jagannath Mishra was my father." So they had a friendly assembly, and then Shri Ranga Puri set out to visit Dwáraká. The Master was detained for some four days by His Brahman host. He bathed in the Bhimarathi and visited the shrine of Vithal. Then He walked by the bank of the Krishna-binna, visiting the temples at the many holy places there. The Brahmans of the country were Vaishnavs and studied the *Krishna-karnámrita*, of which book the Master joyfully made a copy. The world has nothing like the *Karnamrita*, which kindles pure devotion to Krishna. He only knows the fulness of the beauty and sweetness of Krishna's exploits, who ceaselessly reads the *Karnamrita*. He carried with Himself the manuscripts of the *Brahma Samhita* and the *Karnamrita* like two precious jewels.

After bathing in the Tápti, He went to the city of Máheshwati, and then visiting many holy places on the way, reached the bank of the Narmadá. After visiting the Shrine of the Bow (*Dhanu-tirtha*), He bathed in the Nirbindhyá, and then passed on to the Rishyamukha mountain and the Dandaka forest, where He beheld a *saptatál* tree, very old stout and high. As the Master embraced the *saptatal*, the tree disappeared bodily, at which the people marvelled and cried out, "This *sannyasi* is an incarnation of Rám, for lo! the *tál* tree has flown up to Vishnu's heaven. Who but Ram can work such a miracle?"

Then the Master bathed in the lake of Pampá, and rested in the Panchavati wood. From Násik and Trimbak He passed on to Brahma-giri, to Kushávarta (the source of the Godavari), the seven (branches of the) Godavari, and many other shrines, and finally returned to Vidyá-nagar.

On hearing of His arrival, Ramananda Ray joyfully hastened to Him and prostrated himself; but the Master raised him and clasped him to His bosom. Both wept in delight and their minds were unstrung by rapture. After recovering composure they talked of many things together. The Master gave a narrative of His pilgrimage, and showed him the *Karnámrita* and the *Brahma Samhitá,* saying "These two books bear out the theories of devotion (*prem*) which you had expounded to me." The Ray in delight tasted the books in the Master's company and took copies of them.

The whole village was agitated by the news of the *sannyasi's* return and all men flocked to see Him. At this Ramananda went back to his own house. At noon the Master rose for His meal. Ramananda returned at night and the two kept a vigil discoursing of Krishna. Thus five or six days were spent blissfully, the two holding forth on Krishna day and night. Ramananda said, "With thy leave, Master, I petitioned my king, and he has permitted me to visit the Niláchal. I have already begun my preparations for departure." The Master replied, "I have come here only to take you to the Nilachal." But the Ray objected, "Master, go you in advance. A noisy throng of elephants, horses and soldiers surrounds me. Let me first dispose of them, and then after ten days I shall follow you." The Master consented and returned to the Niláchal by the route He had previously followed, the people everywhere chanting Hari's name as they saw Him. He rejoiced at it. From Alalnath he sent Krishna-das in advance to call Nityánanda and others of His own folk. At the news, Nityánanda went to meet the Master, his devotion knowing no bounds. Jagadánanda, Dámodar, Gopinath Acharya and Mukunda Pandit went along dancing, unable to contain their delight. They all met the

Master on the way, and He lovingly embraced them, all weeping in delight. Sárvabhauma Bhattacharya joined the Master on the beach of the ocean and fell at His feet ; but the Master raised him up and held him to the bosom, Sarvabhauma weeping in rapture. The whole party went to visit Jagannath's shrine, where the Master had a transport of devotion, trembling, perspiring, weeping in delight, dancing and singing again and again. The servitors of the temple offered Him the dedicated garlands and food of the god, at which the Master regained composure. The attendants of Jagannath joyfully flocked together. Káshi Mishra (the high priest) fell at His feet, but the Master did him honour and embraced him. The *Parichhá* of Jagannath, too, did Him obeisance.

Sarvabhauma took the Master to dinner at his own house, and fed Him and His party at noon on sumptuous dishes from the temple. Thereafter he made the Master lie down and rubbed His feet ; but the Master bade him go and dine ; and He passed the night also in Sarvabhauma's house to please him, narrating the story of His pilgrimage all night to His followers and host, and saying, "In all the holy places I have visited I did not meet with a single Vaishnav who can equal you. Only Ramananda Ray gave me intense delight." The Bhatta replied, "It was just for that reason that I had asked you to see him." [Text, canto 9.]

NOTES ON THE PLACES VISITED BY CHAITANYA IN THE SOUTH.

[In this connection we should bear in mind that no record of Chaitanya's pilgrimage was kept at the time it was made. His disciples heard of it, evidently piece-meal, from his lips long afterwards. A diary constructed on this basis by Govinda-das has been lost. Our author, Krishna-das Kaviraj, frankly admits (at the beginning of canto ix) that he has not been able to name the holy places, of the South in the order in which they were visited by the Master. We should also note that this pilgrimage was performed between April 1510 and January 1512 and that the great and widespread revival of temple building which resulted from the restoration of the Vijaynagar empire under Krishna Dev just began at the time of Chaitanya's visit, but was completed long afterwards. Hence many of the famous shrines of the South dating from the early 16th century were not seen by him, as they were completed after his visit].

Ahobal.—Ahobilam, in the Sirvel taluq of the Karnul district. The most sacred Vishnu temple in the district, it is dedicated to Narasimha. Together with other temples in the neighbourhood, it forms a group known as the Nava (nine) Narasimha, representing nine different forms of Vishnu. The original temple is supported by 64 pillars, each of which is beautifully carved into several miniature pillars. In front is a fine unfinished mantapam with large pillars of white sand-stone, about 3 feet in diameter, elaborately sculptured. (*Kurnool Manual*, 183-184, 145).

Ananta Padmanava.—The famous Padmanava temple in Trivandrum.

Betapani.—Bhutapandi in Travancore, in the Tobala taluq, n. of Nagarcoil, with temple of Bhutanath. [R. M. Ghose.]

Brahma-giri.—There is a Brahmagiri near Sopara (*Bom. Gaz.* xiv. 315); but that is not the place meant in our text. The reference is to the *Brahma mountain*, in the ridge joining which to the Trimbak mountain the Kikvi, a larger and more distant branch of the Godavari (than the one issuing at Trimbak) takes its rise. (*Bombay Gaz.* xvi. 7).

Chamtapur.—*Chenganur* in Travancore State. [R. M. G.]

Chiyár-talá.—*Shertalá* near Nagarcoil, [according to R. M. Ghose].

Courtallam, 7 m. s. w. of Tenkashi in the Tinnevelly district, 450 ft. above sea-level. The falls of the Chittar (a river which joins the Tamraparni 15 m. n. e. of Tinnevelly) at this place are famous among the Hindus for their virtue of cleansing from sin. [*Tinn. Man.* 96.]

Dhanu-tirtha.—*Dhanus-kodi*, terminus of the S. I. Railway, 12 m. south-east of Rameshwaram. [R. M. G.]

Durbesan.—*Darvashayan*, on the sea-coast seven miles east of Ramnad. [R. M. G.]

Gajendra-mokshan.—Probably *Devendra-mokshan* or Suchindram, 2 m. s. of Nagarcoil. Here Indra was cleansed of his sin and built a temple to Sthanu-linga Shiva. [R. M. G.]

Ganga Gotami.—The Godavari river. At Kobur, opposite Rajmahendri, was the hermitage of the sage Gautama, from whom this river is named.

Gokarna.—On the west coast, about 20 miles s. e. of Karwar, famous for its temple of Mahabaleshwar and a very popular place of pilgrimage. (*Bombay Gazetteer*, Kanara, xv. pt. 2, pp. 289-301).

Kolhapur.—Out of about 250 temples in this city at present six are well-known, namely, the temples of Ambábái or Mahálakshmi, Vithoba, Temblai, Mahákali, Phirangai or Pratyangiras, and Yallamma. (*Bombay Gaz.* xxiv. 309-311).

Kumbha-karna.—*Kumbakonam* in the Tanjore district, 20 miles north-east of Tanjore town. It contains 12 principal Shaiva and 4 Vaishnav temples and one dedicated to Brahmá. (*Tanjore Gaz.* 217-219).

Madura—on the river Vaigai, the minor basin of which is called *Kritimá-nadi* (the *Krita-mala* of our text). Its temples are described in the *Madura Gazetteer*, 267-274.

Mahendra hill.—There is a peak of this name in the Travancore State, but too far from Cape Comorin.

Malay mountain (Agastya).—(i) There is a temple to the sage Agastya in the village Agastyampalli, close to Vedaranniyam, near Point Calimere in the Tanjore district; but it cannot be the place meant. (ii) *Palni* in the Madura district contains a famous temple to Subrahmanya on the top of a hill (Shivagiri) created by Agastya.

But there is no temple to Agastya here. (*Madura Gaz.* 304-306). (iii) R. M. Ghose is inclined to identify it with *Pothia* hill (near Cape Comorin), the reputed abode of Agastya (K. Pillai's *Tamils 1,800 Years Ago*, 21.) (iv) The Tamraparni rises on either side of a fine conical peak known as *Agastiar-malai* or Agastya's hill. (*Tinn. Man.* 91).

Mallar land.—Malabar.

Mallikarjun.—*Shri-Shailam*, on the south bank of the Krishna, 70 miles below Karnul......In the centre of the enclosure is the temple of Mallikarjun Shiva, the chief deity worshipped here, and considered as one of the *jyotir-lingas*. (*Kurnool Manual*, 181-183, 144). There is another and much less famous temple to Mallikarjun at Bezvada on the Krishna river.

Matsya-tirtha.—Either (1) *Mahé*, the French possession on the coast of the Malabar district. Or (2) *Matsya-gundam*, a curious pool on the Macheru river, near the village of Matam, six miles north-north-west of Paderu (in the Padwa taluq of the Vizagapatam district). A barrier of rocks runs right across the river there, and the stream plunges into a great hole and vanishes beneath this, reappearing again about a hundred yards lower down. Just where it emerges from under the barrier it forms a pool which is crowded with *mahseer* of all sizes. (*Vizagapatam Gaz.* 285).

Nine Tripadi.—*Alwar Tiru-nagari*, 17 m. s. e. of Tinnevelly. Around it are 9 temples to Vishnu (*Tirupati*), the idols of which are assembled in this town on holy days. [R. M. G.]

Paksha-tirtha.—*Pakshi-tirtham* or *Tiru-kadi-kundram*, 9 miles south-east of Chingleput. [R. M. G.] "The hill of the sacred kites." It is a ridge terminating in a spiked hill, some 500 feet above sea-level, on which stands a Shiva temple. The name of the hill is Vedagiri or Vedachalam, and the idol is called Veda-girishwar. Every day two birds of the kite species come to the mountain and are fed by an attendant Brahman. The same two are believed to have come from Benares to receive this daily dole from time immemorial. (*Chingleput Man.* 106-107).

Pampá.—The ancient and Puranic name of the Tungabhadra. The village of Hampi (the site of the famous capital Vijaynagar) was originally known as Pampa-tirtha. This name (also (*Pampá-*

saras) is now borne by a tank on the Haidarabad side of the Tungabhadra near Anegundi. (*Bellary Gazetteer*, 6, 261).

Pána.—Panakal Narasimha at Mangal-giri, 7 m. south of Bezvada. But it is too far to the north. [R. M. G.] When visitors offer a draught to Narasimha-swami, the image in the temple refuses to drink more than half of it. (*Kistna Dist. Man.* 179).

Pâná-garhi.—*Panagodi*, 30 m. s. s. w. of Tinnevelly on the road to Trivandrum. [R. M. G.] But the temple there is to Ramlinga-swami Shiva and not to Ram.

Panchavati.—Identified with *Nasik* in the Bombay presidency. Nasik and Trimbak (at the source of the Godavari) are described in *Bombay Gazetteer*, xvi.

Pandupur.—*Pandharpur*, on the Bhima river, 38 miles due west of Sholapur; famous for its temple to Vithoba. (*Bombay Gaz.* xx. 415-481).

Papa-nashan.—Eight miles s. w. of Kumbakonam (*Tanjore Gaz.* 221). There is another city of this name 29 miles west of Palamkota, (in the Tinnevelly district). Here near a pagoda the Tamraparni river takes its last fall from the hills to the level country. (*Tinn. Man.* 91).

Payaswini.—*Tiru-vattar* in the Travancore State. [R. M. G.]

Pitambar.—Evidently *Chidambaram*, 26 miles south of Cuddalore. Famous for its great pagoda, covering 39 acres in the centre of the town, and sourrounded on all four sides by a street 60 feet wide. It contains the Akasa-linga. (*S. Arcot Manual*, 400-407).

Rishava peak.—*Anagarh-malai*, 12 miles north of Madura. [R. M. G.]

Rishyamukh.—Identified with the hill on the Nizam's side of the narrowest of the gorges in the Tungabhadra near Hampi. (*Bellary Gaz.* 261).

Shiva image.—Either Vedagiris at Pakshi-tirtham or the *lingam* in the shore temple at Mahavalipuram (Seven Pagodas).

Shiva Kanchi.—The modern *Conjeveram*, also called the Southern Benares, 56 miles south-west of Madras. The Shiva temple is dedicated to Ekambara-swami. South-east of it stands *Vishnu Kanchi* or Little Conjeveram, with its temple to Vishnu under the name of Varada-ráj.

Shiva-kshetra.—There is a Shiva-ganga tank at Tanjore. The great

Brihatishwar temple of this town seems to be meant in our text. (*Tanjore Gaz.* 269-271).

Shiyali.—The head-quarters of a taluq of that name in the Tanjore district, about 48 miles n. e. of Tanjore town. It has a famous Shiva temple with a large tank, a shrine dedicated to the Tamil saint Tiru-jnan Sambandhar, and some other separate shrines, and evidently an image of Shiva's consort who is said to have given suck to this saint when he visited this temple as a child. (*Tanjore Gaz.* 258).

Shri Janardan.—Near the Varkala railway station, 26 miles north of Trivandrum.

Shringeri.—In the Kadur district of Mysore. Situated 13° 25′ N. 75° 19′ E., on the left bank of the Tunga, 7 miles s. of Hariharpur. Its full name is Rishya-shringa-giri. It is the head-quarters of the Jagat-guru or successor of Shankaracharya in the headship of the Smartas. (Rice, *Mysore Gazetteer*, ii. 443-445).

Shri-rangam.—The famous Vishnu temple in an island between the Kolerun and the Kaveri, north of Trichinopoly. (*Trichinopoly Manual*, 337-340 and *Gazetteer*, 45-51, 91-126, 319).

Shri-Shaila.—The most famous place of this name is the one in the Karnul district, described above under Mallikarjun. But that place cannot be meant in this context, which suggests some hill between Trichinopoly and Madura, sacred to Shri or Lakshmi.

Shri-Vaikuntha.—*Shri Vaikuntham*, four miles n. of Alwar Tirunagari. [R. M. G.], on the left bank of the Tamraparni and 16 m. s. e. of Tinnevelly.

Siddha-bat.—*Sidhout*, 10 miles east of Cuddapa town. Sometimes known as the Dakshina Kashi or the Southern Benares. The name is derived from *Siddha-vatam* or 'the hermit's banyan tree.' Eight miles south of it is Ontimetta ('the solitary hill') with a large and very holy pagoda and a tank. The pagoda is dedicated to Kodanda-Ram-swami. (*Cuddapah Manual*, 48-49).

Supárak.—Sopara (in the Thana district), 26 miles north of Bombay. It was the capital of the Konkan from very ancient times to 1,300 A.D. (*Bombay Gaz.* xiv. 314-342).

Tamal-kartik.—Tobala, 44 m. s. of Tinnevelly, 2 m. s. of Aramvali pass, temple of Subrahmanya. [R. M. G.]

Tamraparni.—A river on the left bank of which Tinnevelly stands.

Til Kanchi.—Probably *Tenkashi*, 30 m. n. w. of Tinnevelly town.

Tirupati.—A very famous holy city in the Chandra-giri taluq of the N. Arcot district. In Lower Tirupati, which stands in the plain, there are 15 temples; the chief of them being dedicated to Govinda-raja-swami (the brother of Venkateshwar) and Ram-swami. Upper Tirupati, usually called *Tirumala* (from *Tiru-malai*, holy hill), stands on the top of the range, six miles north-west of Lower Tirupati. Its chief divinity is Venkateshwar. (*North Arcot Manual*, 142-153).

Tri-kal-hasti.—Shri Kalahasti, popularly called *Kalahastri*, on the right bank of the Suvarnamukhi river, 22 miles n. e. of Tirupati. Famous for its shrine of the Vayu-linga Shiva. (*N. Arcot Man.* 220-222).

Udipi.—36 miles north of Mangalore (in the South Kanara district), the principal seat of the Madhavacharya priests. The temple of Krishna is said to have been founded by Madhavacharya himself, who set up in it an image of Krishna originally made by Arjun. There are also eight ancient *maths*, each with a swami. (*S. Canara Manual*, ii. 263. For a full description, see *Bombay Gazetter*, xxii. 56).

Vedaban.—*Vedáranniyam* or 'the forest of the Vedas,' in the south-east corner of the Tirutturaippundi taluq of the Tanjore district and five miles north of Point Calimere. Orthodox Brahmans consider it second only to Rameshwaram in sanctity. (*Tanjore Gaz.* 284).

Vriddha-kal.—Varaha-swami temple, a monolithic pagoda, n. w. of "Arjun's Penance" and ¾ m. s. of Valipitham, at Mahavali-puram or Seven Pagodas; image of Vishnu with a huge boar's head, overcanopied by the Shesha Nag.

Vriddha-kashi.—*Vriddhachalam*, on the Manimukta (an affluent of the Vellar), in the S. Arcot district. Sometimes called Vriddha-kashi. (*S. Arcot Manual*, 438-440). It cannot be the place meant, if the order of holy places given in our text be correct.

CHAPTER VIII

The Reunion of the Vaishnavs

After the Master had set out for the South, King Pratap Rudra summoned Sarvabhauma, seated him after due salutation, and asked him concerning the Master, saying, "I hear that a very gracious person has come to your house from Bengal. People say that he has shown you much kindness. Do please help me to see him." The Bhatta replied, "True is what you have heard. But you cannot see him ; he is a *sannyasi* withdrawn from the world, living in seclusion, and not visiting kings even in dreams. I could, however, have contrived somehow an interview between him and you : but he has recently gone to the South." The king asked, "Why did he leave Jagannath's shrine?" The Bhatta replied, "Such is one of the deeds of saints. They visit holy places on the plea of making pilgrimages, but they thereby bring salvation to worldly men. *Vide Bhágabat,* I. xiii. 8. Such is the unalterable character of a Vaishnav : he is not a man but rather a particle of God." The Raja rejoined, "Why did you let him depart? You ought to have clasped his feet and importuned him to stay here." Bhattacharya answered, "He is a god and a free being. He is Krishna's self and not a dependent creature. Still I had tried to detain him, but could not succeed as God is free."

The Raja said, "Bhatta! you are the chief of wise men. As you call him Krishna, I must believe it. When he comes here again, may I see him once and gratify my eyes?" The Bhatta replied, "He will soon return. We want a suitable place for him to lodge in ;—it must be near the temple and yet secluded. Choose such a lodging for him." The king said, "Kashi Mishra's house is just that sort of place,—close to Jagnnath and yet very retired." The king thereafter remained expectant. Bhattacharya informed Kashi Mishra, who said, "Blessed am I that such a holy Master will lodge under my roof."

Thus did all the people of Puri live in ever-growing expectation of seeing the Master, when He returned from the South. All rejoiced at the news, and they all begged Sarvabhauma thus, "Lead us to the Master, that through thy mediation we may reach Chaitanya's feet." Bhattacharya replied, "To-morrow the Master will go to Kashi Mishra's house, where I shall introduce you to Him."

Next day the Master visited Jagannath in company with Bhattacharya, in great delight. The servitors met Him with the god's food and He embraced them all. After the visit Bhattacharya led Him to Kashi Mishra's house. Kashi Mishra fell at His feet, and gave up to Him not his house only but his soul also. The Master appeared to him in the four-armed shape, and embraced him to make him one of His own followers.

Then the Master took His seat there. Around Him sat Nityananda and other devotees. The Master was pleased with the arrangements of the house, which satisfied all His needs. Then Sarvabhauma said, "Master, this house is worthy of you. Accept it, as Kashi Mishra prays." The Master replied, "My body is under your control. What you bid me, I must do, as in duty bound." Then Sarvabhauma, seating himself at the right hand of the Master, began to introduce one after another all the people of Puri, saying, "All these men have been residing in the Niláchal in eager longing to meet you. They have fared like the thirsty *chátak* bird that cries in anguish for water. All were determined [to see you]. This one is Janárdan, a constant attendant on the person of Jagannath. This other is Krishna-das who holds the golden rod [in the temple]. Here is Shikhi Mahanti, the officer in charge of the [temple] secretariate. This, Pradyumna Mishra, is foremost among Vaishnavs, and he waits on Jagannath during the god's sleep. Murari Mahanti, the brother of Shikhi Mahanti, has no refuge save your feet. [These are] Chandaneshwar, Singheshwar, Murari Brahman, and Vishnu-das, all of whom meditate on your feet. Here are the high-minded Praharáj Mahápátra, and his kinsman Paramánanda Mahápátra. These Vaishnavs are the ornaments of this holy place, and all devotedly intent on your feet." They all prostrated themselves on the ground before the Master, who graciously held them to His bosom.

Just then came there Bhabánanda Ray, with his four sons; and they all fell at the Master's feet. Sarvabhauma introduced them, "This is Bhabánanda Ray whose eldest son is Rámánanda Ray." The Master embraced him and spoke in praise of Rámánanda adding, "One cannot adequately describe to the world the greatness of him whose son is a jewel like Rámánanda. Truly, you are Pándu, your wife is Kunti, and your five high-souled sons are the five Pándav brothers." The Ray replied, "I am a Shudra, a worldling and a wretch. That you have touched me is the only holy thing [about me]. I lay down at your feet myself with my house, belongings, servants, and five sons. This youth Vánináth will constantly wait on you, to do whatever you bid him. Know me as your own, feel no delicacy, but order whatever you desire." The Master answered, "What delicacy can there be? You are not a stranger to me. In birth after birth you with your family have been my servants. In some five days Rámánanda will arrive here. His society will complete my bliss." So saying He embraced the father, while the four sons laid their heads at His feet. They were all sent home, only Vánináth Patta Nayak was retained by the Master.

Bhattacharya sent away the other people. Thereafter the Master called for deaf Krishna-dás, and said "Listen, Bhattacharya, to the story of this man. He had accompanied me to the South, but left me to join the tribe of Bhattamári. But I rescued him from their hands. Having brought him back here I give him his discharge. Let him go wherever he likes; I have no longer any concern with him." At this Krishna-dás set up a lamentation. When the Master went away for His noonday worship, Nityananda, Jagadánanda, Mukunda, and Dámodar laid their heads together, saying, "We have to send a messenger to Bengal to report the Master's arrival to His mother. Adwaita, Shribas and others of the faithful will all flock hither on hearing of His return. Let us send Krishna-dás (for the purpose)." With this they consoled Krishna-dás.

Next day they prayed to the Master, "Allow us to send a man to Bengal, as mother Shachi, Adwaita and other devotees have all been plunged in concern since they heard of your setting out for the South. Let a man go and give them the glad tidings (of your safe return)." The Master assented, "Do as you like." So they sent

Krishna-das to Bengal, with a present of the *mahá-prasád* for the Vaishnavs there.

Deaf Krishna-dás reached Bengal, saw mother Shachi at Navadwip, bowed, and gave her the *mahá-prasád* and the news of the Master's return from the South. The mother rejoiced at the news, and so did the faithful led by Shribas. Then Krishna-dás went to the house of Adwaita Acharya, gave him the *prasád,* bowed, and told him all about the Master. The Acharya in rapture danced, sang, and shouted for a long time. How shall I name all the flock who exulted at the news,—Haridás Thákur, Vásudev Datta, Murári Gupta, Shivananda, Acharya Ratna, Pandit Vakreshwar, Acharya Nidhi, the Pandits Gadadhar, Shrirám, Dámodar, Shrimán, and Rághav, Vijay, Shridhar, and Acharya Nandan. They all went in a body to Adwaita, bowed at his feet, and were clasped to his bosom. Two or three days were spent by the Acharya in great rejoicing (with them), and then he confirmed the desire to make a pilgrimage to the Niláchal. Gathering together at Navadwip, they set off for Jagannath with mother Shachi's leave. At the report about the Master, Satyaráj and Rámánanda from the Kulin village joined them, and so did Mukunda and Narahari from Raghunandan Khand. Just then Paramánanda Puri arrived at Nadia from the South, travelling along the banks of the Ganges. He lodged in comfort in the temple of mother Shachi, who honourably fed him. On hearing there of the Master's return, the Puri too wished to hasten to the Niláchal. He set off thither with the Master's devotee, the Brahman Kamalákánta, and soon arrived in the Master's presence, who rejoiced at the meeting and lovingly saluted his feet, while the Puri embraced Him.

The Master said, "I long to live in thy company. Make the Niláchal thy abode, as thou lovest me." The Puri replied, "It is because I desire your society that I came hither from Bengal. The news of your return from the South has gladdened the heart of Shachi. The other devotees are coming to see you, but as they made delay I had started quickly (before them)." The Master assigned to the Puri a retired room in Káshi Mishra's house and an attendant.

Next day arrived Swarup Dámodar, who had touched the inmost recess of the Master's spirit. His name in the world was Purushottam Acharya, and he waited on the Master at Navadwip. Wild at the Master's renunciation of the world, he went to Benares and turned monk there. His *guru*, Chaitanyánanda, bade him study the *Vedanta* and expound it to the people. He was totally withdrawn from the world and a deep scholar, having taken refuge in Krishna with all his body and soul. He had turned *sannyasi*, in a wild longing to worship Krishna in freedom from every (earthly) thought and care. As a *sannyasi* he cast off his sacred thread and took the tonsure, but did not put on the *yogi's* dress. Swarup was the new name given to him. With his *guru's* permission he came to the Niláchal, being day and night out of his senses in the bliss of loving Krishna. He was a perfect scholar, holding converse with none, and living in seclusion unknown to the world. He had known the mystery of the love of Krishna ; his very body was a picture of love ; he seemed the exact second self of the Master. Every book, verse, or song brought to the Master had to be first examined by Swarup before He would hear it. The Master took no delight in compositions that clashed with the theory of *bhakti* and lacked the spirit of delight (*ras*). So, Swarup Goswami tasted books and read to the Master only such as were correct. Vidyápati, Chandidás and *Git-Govinda* were the poetry that delighted the Master. Damodar surpassed others, as he was a veritable *gandharva* in musical skill and a Vrihaspati in Shastric lore. He was a darling to Adwaita and Nityananda, and the very life of Shribas and other faithful ones.

Such was Dámodar who came and prostrating himself clasped the Master's feet while he recited stanza 20 of Act VIII. of the drama *Chaitanya-chandrodaya*.

The Master raised and embraced him. The two swooned away in ecstasy. After a while regaining composure the Master began thus: "I have dreamt that you would come to-day. It is good (that you have come); I am like a blind man who has got back his two eyes." Swarup answered, "Pardon my sin, Master I erred grievously when I left you and sought another (*guru*). I had not a particle of faith in your feet, but, sinner that I was, I had left you to go to another country! I had no doubt left you, but *you* did not forsake me. Thy grace has been a chain round my neck, dragging me to thy feet."

Then Swarup bowed at Nityananda's feet, who lovingly embraced him. He also did due courtesy as he met Jagadánanda, Mukunda, Shankar, Sárvabhauma, and Paramánanda Puri. The Master gave him a quiet room with a servant to draw water and do other services.

One day the Master sat surrounded by Sárvabhauma and other faithful ones, holding sweet discourse on Krishna, when Govinda arrived, prostrated himself, and said, "I am Govinda, a servant of Ishwar Puri, at whose bidding I have come to you. The Puri, when attaining to *siddhi* (death) told me to go and serve Krishna-Chaitanya. Káshishwar will come (here) after visiting holy places. At my master's bidding I have hastened to your feet." To this the Master replied, "Ishwar Puri loved me like a son, and has sent you to me as a favour." At this Sárvabhauma asked, "How could the Puri retain a Shudra attendant?" The Master answered, "God is supremely independent. His mercy is not bound by (the rules of) the Vedas. God's grace defies caste and family distinctions." Witness how Krishna dined at the house of Bidur. Love and service are mere instruments of Krishna's mercy. When actuated by mercy He acts independently [of the conventions of religion]. Loving treatment is a million times more blissful than dignity. The very hearing of it gives intense delight."

So saying the Master embraced Govinda, who then bowed at the feet of all. The Master spoke, "Bhattacharya, solve this problem: the very servant of my *guru* is honourable to me, and it is not seemly that he should serve me. And yet the *guru* has commanded it. What should I do?" The Bhatta answered, "A *guru's* command is most strong, and the Shastras direct us not to violate it. Witness the *Raghuvamsa,* xiv. 53, and Valmiki's *Ramayan,* Ayodhya-kanda, xxii. 9."

Then the Master consented and permitted Govinda to serve His body. All honoured him as the Master's favourite attendant, while Govinda made arrangements for all the Vaishnavs. He was accompanied by the two Haridáses (who were surnamed the greater and lesser chanters),—Rámái and Nandái,—in tending the Master. Govinda's good fortune baffles description.

One day Mukunda Datta said to the Master, "Brahmánanda Bhárati has come to see you. Permit me to bring him hither." But He replied, "The Bhárati is my *guru*. It is I who should go to him." So saying, He went to Brahmánanda, with all His followers. At the sight of Brahmánanda clad in deer skin, the Master grieved at heart, pretended not to have observed him, and asked Mukunda where the Bhárati was. Mukunda replied, "Here, before you!" But the Master objected, "You do not know. It is not he, but somebody else whom you are ignorantly pointing out. Why should the Bhárati Goswami wear a skin?" At this Brahmánanda inly reflected, "He likes not my robe of deer skin. He has spoken well. A skin is worn as a mark of pride (of asceticism). The wearing of it cannot give me salvation from the world. Henceforth I shall renounce this garment." The Master learnt of his thought, and had a cloth brought, which Brahmananda put on after discarding the skin. Then the Master bowed at his feet, but the Bhárati objected saying, "These your acts are for instructing the people. Never bow down to me again, it frightens me. Here are now two gods, *viz.*, Jagannath the stationary, and you the moving god. You are the fair god, while Jagannath is the dark deity. These two (between them) have redeemed the world." The Master demurred, "The truth is that *your* coming has revealed two Brahmas at Purushottam: your name is Brahmánanda, and (you are) the fair-coloured moving Brahma, while Jagannath is the dark and motionless one." The Bhárati cried out, "Be thou the judge between us, Sárvabhauma, and attend to my logical dispute with Him. The Shastras tell us that creation is *vyápya*, while Brahma is *vyápak*.

He has reformed me by taking away my skin robe. This shows that one is *vyápya* and the other is *vyápak*. *Vide Mahabharat*, Dán-parva, ch. 149, stanza 1091. To the Master truly belong these (divine) epithets,—sandal-pasted *prasád, dor*, two-armed *Angad*." Bhattacharya replied, "O Bharati, the victory is thine, as I see." The Master said, "Whatever you say must be true. In a logical disputation, the disciple must always yield to the *guru*." But the Bharati objected, "No, no, the reason (of my victory) is otherwise. It is thy nature to admit defeat at the hands of thy *bhaktas*. Listen to another feat of thine. All my life I had worshipped the formless Deity, but when I saw thee, Krishna became manifest before my eyes. Krishna's name broke forth from my lips, Krishna's image was stamped on my heart and eye. My soul thirsts for thee as thou resemblest Krishna. My condition is truly like that of Billamangal, as described in the *Bhakti-rasámrita-sindhu*."

The Master rejoined, "Deep is your love of Krishna, so that whatever your eye glances on, you see a Krishna there." Bhattacharya replied, "Yes, but only after Krishna had first revealed himself in the flesh. Love alone can enable us to see him. His favour is the (only) means of seeing him." The Master cried out, "Holy God! Holy God! what art thou saying, Sárvabhauma? Your praise in hyperbole is satire in disguise." So saying He led the Bharati to His own house and lodged him there. Rám Bhattacharya and Bhagabán Acharya waited on the Master, leaving all other works.

Another day Kashishwar Goswami arrived and was honourably lodged by the Master with Himself. He used to escort the Master to the temple of Jagannath, removing the crowd from before Him. As all rivers and brooks unite in the ocean, so did the Master's worshippers, wherever they might have been, all come together at His feet. He graciously kept them at His house. Thus have I described the Master's assembling of Vaishnavs. [Text, canto 10.]

CHAPTER IX

The Grand Chanting (Bera Kirtan)

One day Sarvabhauma said, "Master, may I make bold to submit a thing?" He replied, "Say thy say without hesitation. If it is a proper request, I shall keep it, if not, not." Sarvabhauma said, "Here is Pratap Rudra Ray, eager to meet you." The Master clapped His hands to His ears, murmured an appeal to God, and replied, "Why such an improper speech, Sarvabhauma? I am a hermit withdrawn from the world. For me to meet a king or a woman is fatal like a draught of poison."

Sarvabhauma entreated, "True are thy words. But this Raja is a votary of Jagannath and the chief of devotees." "Still, a king is only the deadly snake in another form,—just as the touch of even the wooden statue of a woman causes mental perturbation. Say not so again. If you do, you will miss me from this place." Alarmed, Sarvabhauma retired to his own house.

At this time King Pratap Rudra of the Gajapati dynasty arrived at Puri. With him came Ramananda Ray, who first of all interviewed the Master in great delight. The Ray prostrated himself, the Master embraced him, and the two shed tears of joy. At this loving intercourse, all the *bhaktas* wondered. The Ray said, "I reported your behest to my king, who relieved me of my office, as you wished. I told him that if he would let me I should remain at Chaitanya's feet, as I no longer wished to manage affairs (of state). At the mention of thy name the king in delight rose from his throne and embraced me. On hearing thy name he was enraptured; he held my hand and very graciously told me, 'Enjoy your salary as before, and adore Chaitanya's feet in freedom from all cares. I, worthless wretch, am unfit to behold Him. Blessed are they in life that adore Him. Right gracious is He, the son of Braja's lord. In some other birth He will certainly grant me the sight of Him.' I myself have not a tithe of the passion of devotion which I saw in the Raja."*

The Master replied, "You are the foremost of the adorers of Krishna. He is fortunate who loves you. Krishna will accept the Raja because of the great favour he has shown to you. *Vide Bhágabat,* XI. xix. 21, III. vii. 20, and two verses from the *Adi Puran* and the *Padma Puran.*"

The Ray bowed at the feet of the four apostles, *viz.*, the Puri, the Bharati, Swarup and Nityananda, and properly met Jagadánanda, Mukunda, and the other faithful ones. The Master asked, "Ray! have you visited Jagannath?" The Ray replied, "I am going to see the god now." At this the Master cried out, "What hast thou done, Ray? Why did you come to me before visiting the god?" The Ray answered, "My feet are my carriage, my heart is the driver; wherever they take me I, as rider, must go. What can I do? My heart brought me hither, and did not suggest the idea of visiting Jagannath first." The Master replied, "Hasten to see the god; go to your kindred and home afterwards." At the Master's command the Ray went to see the god. Who can fathom the mystery of the Ray's devotion?

On reaching Puri, the king summoned Sárvabhauma,

and after bowing to him asked, "Did you submit my prayer to the Master?" Sárvabhauma replied, "I have entreated Him hard, but He still refuses to grant interview to kings. If we press Him further He will go away from this place." At this the king lamented, "His advent is for redeeming the sinful and the lowly. He has saved Jagái and Mádhái. Has He incarnated Himself with the determination to deliver the whole world excepting Pratap Rudra, alone? Well, He has vowed not to see me, and I now vow to give up this life if I cannot see Him. If I am not rich in the great Master's grace, what boots my kingdom, my body? Everything is useless to me."

Hearing this Sarvabhauma grew alarmed, and he marvelled at the ardour of the king's devotion. So he said, "My liege! grieve not. The Master will surely take pity on you. He can be compelled by love, and your love is most profound; He cannot help doing you grace. Still, I suggest a device by which you can see Him. At the Car Festival, the Master with all His followers will dance in rapture in front of Jagannath's car, and enter the garden in an ecstatic mood. Just then, clad in a plain robe and reciting the *Krishna-rása-panchádhyáyi* all alone, you will run and clasp the Master's feet. He will then be oblivious of the outer world, and on hearing Krishna's name will embrace you as a Vaishnav. To-day Ramananda Ray has lauded your devotion to the Master, whose mind has been turned by it."

At these words the king rejoiced and accepted this plan of meeting with the Master. He learnt from the Bhatta that the Bathing Festival would occur three days afterwards. Thus consoling the king, the Bhatta returned home.

At the Bathing Festival, the Master greatly rejoiced to see the ceremony ; but when Jagannath withdrew to retirement, He deeply mourned for it, and in anguish of separation, like the milkmaids during Krishna's absence, He retired to Alalnath, leaving His followers behind. They afterwards joined Him, and reported that many of the faithful had arrived from Bengal. Sárvabháuma brought the Master back to His quarters in Puri, and informed the king of the fact. Just then Gopinath Acharya arrived at the Court, blessed the king, and said, "Hark thee, Bhattacharya, two hundred Vaishnavs are coming from Bengal,—all of them followers of the Master and very spiritual personages. They have appeared in the city. Arrange for their being given lodgings and consecrated food." The king replied, "I shall order the *Parichhá*, to assign them lodgings &c., as they require. Show me, Bhattacharya, the Master's followers arrived from Bengal, one by one." The Bhatta said, "Climb to the roof of the palace. Gopinath will point them out as he knows them all, I know none, though I long to do so. Gopinath will introduce each." So saying the three ascended to the roof, while the Vaishnavs came near them. Damodar Swarup and Govinda, sent on by the Master, welcomed the Vaishnavs on the way with the god's garlands and *prasád*. To the Rajah's query Bhattacharya said, "This one is Swarup Damodar, the *alter ego* of the Master. That is His servant Govinda. By their hands has He sent the garlands as a mark of honour." Swarup and Govinda successively garlanded Adwaita and bowed to him. But the Acharya knew not Govinda and asked who he was. Damodar Swarup answered "He is Govinda, a highly meritorious servant of

Ishwar Puri, who had ordered him to tend our Master, and by Him is Govinda now retained."

The king asked, "Who is the high spiritual chief to whom both have given garlands?" The Acharya replied, "He is Adwaita Acharya, respected by our Master and highly honoured by all. That one is Shribás Pandit, and those are Vakreshwar Pandit, Vidyánidhi Acharya, Gadadhar Pandit, Acharya Ratna, Purandar Acharya, Gangadas Pandit, Shankar Pandit, Murari Gupta, Narayan Pandit, Haridas Thakur (the purifier of the world), Hari Bhatta, Nrisinghánanda, Vásudev Datta, Shivánanda, —Govinda, Mádhav, Vásu Ghosh (three brothers, whose chanting delights the Master), Rághav Pandit, Acharya Nandan, Shrimán Pandit, Shrikánta Narayan, Shridhar (the white robed), Vijay, Vallabh Sen, Sanjay, Satyaraj Khan (a resident of Kulin village), Rámánanda, Mukundadas, Narahari, Raghunandan, Chiranjib (of Khanda), Sulochan, and many more. How can I name them all? They all follow Chaitanya and hold Him as their life."

The king answered, "The sight fills me with wonder. I have never before beheld such radiance among Vaishnavs. They are all resplendent of hue like a million Suns. Never before have I heard such entrancing street singing. Nowhere else have I seen such devotion, such dancing, such shouting of Hari's name, and nowhere else have I seen or heard the like of it."

Bhattacharya said, "True are thy words. Chaitanya has created this devotional procession-singing (*sankirtan*). His incarnation is for preaching religion ; in the *Kali* age the *sankirtan* of Krishna's name is the (only) religion. Wise are those who worship Krishna by means of *sankirtan*; all other men are overpowered by the spirit of Kali. *Vide Bhágabat*, XI. v. 29.

The king asked, "The Shastras prove that Chaitanya is Krishna (incarnate). Why then do scholars turn away from Him?" The Bhatta answered, "He alone whom Chaitanya favours even a bit can know Him as Krishna. He who has not Chaitanya's grace is nowise a scholar, as he sees and hears Chaitanya without recognizing the God in Him. *Vide Bhágabat*, X. xiv. 28."

The king asked, "Why are they all hastening to Chaitanya's lodgings without first visiting Jagannath?" The Bhatta replied, "Such is the natural consequence of devotion. Their hearts are yearning to see the Master. They will see Him first, and then led by Him will visit Jagannath." The king next said, "Vánináth, the son of Bhabánanda Ray, is conveying the *mahá-prasád* by five or six porters to the Master's house. Why is such a huge quantity needed?" The Bhatta answered, "Knowing that the faithful were coming, the Master had bidden him bring the *prásad*." The king objected, "It is the custom for pilgrims to fast on reaching a holy place (before they see the god). But why are these men breaking their fast?" The Bhatta answered, "What you mention is the rule of religion. But in this path of devotion there is a subtle inner meaning. God's indirect (or general) command is that pilgrims should first shave their heads and fast. But the Master's direct (or immediate) order is feasting on the *prasad*. Where the *mahá-prasád* is not available, fasting is the rule; but it is a sin to refuse the *prasád* when the Master bids one eat it; especially when He is distributing it with His own hands, who will reject such blessedness in order to fast? Before this He had one morning offered me the *prasád,* and I had eaten it before rising from my bed! He whose heart receives Chaitanya's gracious call discards the Vedas and conventional religion, and seeks refuge in Krishna alone. *Vide Bhagabat,* IV. xxix. 43."

Then the king descended from the palace terrace. He summoned Kashi Mishra and the *Parichha* officer and bade them, "The Master's followers have come to Him. Give them food and board to their comfort, and make it easy for them to see the god. Heedfully obey the Master's behests. Even when He does not speak out, carry out His hinted purpose." So saying he dismissed them.

Sarvabhauma then went away to visit the temple. Gopinath Acharya and Sárvabhauma from afar beheld how the Master met the Vaishnavs. The Vaishnavs (from Bengal) took the way to Kashi Mishra's house, leaving Jagannath's lion-gate on their right. Just then the Master coming with His attendants met them on the way in great glee. Adwaita bowed at His feet, but He embraced him. In rapture of devotion the two were greatly excited, but in consideration of the occasion the Master composed Himself somewhat. The new arrivals all bowed to Him, and He embraced and addressed each of them in turn, took them inside His house (which was filled with the throng of countless Vaishnavs), seated them by Himself, and personally gave them garlands and sandal-paste. Then Gopinath and Sarvabhauma arrived there and saluted all in proper terms.

Sweetly did the Master address Adwaita, "Thy coming has made me complete to-day." But Adwaita objected, "Such is the nature of God. He is full and the source of all power, and yet He exults in the society of the faithful and ever disports in many ways with them."

The Master, delighted to meet Vasudev, stroked his body and said, "Mukunda has been my companion from my childhood. But the sight of you gives me even more delight." Vasudev replied, "That Mukunda has gained your society is a second birth to him. Therefore is his rank higher than mine, though I am his elder brother. Your grace has made him excel in all virtues." Then the Master added, "I have brought two manuscripts from the South for you. They are with Swarup; take copies of them." Vasudev was pleased to get the books, and every Vaishnav (from Bengal) took a copy of them; so that gradually the two works spread everywhere.

Lovingly did the Master address Shribas and others, "You four brothers have bought me (with your kindness)," to which Shribás replied, "Why do you speak just the contrary of the fact? *We* four are bondsmen purchased by your grace."

Seeing Shankar, the Master spoke to Damodar [his elder brother], "My love for you is mixed with respect, whereas towards Shankar I feel pure affection. Therefore keep him in your company." Damodar replied, "Shankar was born after me, but your grace has made him my elder brother."

To Shivananda He said, "I knew before [this your first introduction to me] that you were ardently devoted to me." At these words Shivananda was enraptured; he prostrated himself on the ground and recited an extempore Sanskrit stanza.

Murari Gupta, without coming to the Master at first, lay prostrate out of doors. The Master searched for him, and many ran out to bring Murari in. Murari presented himself before the Master holding two blades of grass between his teeth as a mark of abject humility. As the Master advanced to welcome him, Murari stepped back shouting, "Touch me not, Lord, I am a sinner, my body is unworthy of your touch." The Master replied, "Away with your lowliness, Murari; the sight of it pierces my heart." So saying He embraced Murari, seated him by His side and patted him on the back.

Similarly, with words of praise and repeated embraces did the Master receive Acharya Ratna, the Vidyanidhi, Gadadhar Pandit, Gangadas, Hari Bhatta, and Purandar Acharya. Then He asked, "Where is Haridas?" But Haridas lay prostrate far away on the edge of the public road, whence he had first beheld Chaitanya. He had not resorted to the Master's reception, but stopped at a distance. The devotees hurried there to lead him in, but Haridas said, "I am a low person, of no caste, and debarred from going close to the temple. If I can get a little retired space in the garden, I shall lie there and pass my time in loneliness, so that no servitor of Jagannath may have any occasion to touch me. That is my prayer."

At the report of this speech the Master was pleased. Just then Kashi Mishra and the *Parichha* arrived and did obeisance to the Master. Delighted to see so many Vaishnavs, they were introduced to all with due courtesy. Then they entreated the Master, "Permit us to make arrangements for these Vaishnavs. We have chosen lodgings for all and shall serve them with the *mahá-prasád*." The Master replied, "Gopinath! take the Vaishnavs with you and bestow them in the lodgings chosen for them. Deliver the *mahá-prasád* to Vánináth, who will distribute it to all. Close to my place is a very lonely house in this flower-garden. Let me have it, as I need it for lonely meditation." The Mishra said, "All is thine, and this begging is needless. Take whatever houses you please. We two are slaves waiting for your bidding. Be pleased to command us in whatever you wish for."

The two now left with Gopinath and Vaninath; the former was shown all the lodging-houses, and the latter was given immense quantities of the *mahá-prasád* (for the whole party). Thereafter Vaninath returned with the consecrated rice and cakes, and Gopinath after cleaning the lodgings. The Master said, "Hear, all ye Vaishnavs! Go to your respective lodgings. After bathing in the ocean and gazing at the pinnacle of the temple, come here for your dinner." After bowing to the Master, they were led away to their quarters by Gopinath.

Then He came to receive Haridas, who was chanting God's name in rapture. Haridas fell flat at the Master's feet, who clasped him to His bosom. Both wept in fervour of love,—the Master overcome by the disciple's merits and the disciple by the Master's. Haridas cried, "Touch me not, Master, I am a low untouchable wretch." But the Master answered, "I touch you to be purified myself, because I lack your pure religion. Every moment you acquire as much piety as by bathing in all holy places, or by performing sacrifice, austerities, and alms-giving, or by reading the Vedas. You are holier than a Brahman or a *sannyasi*! Vide *Bhágabat* III. xxxiii. 7." So saying He took Haridas into the garden and gave him a room all apart, adding, "Live here, chanting His name. Daily will I come and join thee. Bow to the discus on the top of the temple of Jagannath (which you can see from here). The *prasad* will be sent to you here." Nityananda, Jagadananda, Damodar, and Mukunda rejoiced on meeting with Haridas.

After bathing in the sea the Master returned to His quarters. Adwaita and his party also bathed in the sea, gazed (reverently) at the pinnacle of the temple, and came to the Master's house for dinner. Chaitanya seated them in proper order and Himself distributed the food. So lavish was His hand that He gave two or three men's food to each. But all the faithful held their hands back from the dinner so long as the Master fasted. Swarup reported this to Him, saying, "Unless you sit down to meal, none else will dine. Gopinath Acharya has invited the party of *sannyasis* to dine with you. He has brought the *prasad*, and the Puri and Bhárati were waiting for you. Do you sit down to dinner with Nityananda, while I serve the Vaishnavs." Then the Master carefully sent the *prasad* to Haridas by the hand of Govinda, and Himself sat at meals with all the *sannyasis*, while the Acharya served them in delight. Swarup Damodar and Jagadánanda served the Vaishnavs, who ate all sorts of cakes and syrups, joyously shouting Hari's name every now and then.

After they had dined and washed their hands, the Master gave each a garland and a sandal-paste mark. They then retired to their lodgings for rest. In the evening they came to Him again, when Ramananda also arrived. The Master introduced him to all the Vaishnavs. With the whole party He went to Jagannath's temple, and began to chant (*kirtan*). After the burning of evening incense He began a *sankirtan*. The *Parichhá* presented Him with a garland and sandal-paste.

Four parties sang on four sides, while in their midst danced Shachi's darling. Eight *dholes* and 32 cymbals were played on. All shouted "Hari! Hari!" and cheered. The blissful sound of *kirtan* penetrated through the 14 regions to the empyrean. As the *kirtan* began, devotion welled out; the people of Puri ran thither and marvelled at the singing, having never seen such transports of love before.

Next the Master went round Jagannath's temple, dancing and singing, while the four parties of chanters preceded and followed Him. As He was falling down, Nityananda held Him up. Men wondered as they beheld His weeping, tremour, perspiration, and deep shouting. The tears ran down His cheeks like jets from a syringe and bathed the men around. After dancing round the temple for a long time, He performed *kirtan* behind it, the four parties singing in a high pitch, while Chaitanya danced wildly in the middle. After dancing long He stopped and permitted the four Apostles to dance with the four parties,—Nityananda, Adwaita Acharya, Vakreshwar Pandit, and Shrinibas—while the Master from the centre gazed on. Here He manifested a miraculous power: every one who danced around Him saw that the Master was gazing only at him! He manifested this power only because He wished to behold the dance of the four. Every one noticed His attentive gaze but did not know how He could gaze on four sides! Just as at the feast on the Jamuna's bank, Krishna in the midst of his comrades seemed to be gazing at every one of them at the same time.

As each came up to Him dancing, the Master firmly clasped him to His bosom. The people of Puri swam in a sea of delight as they beheld such grand dancing, devotion, and *sankirtan*. The king himself on hearing of the splendour of the *kirtan*, ascended to the terrace of his palace with his Court to gaze at it. The sight increased his admiration and his eagerness to be introduced to the Master.

After finishing the chanting and beholding the ceremony of showering flowers on Jagannath, the Master returned home with all the Vaishnavs. The *Parichhá* brought to Him plenty of *prasád* which He divided among all. Then he dismissed them and retired to bed. All the time they were with Him, they daily performed *kirtan* in this style. [Text, canto 11.]

CHAPTER X.

Cleansing Jagannath's garden-house

Before this, when the Master returned from the South, King Pratap Rudra Gajapati, eager to see Him, wrote to Sárvabhauma from Katak to get the Master's consent to an interview. On Bhattacharya replying that the consent was withheld, the king wrote again, "Entreat the *bhaktas* of the Master to intercede with Him for me. Through their favour I may reach His feet. I like not my kingship if I cannot gain His grace. If Chaitanya does not take pity on me, I shall give up my throne and turn a religious mendicant." Bhattacharya in great alarm went to the *bhaktas*, told them of the king's plight and showed them the letter.

They marvelled at the king's devotion to the Master and said, "He will never receive the king. If we entreat Him, it will only grieve Him." But Sárvabhauma said, "Let us all go to Him. We shall tell Him about the king's conduct without pressing Him to grant an interview."

So they all repaired to the Master's presence, eager to speak and yet silent. He asked, "What is it that you have all come to say? I see you have got something in your minds. Why then do you not speak it out?" Nityananda replied, "We have a prayer to make. We cannot keep it back, and yet we fear to speak. Proper or improper we shall report it all to you. If you do not see him the king wishes to turn hermit." The Master's heart was secretly softened by the speech, but with a show of harshness He said, "I see that you all wish to take me to see the king at Katak! Not to speak of the next world, even the people (of the earth) will blame me. Not to speak of other people, even Damodar will condemn me. If I ever receive the king it will be with Damodar's approval and not at your request." Damodar said, "You are God and a free being. You know best what is proper (for you) and what is not. How can a petty creature like me lay down the rule to you? I shall witness your granting him an audience of your own accord. The king loves you, love compels you, therefore his love will make you touch him. A free God as you are, it is your nature to be swayed by love."

Nityananda broke in, "Where is the man that dares bid you interview the king? But it is the nature of devoted ones that they give up their lives if they fail to obtain the object of their adoration. Witness how the sacrificing Brahman's wife gave up her life on failing to go out and see Krishna [*Bhagabat,* X. xxiii]. There is one way, however, if you will only listen to it, by which you will not meet the king and yet his life will be saved: give him of thy grace thy wearing apparel, by getting which he will hold to life."

The Master replied, "You are all highly learned. Do whatever you think fit." Then Nityananda begged from Govinda, one of the *dhotis* of the Master, and sent it by Sarvabhauma to the king, who gleefully adored the cloth as if it were the Master Himself.

Thereafter when Rámánanda Ray came back from the South and entreated the king to let him stay with the Master, the king gladly consented, and pressed him to entreat the Master, whose favourite he was, to grant him an interview. Then the two arrived at Puri, and Ramananda waited on the Master and reported to Him the king's love and devotion. He repeatedly took occasion to mention the subject, being a minister expert in diplomacy, and succeeded in softening the Master's mind.

Pratap Rudra could not contain himself in his eagerness, and again pressed Ramananda, who begged the Master to show His feet only once to the king. But the Master replied, "Judge for yourself, Ramananda, whether a hermit ought to receive a king. Such an interview ruins a hermit in this world and the next, and makes him a butt of ridicule." Ramananda pleaded, "You are God and your own master; whom fear you? You are subject to none!" The Master replied, "I am a *sannyasi* living in human habitations, and I fear worldly dealings with all my soul and body. Even the most trifling failing of a *sannyasi* is talked of by all men, just as a spot of ink on a white cloth cannot be hidden." The Ray urged, "You have saved (by your touch) many a sinner, while this king is a devotee of God and your *bhakta*!" The Master parried the argument thus, "Just as a jar full of milk is shunned if it contains even one drop of wine, so is Pratap Rudra, clad in all the virtues, defiled by his title of King. Still, if you are keen about it, introduce his *son* to me. The Shastras say, the *son is one's own self born again.* My interview with the son will be equivalent to a meeting with the father."

The Ray reported it to the king and conducted the Prince to the Master. The royal youth was handsome and dark, clad in a yellow robe and jewels,—so that he reminded one of Krishna. On seeing him, the Master thought of Krishna, lovingly received him, and said, "A very pious personage is this youth, the sight of whom makes all men remember the Darling of Braja's lord. Blessed am I that I have seen him." So saying He repeatedly embraced the Prince, who was transported by the touch and began to perspire, tremble, weep, exult and stand inert, and (then) danced and wept chanting Krishna's name. The *bhaktas* present praised his good fortune. Then the Master composed him and bade him come there daily.

The Ray took the Prince away to the king who rejoiced at his son's exploit, and in embracing his son felt the touch of the Master's person as it were. Thenceforth the lucky Prince was numbered among the Master's *bhaktas*.

So did He pass His time blissfully in ceaseless *sankirtan* with His followers. He was feasted with His companions by the Acharya and others successively. Thus some time passed and the day of the Car Festival approached. At the outset He called for Kashi Mishra, the *Parichhá* minister and Sarvabhauma, and smilingly said, "I beg to undertake the service of cleansing the Gundichá temple." The *Parichhá* replied, "We are all your servants, bound to do whatever you wish for. On me has been laid the special command of my king to quickly perform whatever you bid. Cleaning the temple is not a task worthy of you ; but it is one of your playful acts ; do whatever you like. But many pitchers and brooms will be required. Permit me to bring them here to-day." So he delivered to the Master a hundred new pitchers and brooms.

Next morning the Master rubbed His followers over with sandal-paste, gave each a broom and went with them to the Gundicha temple to clean it. First He swept and cleaned the inside, the roof, and the throne. The two temples, large and small, were swept and washed, and then the dancing-hall in front. The hundred *bhaktas* plied their brooms, the Master in the middle guiding them by His own manner of sweeping. Following Him they gleefully chanted Krishna's name while at work. The dust covered His fair form ; now and then His tears washed the ground. The god's dining-hall was swept and then the court-yard. At last all the rooms were cleaned. He made a bundle of the collection of straw, dust and pebbles in His outer clothing and threw them outside. So did His followers, too. The Master said, "I shall learn the amount of the labour done by each from the size of his bundle of sweepings." So their bundles were heaped together, but the Master's own bundle was seen to exceed the entire heap.

After cleansing the interior, He divided the work again among them, telling them to make the place thoroughly tidy by removing all the fine dust, small straws and gravel. He rejoiced to see the cleansing finished a second time by His party of Vaishnavs. A hundred other followers had been waiting with a hundred pitchers of water from the outset, for their turn. As soon as the Master called for water they placed the hundred pots before Him. He first washed the temple,—top-floor, wall, and the throne in the interior. The water was dashed in earthen cups on to the top, and thus the upper walls were washed. He Himself washed the throne, while the *bhaktas* washed the inner shrine, and scrubbed it with their own hands. Some poured water on the Master's hands, some on His feet, and some covertly drank up the water (so consecrated). Some begged this water from others. After the temple had been cleansed they poured water into the drain and thus the court-yard was submerged. With His own cloth the Master wiped the building and the throne. It took a hundred pitchers of water to wash the temple.

The purified temple became spotless, cool and delicious, like His own mind laid bare to view. A hundred filled their pitchers at the tank, or, if crowded out, at the well. A hundred *bhaktas* brought the filled pitchers in, while another hundred ran off with the empty ones. Only Nityananda, Adwaita, Swarup, the Bhárati, and the Puri did not draw water. (In their hurry) many pitchers were knocked together and broken, but men brought hundreds of new pots to replace them. They shouted *Krishna! Krishna!* as they filled their pots, or broke them, delivered the filled pitchers or begged for new ones. No other word was uttered there; Krishna's name became a mystic word to express all their different purposes. In ecstasy of devotion the Master chanted Krishna's name and did alone the work of a hundred men, as if He had put forth a hundred arms in washing and scrubbing. He also went up to each to instruct him, praising those whose tasks were well done and gravely chiding those who were slovenly. "You have done well, teach others to do the like,"—at these words of His they were put on the alert and did their work with all their heart. Then they washed the *Jagmohan,** the

* A quadrangle in front of the inner shrine, where the worshippers stand when gazing on the idol.

dining room, the dancing-hall, the court-yard, the kitchen, the environs of the temple, and all nooks and private places.

Just then an honest simple Bengali emptied his pitcher at the Master's feet and drank the water. At this the Master turned angry and sorry. He inly felt pleased, but for the instruction of others outwardly professed anger, calling out to Swarup "Look at the conduct of your *Gauriyá*. He has washed my feet in God's temple and drunk the water. From this sin where can I hope for salvation? Your Bengal man has caused me this misery." Then Swarup took the man bv the nape of his neck, shoved him out of the temple, and on his return entreated the Master to pardon the man. The Master was now satisfied. He seated all in two rows and sat in the middle, picking up straws and brambles with His own hands. "I shall see what a heap the gleaning of each can make. He whose collection is small must forfeit his cake and syrup to me!" Thus was the temple made clean, cool and pure, like His own mind. The water running down the drain looked like a new river flowing to the ocean.

He then cleansed the Man-lion temple in and out, rested a little, and then set up dancing. And in the same manner He swept the roads in front of the temple. The *bhaktas* danced around, while the Master danced in their midst like a raging lion, perspiring, trembling, turning pale, being thrilled, and roaring. After washing His body He marched in advance, showering down tears, while the *bhaktas* washed themselves clean, like unto the deluge of rain from the clouds in the month of *Shrávan*. The loud *sankirtan* filled the sky, the vigorous dance of the Master shook the earth. The resonant singing of Swarup pleased the Master, who danced wildly in delight. After dancing thus, He took rest at the proper time.

Shri Gopal, the son of the Acharya, when allowed by the Master to dance, was so overcome by devotion that he fell down in a fit. The father hurriedly took him up in his arms, and was afflicted to see his breathing stopped. Uttering with a sky-splitting roar the "spell of Nrisingha" he dashed water on the youth's face. But the youth did not regain consciousness, in spite of all their efforts. The Acharya wept, the *bhaktas* wept too. Then the Master laid His hand on the youth's breast and cried out, "Rise Gopal!" and lo! at the cry Gopal came round. The *bhaktas* danced chanting Hari's name.

After a short rest, the Master disported with His followers in the tank. On rising from the water He put on dry clothes, bowed to Nrisingha, and went to sit in the garden, with His followers around Him. Then Vaninath, accompanied by Kashi Mishra and Tulsi *Parichhá*, brought to Him the *maha-prasad*, rice, cakes, and syrup, enough to feed five hundred men. The Master delighted at the sight. On the terrace He sat down to meal with the Puri, Brahmananda Bharati, Adwaita Acharya, Nityananda, Acharya-Ratna, Acharya-Nidhi, Shribas, Gadadhar, Shankar Nyáyáchárya, Raghav, Vakreshwar and Sarvabhauma. Then the *bhaktas* sat down in the successive terraces below them, in due order. The garden was filled with them. The Master repeatedly called for Haridas, who from afar off replied, "Partake of thy repast with the *bhaktas*, Master. I am all too unworthy to sit with thee. Govinda will afterwards give me *prasad* outside the gate." Knowing his intent, the Master did not press him further. The food was served up by Swarup, Jagadananda, Damodar,

Kashishwar, Gopinath, Vaninath and Shankar, while the *bhaktas* shouted *Hari! Hari!* at intervals. The Master remembered the picnic on the Jamuna bank which Krishna had held of yore. He checked, as inopportune, the rapture of devotion which seized His mind (at the thought), and said, "Serve me with sauce and fry only, and let the *bhaktas* have the sweets." Being omniscient He knew who liked which dish, and directed Swarup to serve each according to his taste. Jagadananda, in the course of his serving, dropped sweet things unawares on the Master's plate, and though the Master angrily protested, he supplied more by force or cunning, as such serving was his delight. As Jagadananda came there on his rounds again and gazed at the sweets he had served before, the Master in fear of him ate a little of them, lest Jagadananda should himself fast! Swarup with his hands full of sweet *prasád* stood before the Master praying "Taste a little of this *maha-prasád* and see what Jagannath has eaten!" He placed them on the plate, and the Master moved by his kindness, ate a little. Thus did these two *bhaktas* repeatedly show their wonderful tender regard for Him. Sarvabhauma, who sat at the Master's side, smiled at their loving conduct. The Master ordered sweets to be served to Sarvabhauma and repeatedly pressed him to eat. Gopinath Acharya placed nice dishes before Sarvabhauma and said sweetly, "Bhattacharya! where is your former line of conduct now? Whence do you feel such supreme bliss? Answer me that." Sarvabhauma replied, "I was a sophistical disputant. Your grace has made me attain to this fortune. The Master is the only Gracious One. Who else could have turned a crow (like me) into a *garuda* (the favourite bird of Vishnu)? Formerly I used to howl with the sophist jackals, and now out of the same mouth I utter Krishna's name! What was my former concourse with externalist logician disciples, and what is this society of saints like merging in the ocean waves!" The Master said, "Your devotion to Krishna had already matured (before I met you). It is *your* society that has made *us* all devoted to Krishna!" There is none like the Master, in the three worlds, to exalt the glory of the *bhakta* and to soothe a *bhakta's* heart. Then the Master sent cakes and syrup from the leavings of His plate, to each *bhakta* by name.

Adwaita and Nityananda, sitting together began a mock quarrel, the former saying, "I have dined in the same row with a hermit (*abadhut*). Who knows what my fate will be in the next world? The Master Himself is a *sannyasi*, and as such is above defilement from food-contact (with a casteless man like an *abadhut*), for so the Shastras say. But I am a Brahman householder, and therefore liable to defilement. It has been a great sin on my part to dine in the same row with a man whose birth, pedigree, conduct and character are unknown to me!"

Nityananda replied, "You are Adwaita Acharya. According to the theory of *Adwaita* system (Monism), the duty is abstract *bhakti*. He who accepts your theory recognizes only one principle and no second. With such a person as you have I dined! I know not what led me to join your company." So they wrangled, really praising one another in the garb of abuse.

After the dinner, the Vaishnavs rose up shouting *Hari* loudly enough to split earth and heaven. The Master gave to each of them a garland with His own hand. Next the waiters, Swarup and the other six, sat down to their repast within the room. Govinda laid aside the leavings of the Master's plate, to be given to Haridas. The *bhaktas* and even Govinda himself took a little of this hallowed food. Various are the sports of the free God, such as this ceremony of washing and cleaning.

For a fortnight the people had been denied sight of the god Jagannath [while his image was being painted anew]; and their grief changed into joy when, at the expiry of the period, the eye-painting (*i.e.*, the last stage) being over, they could again see him. The Master went thither with all His followers. First marched Kashishwar, making a lane through the crowd, next went Govinda with a bowl of water. In front of the Master walked the Puri and the Bharati, and by His side Swarup and Adwaita, the other *bhaktas* bringing up the rear. Anxiously did He go to Jagannath's temple and in passion of longing stepped beyond the rules, asking to see the fair face of the god in the dining room. The thirsty eyes of the Master ardently drank in the face of Krishna, like a pair of bees sucking in a lotus. The god's eyes surpassed the blooming lotus in beauty, his cheeks flashed radiance like a polished turquoise mirror, his lower lip was sweet as the *Bándhuli* flower, a light smile spread a ripple of nectar over his form. As the *bhaktas* gazed on, the charm of the god's countenance increased every moment; their thirst increased with its gratification; their eyes could not move from that face. Thus did the Master with His following gaze at the god till noon,—perspiring, trembling, weeping incessantly, and again checking these outbursts in order to have a clearer view of the deity. At the time of *bhog* He began to sing *kirtan*, forgetful of everything else in the bliss of gazing. The *bhaktas* led Him back to His quarters at noon. The servitors offered to the god a double quantity of *prasád*, knowing that the Car Festival would take place next morning. [Text, canto 12.]

CHAPTER XI

The Dance before Jagannath's Car.

Next dav the Master took care to bathe with His followers before it was dawn. Pratap Rudra himself accompanied by his Court showed the Master's *bhaktas* the ceremony of Jagannath leaving his throne to take his seat in the car. Girt round by Adwaita, Nityananda and other *bhaktas*, the Master delightedly witnessed the scene. The stout *pándás* [attendants on an idol] like so many wild elephants, conveyed Jagannath in their arms, some holding the god's neck and some his feet. A strong thick rope was fastened to his waist, and the *pándás* raised the image by pulling at the two ends of the rope. Thick and high heaps of cotton were placed at different points, and the god was raised from one and quickly rested on another of them ; but the touch of his feet broke up the heaps and scattered the cotton with a loud sound. (In fact) Jagannath supports the universe ; who can move *him*? He moves of his own will, to disport himself. Shouts of "Great Lord ! Master ! Master !" rose up, but nothing could be heard amidst the clang of many instruments of music. Then Pratap Rudra, with his own hands, swept the path with a golden broom-stick, and sprinkled sandal water on the ground. He was a king accustomed to sit on the throne, but in as much as being so high he did such lowly services, he gained Jagannath's grace. The Master rejoiced at the sight, and this lowly service of the king gained for him the Master's regard.

Men marvelled as they beheld the trappings of the car. It was covered with fresh gold and high as the Sumeru mountain. Hundreds of fly-whiskers and polished mirrors hung from it ; above were flags and a pure canopy. The *ghágar* rattled, bells jingled on it. Many coloured silk cloths covered it. Jagannáth mounted one car, Subhadrá and Balarám two others.

For fifteen days had Jagannath remained (behind a screen), dallying in secret with Lakshmi, and now with her leave he came out for a ride in his car to give delight to his adorers. The fine white sand on the road suggested a river bank, and the gardens on both sides made the place look like Brindaban. Jagannath went along in his car, pleased with what he saw on both sides. Bengali athletes dragged the car joyfully. It sped at one time, slackened at another, and sometimes stopped altogether. In fact it moved of its own will, and not under the force of men.

Then the Master with His own hands gave to the *bhaktas* sandal paste and garlands......Then He divided the chanters (*kirtaniás*) into four parties,—consisting in all of 24 singers and eight men playing on the *khol,* their chiefs being Swarup and Shribas. Then He bade Nityananda, Adwaita, Haridas, and Vakreshwar dance. In the first party Swarup was the leading singer, while the other five were Damodar, Narayan, Govinda Datta, Raghav Pandit and Shri Govindananda ; with them danced Adwaita. Of the second party the spokesman was Shribas, his followers being Gangadas, Haridas, Shriman, Shuvananda, and Shri Ram Pandit. Here danced Nityananda. Mukunda led the third party, consisting of Vásudev, Gopinath, Murari, Shrikánta, and Vallabh Sen, with Haridas Thákur as the dancer. The fourth party was composed of Haridas, Vishnudas, Raghav, Madhav Ghosh and his brother Vásudev Ghosh, their leader being Govinda Ghosh, and their dancer Vakreshwar Pandit. Other parties of *kirtan* singers were formed by the pilgrims from the Kulin village, (with Rámánanda and Satyaráj as their dancers), the Acharyas of Shantipur (with Achyutánanda as their dancer), the men of Khand (with Narahari and Shri Raghunandan as their dancers). In short four parties preceded the car of Jagannath, two walked on the flanks, and one in the rear. These seven parties played on 14 *khols* in all,—the music of which maddened the Vaishnavs present. The cloud of Vaishnav enthusiasm melted in showers,—their eyes dropped tears along with the nectar of *kirtan*. The shout of *kirtan* filled the three worlds and drowned all other sounds. The Master visited the seven positions shouting "Hari" and "Glory to Jagannath!" with uplifted arms.

Another miracle did He manifest: at the same moment He was present with all the seven parties, so that each cried out, "The Master is with us. Out of His grace for us He has not gone elsewhere." No one can describe the inscrutable power of the Master, only the pure-souled esoteric *bhakta* can know it.

Jagannath, pleased with the *sankirtan*, stopped his car. At this Pratap Rudra marvelled exceedingly and became overcome with excess of devotion. He spoke of the Master's greatness to Kashi Mishra, who replied, "You are, O King, fortunate beyond limit." The king and Sarvabhauma exchanged glances, as none else knew the secret manipulation of Chaitanya;—only those whom He favours can know Him; without His grace even Brahmá cannot recognize Him. He had been delighted with the lowly service done by the king, and for that reason had revealed His mystery to him. True, He had shown Himself to the king only indirectly ; but who can pierce through this illusion of Chaitanya? Sarvabhauma and Kashi Mishra were amazed at the grace shown to the king.

Thus did the Master play for some time, singing and making His followers dance,—now assuming one form, now many, ever putting forth His powers according to the work to be done. In the ardour of play He forgot Himself, and wished not to put a stop to it. Every moment did He do supernatural feats, as He had in a preceding birth performed *rása* and other sports at Brindaban...........

Dancing thus, the Master swept the people away on the wave of enthusiasm......... As Jagannath was going to the Gundichá garden-house, the Master performed *kirtan* before the god for a long time. First He made His *bhaktas* dance, and then, wishing to dance Himself, united the seven parties, placed nine men (Shribas, Rámái, Raghu, Govinda, Mukunda, Haridas, Govindánanda, Madhav, and Govinda) under Swarup to sing and move in the Master's company, while the other parties sang around Him. After bowing to Jagannath, with folded palms and uplifted face the Master prayed:

Salutation to Shri Krishna! who is the divine God, the protector of Brahmans and kine, and benefactor of the universe. To Krishna, to Govinda, I bow again and again!" (*Vishnu Puran*, pt. I. xix. 48.)

"Victory attend Devaki's son, the Lamp of the Vrishni race, the lord! Deep blue like the clouds is his colour, tender are his limbs. He is the Redeemer of the

world from its load of sin. Victory to him! Victory! (*Padávali*, c. 108.) Also *Bhagabat*, X. xc. 24 and *Padavali*, c. 63.

Reciting these verses the Master bowed low again, while the *bhaktas* with folded palms adored God. Dancing impetuously with loud roars, He moved in circles, like a lathe. Wherever His feet touched the ground, the earth with its hills and oceans trembled. He manifested stupor, perspiration, joyous weeping, tremour, turning pale, all sorts of helplessness, pride, exultation and humility. Stumbling He rolled on the ground, like a golden hill thrown on the earth. Nityananda and Adwaita hastened to raise Him up in their arms, shouting *Hari! Hari*. Three circles were formed to keep the crowd back. The first was formed by Nityananda, the second was composed of Kashishwar, Mukunda and other *bhaktas* locking their hands together. Outside Pratap Rudra with his ministers formed another ring to keep the spectators in check. The king, with his hand resting on the shoulder of his prime-minister, was gazing in absorption at the Master's dance. As Shrinibas, sunk in devotion, was standing before the king, the prime-minister touched him and said "Step aside." But Shrinibas in the ardour of his dancing was forgetful of all else. He was pushed repeatedly and at last grew angry and slapped the minister to stop his pushing. At this the minister in anger wanted to rebuke him, but Pratap Rudra checked him saying, "Blessed art thou, to be touched by him. Such happiness has not been my share!"

Not to speak of the people, even Jagannath himself wondered at the dancing of the Master, stopped his car, and gazed at the dance with winkless eyes. Subhadrá and

Balarám smiled in delight at the sight of the dance. A strange change came over the Master while dancing with all His might: all the eight spiritual phases (*sátwik bháb*) manifested themselves at the same time. His hair stood on end, with their roots in the skin bulging out,—like a *Shimul* tree girt round with thorns. His teeth clashed together fearfully, as if they would be dislocated. Blood and sweat ran over His body. He lisped *ja—ja—ga—ga* inarticulately. His eyes poured down tears like syringes, and moistened the men around. Fair was His complexion, at times turning into rosy, at times resembling the *Mallikâ* flower. At times He stood inert, at times He rolled on the ground; at times motionless like a dry wood, at other times prostrate on the ground and breathing faintly, to the alarm of His *bhaktas*. At times water oozed out of His eyes and nostrils and foam out of His mouth,—as the moon sheds bubbles of nectar. Shuvânanda, mad with passion for Krishna, collected and drank up that froth; highly fortunate was he.

After dancing violently for some time the Master wished to manifest another mood. Leaving the dance He bade Swarup sing. Swarup, knowing His taste, began,—

"I have met the lord of my life,
For whose sake I had been withering in the fire of Cupid."

Loudly did Swarup sing this burden, while the Master in delight danced tenderly. Slowly Jagannath's car moved on, Shachi's son dancing before it. With eyes fixed on Jagannath all danced and sang. (At times) the Master walked behind the car with the party of *kirtan* singers, —His arms making the action of song. When Chaitanya lagged behind, Jagannath stopped his car; when the

Master walked ahead the god propelled his car slowly. Thus did the two urge each other on!

In the course of dancing another change of mood came over the Master: with uplifted arms He loudly recited the following stanza. (*Kavya-prakash*, I. canto 4 and also *Padávali* c. 380).

Again and again did He read the stanza, of which the meaning was known to Swarup only. It meant in effect that as the milkmaids at Kurukshetra were delighted to see Krishna, so was the Master gratified at the sight of Jagannath. Under that emotion He had the burden sung (by Swarup). At last Radhá prays to Krishna, "You are the same [beloved] and I am the same [lover, as during your incarnation as Krishna], and yet Brindaban steals my heart. Appear at Brindaban again! Here there are crowds and the din and bustle of elephants, horses and chariots;—there only flowery woodlands, the bee's murmur, the cuckoo's cooing! Here you are dressed as a King girt round by warriors,—there you were a cow-boy, in the company of flute players! Here I have not a drop of the ocean of bliss I used to taste in thy society at Brindaban. Take me with thee to dally at Brindaban again. Thus only can my heart be gratified." In the ardour of His devotion the Master recited the stanzas of the *Bhágabat*, voicing Radhiká's longing. But other people could not understand the verses; Swarup alone knew their meaning but spoke not. (Afterwards) Rup Goswami proclaimed the sense. (*Vide Bhagabat* X. lxxxii. 35 and 31).

In Swarup's company had the Master day and night enjoyed the sense of these verses in His house. During His dance the same emotion overcame Him; so He recited the stanzas and danced gazing at Jagannath. Swarup,—fortunate beyond expression in being absorbed body and soul in the Master,—sang, while the Master drank in his music in abstraction. Under passion's sway the Master sat down and with bowed head traced letters on the ground with His finger. Lest His finger should be hurt, Swarup prevented Him. Swarup's song was in exact accord with the Master's emotion ; he gave a vocal shape to every mood of the Master's heart.

As He gazed at Jagannath's lotus-like face, flashing in the sunlight, his beautiful eyes, his perfumes, robes, garlands and ornaments, the ocean of joy surged up in the Master's heart,—a wild storm swept through Him ; rapture and wildness raised a tumult, the different emotions fought in Him like hostile armies. A passion rose, a passion subsided, it came to terms with another, and at last His normal mood of spirituality (*sátwik*) asserted itself. The Master's body was a pure hill of gold ; His emotion a tree with every flower in bloom. The sight drew the hearts of all ; with the nectar of love He moistened their minds. All the servitors of Jagannath, all the courtiers of the king, the pilgrims, and the residents of Puri,—all marvelled at the Master's dance and rapture, and all felt devotion to Krishna. In enthusiasm they danced, sang, and set up a din. The pilgrims by joining the dance increased the happiness fourfold. Jagannath himself moved on slowly to witness the Master's dance.

Thus dancing, the Master advanced to where Pratap Rudra stood, and was about to fall down when the king held Him up. On seeing him the Master recovered composure and cried shame on Himself for having touched a

King, a worldling, adding, "In his rapture Nityananda has ceased to be heedful [of me]. Kashishwar, Govinda and others, too, are at a distance." True, the Master had been pleased to see Pratap Rudra humbly serving Jagannath as a sweeper, and had meant to meet the king, yet He professed anger in order to warn His followers against consorting with worldly-minded men. The king grieved at the Master's speech, but Sarvabhauma told him not to lose heart, "The Master is pleased with you ; He is only instructing His followers by means of you. I shall seize a proper time for entreating Him. You will then go and meet Him."

Then the Master walked round the car, and standing behind it pushed it with His head. At His push the car ran on with a clatter ; the people around shouted *Hari! Hari!* Next the Master led His followers away to dance before the cars of Subhadrá and Balarám, and when that was done He returned to dance before Jagannath's car. So the cars reached Balgandi, where they stopped, and Jagannath looked on both sides: on the left were the abodes of Brahmans in cocoanut groves, on the right a flower garden resembling Brindaban.........It is the rule that Jagannath breakfasts here on ten million dishes. Every devotee of Jagannath, whatever his position, offers his best food to the god. The king, his wives, ministers and courtiers, all citizens of Puri, great and small, the pilgrims from various lands, the people of the province,—all offered him their respective *bhog*. No order was observed, each deposited his offering of food in front, behind, on the two sides of the god, or in the garden, wherever he could find a spot. The crowd grew immense at the time of the *bhog*, and so the Master stopped dancing and entered the garden, where He lay prostrate on the *veranda* of the garden house, overcome with love ; the exertion of dancing made Him perspire copiously and He enjoyed the fragrant cool wind. All the *bhaktas* who had been singing *kirtan* came and rested under the trees. [Text, canto 13.]

CHAPTER XII

The Hora-Panchami Procession of Lakshmi

As the Master lay thus in the trance of love, Pratap Rudra entered the garden alone, casting off his royal robes and dressed as a [common] Vaishnav, according to the advice of Sarvabhauma. With folded hands he took permission of every *bhakta* and then mustered enough courage to fall down clasping the Master's feet. The Master lay on the ground, His eyes closed in love ; the king eagerly nursed His feet. Pratap Rudra recited the stanzas of the *Rása* dance, (*Bhagabat*, X. xxxi. 1). Infinite was the Master's delight as He heard the verses, and He repeatedly cried "Go on." When the king proceeded to the stanza beginning with "*The nectar-like discourse of thee,*" the Master in devotion rose up and embraced the king, saying "You have given me many priceless gems. I have nothing to give in return, save this embrace." So saying He read the verses over and over again, both quivering and showering tears.

"*The nectar-like discourse of thee, O darling! is life to the afflicted, the theme of praise to sages, and the antidote to sin. The hearing of it does good and gives peace. Blessed are they who spread it far and wide on earth, for they are truly givers of much alms.*" (*Bhagabat*, X. xxxi. 9).

Crying 'the giver of much alms,' the Master embraced the king, not knowing now who he was. The king's lowly service had won for him the Master's pity, who now made him a gift of His grace without any inquiry. Lo! the power of Chaitanya's grace, which bears fruit without questioning. The Master asked, "Who art thou, my benefactor, that hast poured by surprise into my ears the nectar of Krishna's deeds?" The king replied, "I am the slave of thy slaves. My only desire is that you may make me the servant of your servants." Then the Master revealed His godhead to the king, forbidding him to tell it to anybody. Though knowing everything at heart, He outwardly showed as if He did not know that the visitor was a king. The *bhaktas* extolled the king for his good fortune. Pratap Rudra took leave after prostrating himself, and then with folded palms bowed to all the *bhaktas,* and went away. At noon the Master with His followers breakfasted on the plentiful *prasád* sent by the king by the hands of Vaninath, Sarvabhauma and Ramananda. The *prasád* from the Balgandi *bhog* was excellent and of infinite variety, but none of them was cooked food. [Details of the dishes.]........

Knowing the fatigue of the *kirtan* singers, Chaitanya resolved to feast them. He seated them in rows and began to serve the food Himself. Each man was given one leaf and ten cups of *Keyá* leaves. Swarup informed Him that as none would dine before the Master, He ought to sit down to meal. Then the Master sat down with His circle and fed all to their fill. The excess of *prasád* that was left over sufficed to feed a thousand men. Govinda, at the Master's bidding, brought in beggars to eat this food. At the sight of the beggars' feast the Master taught them to chant Hari's name, and they were carried away on the stream of love as they shouted *Hari-bol.*

Now came the time for dragging the car of Jagannath.

The Bengal athletes pulled at the rope, but the car did not move. So they gave up the work in despair. The king and his Court hastened thither in alarm. He set the wrestlers to draw the car and applied his own hand to it; but still the car did not move. Then powerful elephants were harnessed to the car, but it did not advance a step in spite of their utmost efforts. Hearing this the Master arrived with His followers and gazed at the furious elephants pulling at the car. The elephants shrieked at the blows of the goad, but the car stirred not, and the people lamented.

Then the Master took away the elephants, gave the ropes to His followers, and Himself pushed the car from behind with His head. The car sped along rattling. The *bhaktas* merely held the ropes; they had not really to pull, as the car advanced of itself. In delight the people shouted "Glory! Glory to Jagannath!" No other sound was heard. In a twinkle the car reached the gate of the Gundichá garden, the people marvelling at the power of Chaitanya. They set up a roar of "Glory to Gaurchandra! Glory to Krishna-Chaitanya!" At the sight of the Master's might, Pratap Rudra and his courtiers swelled with enthusiasm. Then the servitors performed the ceremony of dismounting Jagannath from his car and conveying him to the Gundichá people. The three images were placed on their thrones, and the ceremony of the gods' bath and dinner commenced. The Master began a joyous dance and *kirtan* in the courtyard in delight. His love welled out in blissfulness, and the sight of it swept away the beholders in a torrent of love. In the evening He witnessed the adoration with lamps, and came to the *Ai-totá* garden for reposing. Adwaita and eight other leading followers invited Him for nine days. Among the rest as many got a chance of entertaining Him as there were days in the "four months," while the rank and file of His followers had no day free for each individually ; so two or three of them combined to give Him a joint entertainment on one day.

Thus did the Master play at dining out. After His morning bath He visited Jagannath, where He danced and sang with His followers, now bidding Adwaita dance, now Nityananda, Haridas, Achyutánanda, Vakreshwar or some other *bhakta.* Thrice in the day did He sing *kirtan* in the Gundichá garden, imagining that Krishna had come to Brindaban and that the period of separation was over. Cherishing in His heart the idea that Krishna was then dallying with Radha there, He remained absorbed in that emotion (of gratification), acting in many gardens the feats of Krishna at Brindaban,—disporting in the tank of Indradyumna, splashing His *bhaktas* with water, while they splashed Him from all sides, now forming one circle, now many, and clapping their hands while croaking like frogs. Sometimes a pair of them wrestled in the water, the Master looking on to see who would win. Adwaita and Nityananda tried to overwhelm each other with water ; the former was beaten and vented his feelings in abuse. Vidyanidhi struggled with Swarup, Shribas with Gadadhar, Raghav Pandit with Vakreshwar, Sarvabhauma with Ramananda Ray. The gravity of the last two disappeared and they became boys again ! Seeing their excitement the Master smiled and said to Gopinath Acharya, "Both are grave scholars and venerable men, but they are acting like wild boys. Stop them." Gopinath replied, "When the ocean of your grace surges up, a single drop of it can easily drown tall mountains like Meru and Mandár,—what to speak of these two small stones? It is thy grace only that has given the nectar of *lilá* to one whose life was formerly spent in chewing the dry husks of logical disputation." Laughing, the Master brought Adwaita there and made him lie on his back on the water like the *Shesha* serpent, while He Himself reclined on him (like Vishnu). Thus did He act the *lilá* of Vishnu reposing on the serpent. Adwaita, putting forth his strength, began to float on the water bearing the Master.

After disporting in the water for some time He returned with His followers to the *Ai-totá*. At the Acharya's house He dined with His leading followers. The *prasád* brought by Vaninath served to feed the other followers. In the evening He visited the god and danced before him, and at night returned to the garden to sleep.........

In the garden, in company with His *bhaktas* He sported as at Brindaban. The trees and creepers blossomed at His sight, the bee and the black-bird sang, the zephyr blew. Under each tree He danced, Vasudev Datta alone singing. Each (*bhakta*) sang under a different tree; Chaitanya alone danced in supreme rapture. Then He bade Vakreshwar dance, while He sang. Swarup and other *kirtaniás* joined the Master in singing, forgetful of all else in the vehemence of their love.

After performing this woodland sport, He went to the Narendra tank for water-sport. Thence He returned to the garden and dined out with His *bhaktas*. For the nine days that Jagannath remained at Gundichá, such was the Master's life. He lodged in the large flower garden named *Jagannath-vallabh*.

When the time came for the ceremony of *Horá-*

Panchami, the king spoke earnestly to Kashi Mishra, "To-morrow is Hora-Panchami, the day of Lakshmi's triumph. Let the celebration be of unprecedented splendour, so that the Master may be filled with wonder. Let extraordinary arrangements be made for the ceremony. Let coloured cloths, bells, fly-whiskers and umbrellas be brought out of my wardrobe as well as Jagannath's, and let the flagstaff, flag, bell, &c. be decorated. Let (Lakshmi's) litter be set forth with varied music and dance. The expenditure should be double (the ordinary), so that the ceremony may eclipse the Car festival. Act so that the Master may be drawn to come out with His followers to behold it."

Next morning the Master with His party visited Jagannath at Gundichá, and then returned to the temple eager to behold the Hora-Panchami festival. Kashi Mishra with great honour seated the Master and His party in a good position. Chaitanya wished to hear about a particular emotion and smilingly asked Swarup, "Though Jagannath lives at Dwaraka, manifesting his natural be- pretext of a ride in his car. From the temple he goes to visit Brindaban. The parks here resemble Brindaban ; he longs to see them therefore, and leaves his temple on the pretext of a ride in his car. From the temple he goes to Gundichá and there disports day and night in the many gardens. But why does he not take Lakshmi with him?" Swarup answered, "Listen, Master, to the reason. Lakshmi has no access to Brindaban, as Krishna's playmates there are milk-maids. So none but the latter can ravish Krishna's heart." The Master continued, "Krishna sets out on the plea of a ride. Subhadra and Baladev accompany him. His dalliance with the milk-maids is done in secret in the parks, unknown to others. Krishna does not overt offence. Why then does Lakshmi fly into a rage at his journey to Gundichá?" Swarup replied, "Such is the nature of a loving mistress. Indifference on the part of her sweetheart rouses her anger."

Just then Lakshmi arrived in an angry mood at the Lion Gate,—riding a golden litter set with many gems, and accompanied by rows of men bearing flags, fly-whiskers, umbrellas and standards, with many musicians, and preceded by the dedicated dancing-girls (*devdási*). A hundred richly dressed hand-maids bearing betel-leaf caskets, goglets of water, fans and fly-whiskers, and much display of wealth and retinue came in her train. Her maids chained the chief servitors of Jagannath and dragged them to her feet, punishing them like thieves and fining them heavily. She beat them till they almost fainted, and abused them in feigned anger. The Master's followers laughed hiding their faces with their hands as they beheld the forwardness of Lakshmi and her maids. [Swarup gave a long explanation of Lakshmi's mood, with illustrative quotations from Sanskrit treatises on love].

At his words Shribas laughed and said "Hark you, Dámodar! behold the vast wealth of my Lakshmi. Brindaban can boast of only flowers, leaves, hills, peacock plumes, and the *Gunchhá* fruit. And yet Jagannath has gone to visit Brindaban! Lakshmi might naturally suspect Krishna's motive in leaving such wealth for poor Brindaban." As he was laughing Lakshmi turned to chastise him, saying "Behold, your god has left such splendour and gone to the Gundichá garden for the sake of flowers, leaves and fruits! Why does the chief of the wise act thus? Bring your lord before Lakshmi!" So saying, Lakshmi's handmaids brought the Master's attendants tied with their waist-bands, made them bow at her mercy. They beat (Jagannath's) car with their sticks, and treated Jagannath's officers like thieves, until they cried with folded hands, "To-morrow shall we produce Jagannath before you." Then Lakshmi was pacified and returned to her abode......[Swarup again shows Lakshmi's conduct as natural in a true lover].

The Master listened with absorption to his exposition of the pure emotion of Radha, and began to dance in rapture while Swarup sang. "Sing on! Sing on!" He cried with ears on the alert. His enthusiasm welled forth on hearing the song of the love-making at Brindaban, and He flooded the village of Puri with devotion. Lakshmi went back to her own place in time, but the Master danced on till the third quarter of the day. The four parties grew tired with singing, but His ardour became doubly intense. Under the influence of Radha's love He became an image of the passion. Nityananda seeing Him from afar prayed to Him, but came not near in consideration of His ecstasy. None but Nityananda could hold the Master [and force Him to stop dancing]. His ecstasy did not cease, and the *kirtan* therefore had to continue. So, Swarup by gesture informed Him how the party was exhausted. At this the Master came to Himself, and returned to the garden. After taking rest He had His midday bath, and dined pleasantly with His party on the many dishes sent from Jagannath's and Lakshmi's *prasád*. In the evening He bathed again and visited Jagannath, dancing and singing before the god.

He sported in the Narendra tank with His *bhaktas*, and held a picnic in the garden. Thus He spent eight days, after which came the return journey of Jagannath in his car to his temple, at which the Master in supreme delight danced and sang as during the outward ride......

When Jagannath again occupied his throne, the Master returned with His followers to His quarters. [Text, canto 14.]

CHAPTER XIII

The Dinner at Sarvabhauma's House

Thus did the Master live at the Nilachal with His followers, engaged in dancing, singing, and delight. In the first year (of His stay) He used to visit Jagannath to whom He bowed, hymned, danced and sang. When the god's *Upala-bhog* was offered, He issued from the temple and took Haridas home with Himself, and there chanted Hari's name.

Adwaita arriving there adored the Master, washed His feet with perfumed water, rubbed Him all over with fragrant sandal-paste, placed a garland round His neck and the tufted *Tulsi* flower on His head, prostrated himself at the Master's feet, and adored Him with folded palms. The Master adored the Acharya with the flowers and *Tulsi* leaves left over on the ritual tray, and recited the verse "I bow to thee, that art what thou art!" Then He made a playful sound with His lips and had a laugh at the Acharya. Thus did the two honour each other. The Acharya repeatedly asked the Master to dinner...... The Master with His party dined at the houses of the different *bhaktas* on successive days. Thus did they spend four months in His company, witnessing all the festivals of Jagannath.

On Krishna's Nativity Day took place the ceremony of Nanda's grand festival, at which the Master with His *bhaktas* personated the cowherds [of Mathura]. On His own shoulders did He carry the loads of milk and curds to the place of the ceremony, shouting Hari's name. Kánái Khuntiá played the *rôle* of Nanda and Jagannath Máhánti that of the queen of Braja. With Pratap Rudra himself, Kashi Mishra, Sarvabhauma, and the *Parichhá* (minister) Tulsi, the Master danced and sported, spattering all their bodies with milk, curds and yellow liquid. Adwaita said, "Bear with me when I tell the truth. I shall know you for a cowherd only if you can brandish a staff!" At this the Master began to play with the staff. He tossed it in the air and caught it repeatedly as it fell. He swung it round His head, behind, before, on the two sides, and between the legs,—spectators laughing. The stick circled round and round like a lathe, all men wondering at the sight. Similarly Nityananda too played with his staff. Who can fathom the deep cowherd mood of these two? At the king's command, Tulsi Parichhá brought out a costly cloth, once worn by Jagannath, and tied it round the Master's head. [Other clothes] were presented to the Acharya and other followers of the Master. Kanai Khuntia and Jagannath Mahanti, in their enthusiasm, gave away all the wealth of their houses. At this the Master was greatly delighted, and bowed to them as his parents (*i.e.*, as Nanda and his wife, the foster-parents of Krishna). In deep spiritual exaltation did He return to His quarters. Thus did Chaitanya play.

On the *Bijaya-dashami*, the day of the storming of Lanká, the Master with His followers played the part of the monkey army [of Ram]. Transported by the spirit of Hanumán, He seized a branch and broke it off as if it were the citadel of Lanka, shouting in a rage, "Where art thou, Rávan! Thou hast kidnapped the Mother of the World. Wretch! I shall destroy thee with thy kith and kin." The people marvelled at His passion and exclaimed "Glory! glory!" So, too, did He witness the celebration of *Rása-yátrá, Dipávali* and *Utthán-dwádashi*. One day He and Nityananda formed a plan in secret, the nature of which His followers afterwards guessed only from the result. Calling all His *bhaktas* together, He said, "Return ye all to Bengal. Come here every year and visit the Gundichá garden with me." On Adwaita Acharya he honourably laid His command, "Teach the lesson of faith in Krishna to all men, down to the Chandáls." Nityananda was bidden, "Go to Bengal. Freely proclaim the gospel of devotion and love. Ramdas, Gadadhar and some others will assist you. Now and then I shall be with you, and standing unseen shall witness your dancing." Embracing Shribas Pandit, He clung to his neck and said tenderly, "In the *kirtan* at your house I shall always dance. You alone of all men will be able to see me. Give my mother this cloth and all this *prasád*; bow to her and beg her pardon for all my faults. I have turned a monk leaving her service; this has been an act of irreligion and not of religion on my part. I am bound by her love; service to her is my religion. It has been madness on my part to quit it. Tell her to have pity on me, as 'No mother finds fault with a crazy child'. What need have I of monachism? Love is wealth to me; I must have gone out of my mind when I turned *sannyasi*. At her command I am staying at the Nilachal. I shall occasionally go home to see her. Daily do I go and behold her feet; she feels a delighted sensation but does not admit it as true. One day [for instance] she cooked rice, five or six vegetable soups, *sák, mochághanta,* fried *patal, nim* leaves, lemon, bits of ginger, curds, milk, and sugar and cream, and offered these many dishes to *Saligrám*. Taking up the *prasád* she lamented, 'All these were Nimai's favourite dishes. He is not here. Who thing. On seeing the empty dish she wiped her tears [at her grief]. So I went there quickly and ate up everything. On seeing the empty dish she wiped her tears and asked, 'Who has eaten the rice and soups? Why is the dish empty? Has the young Gopal (idol) eaten them up? Or has an illusion seized my mind? Has some animal came in and devoured them? Or did I by mistake serve no food on the plate at all?' So thinking she looked again at the cooking-pots and found them full, to her wonder and suspicion [of defilement by some beast or demon]. She then called Ishan, had the place cleaned, and offered rice to the god Gopal afresh. Thus, whenever she cooks nice dishes, she weeps in eager desire to feed me on them. Her affection compels me to eat (the food there); and she is pleased at heart, though outwardly she is disconsolate. This happened on the last *Bijayá-dashami* day. Say unto her and make her believe." Though overcome in making this speech, the Master composed Himself in order to bid farewell to the *bhaktas*.

To Raghav Pandit He spoke feelingly, "Your pure devotion has made me your servant. Hear, all ye, the story of his serving Krishna in the most pious and excellent manner. Let me speak of one thing only, namely his offering of cocoanut as *bhog*. In his place cocoanut sells at five *gandás* [*i.e.*, quarter anna each]. Though his orchards have hundreds of cocoanut palms yielding *lakhs* of fruits, yet wherever he hears of very sweet cocoanuts, he procures them at the price of four annas for one, even from 20 miles' distance. Every day he strips the fibre off five or six fruits and cools them in water. Then at *bhog* he smoothes them and making small holes at the top offers the fruits to Krishna, who drinks the milk within, and leaves the fruits empty or full of liquid at different times. When the fruit is empty of milk, the Pandit rejoices, cracks the nut and spreading the kernel on a hundred dishes, offers them to Krishna, while he meditates outside (the god's dining room). Krishna eats the offering, and leaves the dishes bare, or fills them again with the kernel. At this the Pandit's devotion grows and he swims in the ocean of love.

One day his servant brought ten cleaned cocoanuts to be offered to the god ; but while waiting outside the door he happened to touch the wall above with his hand and then placed the same hand on the fruits. On seeing this the Pandit threw away the fruits as defiled and unworthy of offering to the god, because the dust raised by the feet of people entering at the door sticks to the wall above. By such pure loving service he has surpassed the world.........Similarly whenever he hears of any good fruit like plantain, mango, or jack, in far off villages, he carefully buys them dear, washes, cleans, and offers them to the god. So, too, vegetables, roots, fruits, *chirá, hurum,* confects, cakes, sweet drinks, condensed milk, *káshandi,* pickles, scents, cloth, ornaments, and the pick of all things he offers cleanly to the god. His loving service is unmatched and soothes the eyes of all who behold it."

So saying the Master embraced Raghav, and showed due respect to the other *bhaktas*. To Shivananda Sen he spoke in terms of honour, "Do you look after Vasudev Datta, who is so charitable that every day he spends all his day's earnings, saving nothing. But he is a householder and ought to save, for without saving a man cannot support his kinsmen. You have the charge of the income and expenditure of his house. In your capacity as headman arrange (his affairs properly). Come every year with all the *bhaktas* to the Gundichá garden, taking care of them."

To the pilgrims from the Kulin village He said, "Come here every year with striped silk cloth (for Jagannath). Gunaraj Khan wrote the *Shri Krishna Vijay,* one devotional sentence of which, 'Nanda's darling Krishna is the lord of my life,' has made me the bondsman of his line. Not to speak of you, even a dog of your village is dear to me, above all others."

At this Satyaraj Khan and Ramananda too entreated the Master, "I am a worldly man; how can I practise devotion? I beg thee to lay commands on me." The Master replied, "Ever serve Krishna, ever serve Vaishnavs, ever sing Krishna's name." Satyaraj asked, "How shall I know a Vaishnav? Tell me of his general characteristics." The Master answered, "Whosoever utters Krishna's name even once is to be honoured above all other men......Krishna's name alone washes away all sins and kindles many forms of faith. It does not make a man wait for religious initiation or priestly ministration, but as soon as the word is formed on the tongue, it redeems all men down to the Chandál caste. Along with that, Krishna's name destroys our bondage to the world and draws the heart to the love of Krishna. *Vide* Shridhar Swami's stanza in the *Padávali,* xviii. Therefore, he who utters Krishna's name alone is truly a Vaishnav. Honour him as such."

Of the pilgrims from Khanda the leaders were

Mukunda-das, Raghunandan, and Narahari. To the first, Shachi's son spoke thus, "Tell me truly whether you are the father and Raghunandan your son, or the converse? Dispel my doubt." Mukunda replied, "I verily believe that Raghunandan is my father and I his son, because our devotion to Krishna has been imbibed from him." The delighted Master broke out, "True are thy words. He who gives us faith in Krishna is our *guru*." Bliss it is to the Master to unfold the greatness of *bhaktas,* and He holds forth on the subject through five mouths as it were. Turning to His followers He said, "Hark ye about Mukunda's faith. It is a pure and deep love, like unalloyed gold. Outwardly he is a physician royal and serves his master. But who can fathom his heart's devotion? One day the Musalman king was talking with him about medicine, on a high dais, when a servant held a peacock-feather fan over the Nawab's head. At the sight (of Krishna's crest), Mukunda in a rapture of devotion tumbled down from the height. The Nawab, thinking that he was overcome by death, dismounted, restored him to his senses, and asked where he had been hurt. Mukunda replied that he did not feel much pain. Then to the Nawab's query about the cause of his fall, he replied that he was subject to epilepsy. The Nawab was very wise, he discerned the real reason and thenceforth regarded Mukunda as a great devotee."

Raghunandan served at Krishna's temple, in front of which there was a tank with a *Kadamba* tree blooming all the year round on its *ghát*. Daily two flowers blossomed there (as if) derived from Krishna. The Master continued, turning to Mukunda, "Your business is to earn money, Raghunandan's to serve Krishna. His heart has no other desire. Let Narahari remain with my *bhaktas.* Do you three ever perform these duties respectively."

Graciously He addressed the two brothers, Sarvabhauma and Vidyá-váchaspati, "Krishna is at present manifest in the form of wood and water, the sight and ablution of which saves mankind. As the wooden god he lives at Puri, while the deity as water is the river Bhagirathi. Let Sarvabhauma worship the wooden god and Vachaspati the water-deity."

Embracing Murari Gupta, the Master extolled his sincere devotion thus, "Listen, O ye *bhaktas* ! I had formerly often tempted him saying, 'Passing sweet is the lad of Braja's lord, O Gupta ! Krishna is God himself, in all His fulness, the refuge of all. Love is pure, clean, the source of all passions (*ras*), the ocean in which all virtues are stored like gems. He is wise, expert, sedate, the chief of the masters of emotions. Sweet is his character, sweet is his fascination ; his sports are marked by cleverness and skill. Worship that Krishna, seek refuge in him. The heart cannot accept any other object of adoration.' His respect for me somewhat influenced him and he replied that he was my servant, ready to do my bidding, without free will. Going home, he was restless at the thought of giving up his idol Raghunath, and cried, 'How can I quit the feet of Raghunath ? Kill me to-night, O Lord !' So he spent the whole night watching and weeping, sore at heart. In the morning he returned, clasped my feet and cried, 'I have sold my head at Raghunath's feet, and cannot draw it away now, so great would be the pain of it. I cannot leave Raghunath's feet, and on the other hand thy command will be disobeyed. I have no help for it. Take pity, therefore, on me, O Kind One ; and let me die before thee, so that the conflict within me may be ended.' At these words I rejoiced exceedingly, raised and embraced him, saying, 'Excellent! Excellent! firm is your devotion, O Gupta, as my words have not shaken your purpose. It is the devotion of servants of this kind that ought to be offered at the Lord's feet,—when the Lord draws away His feet, the devotee does not let go his grasp. That I urged you repeatedly was only to test this your earnest faith. You are Hanuman himself, the servant of Ram. Why then should you leave his lotus feet?' This is that Murari Gupta [addressing the other *bhaktas*], the very life of me. My heart breaks to see his meekness of spirit."

Then He embraced Vasudev, and dwelt on his merits with a thousand tongues. The Datta, blushing to hear his own praise, begged at the Master's feet, "Thou hast come down to deliver the world. Grant one prayer of mine. It can be easily granted, if thou willest, O Gracious One! My heart breaks to see the sorrows of mankind. Lay thou the sins of the rest of mankind on *my* head; let *me* suffer in hell under the load of their sins, so that, Master, thou mayest remove the earthly pangs [*i.e.*, birth on earth] of all other beings." These words melted the Master's heart. Trembling and weeping He answered in broken accents, "This request is no surprise, coming from you who are a Prahlád. Full is Krishna's grace on you. Krishna brings to fruition whatever his servants ask for; he has no other work than to gratify his servants' wishes. You have prayed for the salvation of all the creatures of the universe. (I say) they will all be delivered, without suffering for their sins. The task is not too much for Krishna, who is omnipotent. Why should he make you (alone) undergo the due chastisement for (their) sins?

Those whose good you desire are Vaishnavs, all of whose sins are removed by Krishńa. Witness the *Brahma Samhitá*, v. 60.

"At your mere wishing, the universe will be redeemed. It is no labour for Krishna to deliver all men. Ten million figs (*dumbur*) can grow on one tree ; similarly ten million universes float in the water of the Pure. The tree knows not the loss, if a fruit drops and perishes. So, too, if one universe is set free [from re-birth], Krishṇa does not regard it even as a trifling loss. Endless are Krishna's possessions. Vaikuntha and other places belong to him. They are girt round by the ocean of the Cause of Creation. Countless illusive universes float in that ocean, just as a pot of oil-seeds may float in the ditch round a city. The loss of one seed-grain out of it matters nothing. So, too, Krishna does not feel the loss if one universe is gone. Even if illusion and *all* the universes subject to it perish, Krishna does not mind the loss. The illusion [-created world] is no more to Krishna than a she-goat is to the owner of ten millions of cows giving inexhaustible milk. *Vide Bhagabat*, X. lxxxvii, 10."

In such terms did the Master speak of the different merits of all His followers, embrace and give them leave. They wept at parting from Him, while His mind, too, was saddened. Gadadhar Pandit stayed with Him and was settled by Him at Jaleswar [in Jagannath-Puri]. The Puri, Jagadánanda, Swarup Damodar, Damodar Pandit, Govinda, and Kashishwar,—these lived with the Master at Puri. He visited Jagannath every morning.

One day Sarvabhauma solicited Him with folded palms thus, "Now that all the Vaishnavs have returned to Bengal, I have got an opportunity of entertaining you.

Be pleased to be a guest at my house for a month." The Master replied, "It is opposed to my rules of duty. I can't do it." Sarvabhauma persisted, "Let it be for twenty days only." But the Master objected, 'No, that too is opposed to the rules of a *sannyasi*." Sarvabhauma came down to fifteen days, but the Master insisted on dining with him for one day only. Then Sarvabhauma, clasping His feet, begged for ten days out of which the Master gradually reduced five, and accepted the invitation for five days only. Then Sarvabhauma made another prayer, saying, "There are ten monks with you, out of whom the Puri will dine with me for five days, as I told you before. Damodar Swarup, my friend, will go to my house with you and at times alone. The other eight will be my guests dining singly for two days each. Thus a month is filled up with engagements. I fear lest I should fail to show due hospitality if so many monks come to me together. You, too, will visit my house with your shadow, and sometimes in the company of Swarup Damodar." Glad of the Master's nod [of assent] he invited Him that very day. The Bhattacharya's wife was called *Shâthi's mother*; she was greatly devoted to the Master and a very mother in tenderness. [The cooking, the courses, and the dinner described in great detail].

The Master said, "It is impossible to eat so much rice" [*viz.*, three maunds]. The Bhatta replied, "I know what is a sufficient quantity for you. At Puri you [as Jagannath] eat *bhog* 52 times a day, and the quantity for each time is hundreds of loads. At Dwaraka you [as King Krishna dine daily] at the houses of your 16,000 queens, 18 mothers, and the Yádav clan. At Brindaban you dine twice daily at the houses of your kinsmen and cowherd comrades. At the Govardhan sacrifice heaps of rice were brought for you, in comparison with which my dishes form less than a mouthful. You are God indeed. I am a wretched little creature. Consent to take only a little mouthful of food at my house." Smiling, the Master sat down, the Bhatta serving Him with the *prasád* of Jagannath. Just then there came Amogh, the son-in-law of Bhattacharya and the husband of Shâthi. He was a *Kulin* and a fault-finder. He wished to see the feeding, but could not come, as Bhattacharya kept watch at the door stick in hand! When Bhattacharya was busy serving the *prasád*, Amogh came in and looking at the rice began to criticise, "What! a single monk is eating this rice, on which ten or twelve others can feed to their fill!" Hearing these words Bhattacharya looked over his shoulders, and Amogh fled away......His father-in-law cursed him and his mother-in-law prayed for her daughter's widowhood.

That night Amogh spent in hiding, and next morning he was seized with cholera. At the news that he was dying, Bhattacharya exclaimed, "The gods are on my side, and are doing my work. A sin against God bears immediate fruit. Witness the *Mahabharat*, Bana-parva, ccxli. 17, and *Bhagabat*, X.iv.31."

When Gopinath Acharya went to see the Master, in answer to a question about Bhattacharya, he said, "The couple had fasted at night. Amogh is dying of cholera." At this the merciful Master hastened there, laid His hand on Amogh's breast and said, "Pure by nature is this Brahman's heart,—a fit place for Krishna to sit on. Why have you seated the Chandál Envy here, and thus defiled a very holy spot? Your sins are ended by the society of Sarvabhauma. When sin is gone, men recite Krishna's name. Rise, thou, Amogh! chant Krishna's name. Soon will God have mercy on you." At these words, Amogh rose up with the cry of *Krishna! Krishna!* and began to dance in an ecstasy of devotion,—weeping, trembling, standing stockstill, perspiring, lisping. The Master smiled at seeing the surging up of his love. But he begged the Master, holding His feet, "Gracious Master! forgive my fault." With this he slapped his own cheeks till they were swollen. Gopinath Acharya held his hand to stop him, and the Master stroked his body to console him saying, "You are an object of affection to me, being related to Sarvabhauma. Even the very servants and dogs of his house are dear to me above all others. Thou hast not offended. Chant Krishna's name."

So saying the Master came to Sarvabhauma's house, who clasped His feet, but the Master embraced him, took His seat and began, "Amogh is a child. He cannot offend. Why are you fasting, why are you angry with him? Up, bathe, visit Jagannath, and break your fast soon, if you want to please me. I shall wait here so long as you do not return with the *prasád* (for your dinner)." Clasping His feet Sarvabhauma asked "Amogh was dying. Why did you revive him?" The Master replied, "Amogh is your child. The father, especially if he is the nourisher, does not take note of the offence of his boy. He has now turned Vaishnav; his sin is gone; do you then look kindly on him." The Bhatta said, "Go, Master, to see the god. I shall quickly join you there after taking my bath." But He replied, "Gopinath! stay here. When the *prasád* comes to him, inform me of it." Then He went to see the god, while the Bhatta bathed, prayed, and dined.

This Amogh became extremely devoted to the Master.

A very sedate man, he incessantly recited Krishna's name. [Text, canto 15.]

CHAPTER XIV

The Return to Bengal

Pratap Rudra grew sad when he heard that the Master wished to visit Brindaban ; calling Sarvabhauma and Ramananda, the king entreated them, "The Master's mind is inclined to go away from Puri. Try to keep Him here. Without Him this kingdom is of no delight to me. Try every means to detain the hermit." When the Master was taking counsel with the two about making a pilgrimage to Brindaban, they said, "Wait to see the Car Festival, and set out in the month of Kártik." In Kártik they urged, "It is mid-winter now. Better set out after witnessing the Swinging Festival." So they plied all arts to put off His departure ; and gave not their consent in fear of parting with His company. True, the Master was a free agent, under nobody's control. Yet He did not depart against the wishes of His followers.

In the third year of His stay, the Bengal followers wished to go to Puri. So, they all resorted to Adwaita Acharya, who set out joyfully to see the Master. Nityananda, though charged by Him to stay in Bengal and preach the faith of love, nevertheless went to see Him. Who can understand the display of Nityananda's love? Who can number the *bhaktas* that started?—Acharya Ratna, Vidyanidhi, Shribas, Ramai, Vasudev, Madhav, and Govinda (the three brothers), Raghav Pandit with his casket fitted up, the residents of the Kulin village with their striped silk cloth (for Jagannath), Narahari and

Raghunandan of Khanda,—in short all of the *bhaktas* went; who can count them? Shivananda Sen made arrangements about the stages of the road, and guided the whole party in comfort, supplyirg all their needs and securing lodgings, as he knew all about the road to Orissa.

That year the ladies too set out to visit the Master: With the Acharya went Achyuta's mother, Malini with Shribas Pandit, with Shivananda his wife and son named Chaitanya-das, with Acharya Ratna his wife. All the ladies took from their houses all kinds of choice things formerly dear to Him, to feed the Master with. Shivananda looked after their needs, provided them with lodgings by winning over the officers of the halting stations (*ghátiál*), and everywhere nourished them with provisions.

At Remuná they saw Gopinath (idol), at whose temple the Acharya danced and sang. Nityananda knew all the servitors of the god; so they highly honoured the party. The night was passed there; Nityananda distributed among them the twelve pots of condensed milk (*bhog*) presented by the servitors. Then Nityananda told them the whole story of Madhav Puri, the installation of the Gopal, the begging of sandal by Gopal, the stealing of *kshir* by Gopinath for the Puri,—as he had heard it from the Master. The Vaishnavs rejoiced.

So they wended their way to Katak. After visiting the Witness Gopal they spent the night there. Nityananda told the legend of the god, to the increased delight of the Vaishnavs, who pushed on to Puri, eager at heart to meet the Master. When they reached Athára-nálá (Bridge of 18 spans), Govinda, sent by the Master with two garlands to welcome them, met the party and placed the garlands on the necks of Adwaita and Abadhut Goswami, to their intense bliss. There the two began the *sankirtan* of Krishna and advanced dancing. Next Swarup and other followers, sent by the Master, received them with garlands at the Narendra Tank. When they reached the Lion Gate, Chaitanya Himself came out to meet them all. He took them to see Jagannath, and then led them to His own lodgings. With His own hands He served them the *prasád* brought by Vaninath and Kashi Mishra. They were then sent to take rest in the houses respectively occupied by them in the previous year.

Thus the *bhaktas* spent four months at Puri, joining in His *kirtan*. When the season of the Car Festival arrived, He took them, as on the last occasion, to wash the Gundichá temple, presented to Jagannath the striped silk brought by the people of the Kulin village, danced long before the car, and then returned to the garden. While He was reposing on the bank of the tank, Krishnadas, a Brahman of West Bengal (Rárh) and a disciple of Nityananda, was so fortunate as to pour on the Master's head a pot of water, to His great relief.

The Master dined with all His followers on the numerous dishes of *Balgandi bhog* sent to Him. As before, they witnessed the Car procession and the *Horá-Panchami* procession with Him. The Master was invited to dinner by Acharya Goswami, at which a rain storm burst. Then Shribas invited Him, and the Master's favourite dishes were cooked by Málini, who was His handmaid in devotion, but a mother in tenderness. Acharya Ratna and other leading disciples gave dinners to the Master at intervals. When the four months were over He again took counsel in secret with Nityananda. The Acharya whispered to the Master mystic hints ; he seemed to be muttering and none could know his meaning. Chaitanya laughed at seeing the gestures of his face. This the Acharya took to be a mark of assent, and he began to dance in delight ;—none knew what the request and the consent were. But the Master embraced and dismissed him.

Then He addressed Nityananda, "Listen, Shripád! I pray thee grant this request of mine. Don't come to Puri every year, but stay in Bengal to carry out my will, for I see none else who can do the work. You alone can accomplish my hard undertaking." Nityananda replied, "I am but the body ; you are the life of it. It is admitted that the body cannot live apart from life ; yet you, by your incomprehensible power, are performing such an impossibility. Well, I shall do whatever you make me. I am not subject to any [other] law." The Master embraced and gave him leave, and so to the other *bhaktas* too.

The pilgrims from the Kulin village begged, as before, "Master, appoint us our duty," to which He replied, "Serve Vaishnavs, chant Krishna's name. These two will lead you soon to Krishna's feet." The men asked, "By what signs can a Vaishnav be known?" The Master knew their real thoughts, smiled, and answered, "He is the true Vaishnav, who has Krishna's name ever on his lips. Adore his feet." Next year they put the very same question, and the Master by His answer taught them the gradations of Vaishnavs: "Know him to be the best of Vaishnavs, the sight of whom brings Krishna's name on your tongue." Thus did He describe in succession the three grades of Vaishnavs: good, better, and best.

All the Vaishnavs returned to Bengal. Vidyanidhi alone stayed at Puri that year. He formed a close friendship with Swarup, and the two lived together engaged in discourse on Krishna. He gave *mantra* anew to Gadádhar Pandit. On the day of *Orani Shashthi* he witnessed the procession, and felt contempt at beholding Jagannath wearing a cloth with the size not washed out of it. That very night Jagannath and Balaram visited him [in his sleep] and laughingly slapped his cheeks. Vidyanidhi was inly glad at finding his cheeks swollen.........

Thus did the *bhaktas* of Bengal come every year and witness the god's procession in the Master's company. I shall describe only the years in which something special happened. Four years did the Master pass in this way: two years [after He took the monastic vow] were taken up by the pilgrimage to the South and the return ; the next two years He [stayed at Puri] wishing to go to Brindaban, but unable to stir at Ramananda's opposition. In the fifth year the Bengal pilgrims returned home immediately after witnessing the Car Festival without staying [for four months].

Then the Master embraced Sarvabhauma and Ramananda and said, "Very eager am I to visit Brindaban. At your objection I have not set out these two years. I *must* go now. Do you both consent, for I have no other refuge save you. In Bengal my two refuges are my mother and the river Ganges, both gracious ones. On my way I shall see them. Permit me freely to depart."

At these words they reflected, "It is not good to oppose Him too much," and then told Him, "It is now the rainy season, which makes travel impossible. You will certainly depart on the *Vijayá-dashami.*"

On that day the Master set out, taking with Himself all the *prasád* of Jagannath that had been given Him, and also the sandal wood and coloured threads. Taking leave of Jagannath, He started in the morning, and sent back the Oriya disciples who were following Him. With His men He reached Bhabânipur, Ramananda Ray coming behind in his litter. They spent the night there, feeding on the copious *prasád* sent by Vaninath. Next day the Master reached Bhubaneshwar. At Katak He saw the [Sakshi-] Gopal image. Here a Brahman named Swapneshwar bade Him to dinner, while Ramananda Ray invited His followers. The Master lodged in the outer garden, and after dinner reposed under the *Bakul* tree.

Ramananda Ray went to inform King Pratap Rudra, who hastened thither in joy and repeatedly prostrated himself at the Master's feet in ecstasy, and prayed to Him with tremour and tears. The Master, pleased with his faith, rose up and embraced him. The king hymned and bowed to Him again, his body bathed with the tears of the Master's grace. Ramananda composed and seated the king, and the Master showed His favour to him in body mind and speech. So great was the favour shown that He became famous in the world under the name of "the Saviour of Pratap Rudra." The royal ministers adored the Master, who then dismissed the king. Coming out Pratap Rudra sent letters to all officers in his kingdom, bidding them, "Build new houses in different villages [on the route] ; fill six or seven such rooms with provisions. There lodge the Master and wait on Him day and night with your rods [of authority] in hand." His ministers Harichandan and Mangraj he ordered, "Conduct all this business. Bring a new boat to the river [Mahanadi] bank. When the Master after bathing crosses the river, plant a staff there to mark the spot as a holy *tirtha*. I shall daily bathe there.

May I die there. Hang out fine new cloths at the four gates. Ramananda, go you back to the Master." The king heard that the Master would resume His journey in the evening. So he mounted his wives in covered litters on the backs of elephants, which were drawn up in a line along the route. In the evening the Master proceeded with His followers and bathed at the *ghát* of the Chitrotpala [Mahanadi] river. The queens bowed when they saw Him, and at the sight of Him they were filled with devotion, chanting Krishna's name with tears in their eyes. In the three worlds has not been heard of such another gracious saint, whose very view from a distance inspires love of Krishna.

Then He crossed over in a boat, and in the moonlit night reached "the four gates" (*chatur dwár*). Here He passed the night, and next morning bathed and ate the *mahá-prasád* of Jagannath, which the Parichhá used to send Him daily in huge quantities at the king's command by means of a host of servants.

Then the Master wended His way, served by Ramananda, Mangraj, and Hari Chandan, the three [officers of the king]. He was accompanied by the Puri Goswami, Swarup Damodar, Jagadananda, Mukunda, Govinda, Kashishwar, Haridas Thakur, Vakreshwar Pandit, Gopinath Acharya, Damodar Pandit, Ramái, Nandái and many other *bhaktas*, of whom I have named the chief only, for who can count them all? When Gadadhar Pandit followed Him, the Master forbade him to quit the seat of his monastic devotions. The Pandit pleaded, "Where you are, there is my Puri. Let my 'seat of monachism' go to wrack and ruin." The Master said, "Stay here, worshipping Gopinath;" but the Pandit insisted, "The sight of thy feet is worth ten million worship of gods." The Master argued, "If you give up the worship, mine will be the sin. Stay here and worship, if you want to please me." The Pandit answered, "Let the entire sin rest on me. I shall go alone, and not in your company. I am going [to Nadiá] to see the Mother, and not to bear you company. I am ready to bear the sin of quitting the worship I had vowed to perform." So saying the Pandit proceeded alone. At Katak the Master called him. The Pandit's devotion to Chaitanya passes comprehension: he gave up the vowed worship of Krishna as lightly as a straw. The Master was inly pleased at his conduct, but in loving anger He told him, holding his hand, "Your object of quitting your promised worship has been fulfilled, as you have already arrived far [from the temple of your god at Puri]. By wishing to stay with me, you are seeking your (selfish) pleasure. I grieve to see you losing both your *dharmas* (duties). If you wish to make me happy, return to Puri. I shall swear an oath, if you insist any further." So saying the Master embarked, while the Pandit swooned away on the bank. He bade Sarvabhauma lead the Pandit away. Sarvabhauma said, "Get up! such is the Master's play. You know how Krishna broke his own vow to keep the vow of his adorer Bhishma. *Vide Bhágabat,* I. IX. 34. Similarly the Master has endured separation from you in order to keep your vow sacred." So saying he consoled Gadadhar, and the two returned full of grief to Puri. For His sake His *bhaktas* renounced their religious and earthly duties, but the Master could not bear that they should sin thus.

At Jájpur He dismissed the two royal ministers who had been escorting Him, after talking day and night about

Krishna. At every village (on the way) the royal officers, under orders, entertained the Master with various things in the newly built houses. So faring forth He reached Remuna,* where He dismissed Ramananda Ray. The Ray fell down on the ground in a dead faint ; the Master took him up in His arms and wept.

Then He reached the boundary of the Odhra country, where the royal officer met Him, tended Him for three or four days, and told Him about the path in front, "Before you lies the land of a wine-bibing Muslim king, through fear of whom none can travel on the road. His territory extends to Pichhaldá. None dares cross the river in awe of him. Stay here for some days, while we negotiate with him to secure a safe voyage for you." Just then an Oriya servant of the Muslim had visited Katak in disguise. This Hindu spy, witnessing the wonderful deeds of the Master, reported to his king, "A monk has come from Jagannath, with many pious persons in his train. They sing of Krishna incessantly,—laughing, dancing, singing, weeping. The people flocked in *lakhs* to see Him, but after once seeing Him they could not return home, as they became almost mad, chanting Krishna's name, dancing, weeping and rolling on the ground. He cannot be described in words, but has to be seen, to be understood fully. His power shows that He is God." So saying the spy chanted *Hari! Krishna!* laughing, weeping, and dancing like mad. This turned the Muslim king's mind. He sent his own confidential Hindu minister to the Oriya king's [frontier]

* The author, however, tells us in canto 1 that Ramananda Ray accompanied the Master to Bhadrak. Remuna is 5 miles west and Bhadrak 28 miles south of Baleshwar.

officer. The man bowed to the Master and became overwhelmed with love as he cried *Krishna! Krishna!* Then he composed himself and spoke to the Oriya king's officer, "The Muslim governor has sent me to you to seek your permission for him to come here and meet the Master. He is very anxious to do it, and entreats you. Fear not any attack, it will be a peaceful journey." At this the frontier-officer cried out in wonder, "A Muslim's heart! Who could have done this to it? Surely the Master Himself turned his heart, as the sight and (even) thought of Him saves the world." Then he turned to the confidential minister and said, "He is lucky. Let him come here to see the Master, unarmed and with only six or seven attendants, if I am to trust in him."

On hearing this, the Muhammadan governor arrived in a Hindu dress, and prostrated himself with tears of joy on seeing the Master from afar. The frontier-officer led him forward with due honour, and the governor with folded palms stood before the Master reciting Krishna's name and saying, "Why have I been born in a low Muhammadan family? Why did not Fate send me to earth as one of the Hindu race, for then I could have come near thy feet? My life is useless. Let me die!" The frontier-officer, moved by these words, praised the Master after clasping His feet, "This man has got a view of thee, whose very name when heard purifies a Chandál. What wonder that he will be saved? Such is the efficacy of looking at thee!" Witness the *Bhagabat*, III. xxxiii. 6.

Then the Master looked benignly at the Muslim and in soothing terms told him to repeat Krishna's name. The governor replied, "As I have found acceptance with thee, bid me serve thee. Let me earn deliverance from the sin of hurting Brahmans, cows and Vaishnavs, of which I have been too often guilty." Then Mukunda Datta broke in, "Listen, Sir, our Master wishes to reach the bank of the Ganges. Help Him to go there. It is a great command and a good service."

The Muslim bowed to the Master and His party and set off gleefully. The frontier-officer embraced him, formed a friendship with him, and gave him many presents. Next morning the Muslim governor sent out many decorated boats with his Hindu minister to escort the Master. The Oriya frontier-officer, too, accompanied Him. The Master placed His men in the cabin of a new boat, and dismissed the frontier-officer, who stood on the bank gazing at the voyagers with tears in his eyes. The governor after bowing at the Master's feet, started the flotilla, with ten boat-loads of soldiers as a defence against pirates. He crossed the terrible river Mantreshwar, and proceeded to Pichhaldá, at which (frontier) village the Master sent him back. The new disciple's expressions of devotion on the occasion were indescribable.

In that boat the Master reached Pánihâti, and robed the captain in the robe of His favour. The report of His coming created a sensation: men crowded together on land and water. Raghav Pandit came and led the Master to his house, making their way through the press of men with great difficulty. The Master halted there one day. Next morning He reached Kumárháti, where Shribas dwelt. Thence He proceeded to the houses of Shivananda and Vasudev. When lodging with the Váchaspati, He one night fled to the Kuliá village shrinking from the crowd. Here in the house of Madhav-das millions had a view of Him, and here He stayed a week saving all the sinners. Thence He went to the Acharya's house at Shantipur, where He met mother Shachi for soothing her grief. Thence He visited Rámkeli and the dancing-hall, ...returning to Shantipur for a ten days' halt............ Here Raghunath-das met Him. There were two brothers, Hiranya and Govardhan-das, the owners of Sapta-grám and twelve *lakhs* of Rupees. Both were very charitable and rich Brahmans, well-behaved, high-born, and foremost in piety,—the support of the Brahmans of Navadwip, whom they helped with land and money. Their *guru* was Nilambar Chakravarti, who treated them like his brothers. As they had formerly served Purandar Mishra, they were well-known to the Master. Raghunath-das was the son of this Govardhan, and averse to the world from his childhood.

On the Master's coming to Shantipur after turning hermit, Raghunath had come and fallen down at His feet in a rapture of love. The Master had graciously touched him with His toe. Raghunath's father always did good turns to the Acharya who did Raghunath a favour, helping him to eat the leavings of the Master's dinner. After staying at the Master's feet for a week, he had been sent away by the Master when He went to Puri. Raghunath returned home, turned mad with love, and repeatedly ran away from his father's house to go to Puri. But his father seized him on the way and kept him tied up, with five watchmen to guard him day and night and four servants and two cooks,—in all eleven guards.

Raghunath was brooding over his failure to go to Puri, when he heard of the Master's present visit to Shantipur and begged his father thus: "Let me go and see the Master's feet, or my soul will quit my body." His father then sent him with many men and things and an order to return soon. Raghunath spent a week at Shantipur in the Master's company, ever pondering on his heart's wish, "How shall I escape from my guards? How shall I go to Puri with the Master?" The omniscient Chaitanya, knowing his mind, told him soothingly by way of instruction, "Peace! go home. Turn not wild. It is only gradually that men reach the shore of the world-ocean. Don't ape renunciation of the world, in order to make a show before the people. Enjoy your worldly possessions duly, without setting your heart on them. Cherish piety in your heart, while outwardly you discharge your temporal affairs. Soon will Krishna deliver you. When I return here from Brindaban on my way to Puri, come to me by some device. Krishna will at that time inspire you with the device. Who can hold back one whom Krishna favours?"

Raghunath returned home, followed the Master's advice, outwardly gave up his mania and other-worldliness, and did his proper work without being absorbed in it. His parents were pleased at the change and relaxed their rigour.

Here at Shantipur, the Master embraced Adwaita and other *bhaktas* one by one and said, "Permit me, ye all, to go to Puri. As I have met you all here, you need not go to Puri this year. From this place I will proceed to Brindaban. Grant your permission, so that my journey may be safe." Holding His mother's feet He long entreated her and got her consent to visit Brindaban, and then sent her back to Navadwip.

He then set out for Puri with His followers, being served on the way by the same men as before.........On His arrival at Puri there was a bustle in that village: His joyful *bhaktas* came and were all embraced by Him,—Kashi Mishra, Ramananda, Pradyumna, Sarvabhauma, Vaninath, Shikhi, Gadadhar Pandit and others. To them He said, "I wanted to go to Brindaban by way of Bengal, after seeing my mother and the Ganges. When I arrived in Bengal a thousand followers gathered round me; myriads of people flocked there to see the fun. The crowd blocked the roads. Wherever I put up, the houses and walls were broken down by their pressure. Wherever the eye rested there was a sea of heads. With great difficulty I reached the Rámkeli village, where two brothers Rup and Sanátan came to me. They were foremost of devotees, winners of Krishna's grace, outwardly royal ministers and governors, old in knowledge faith and wisdom, and yet behaving as meeker than grass. Their humility could have pierced a stony (heart). Highly pleased I gave them leave saying, 'It is good to be lowly and curb one's own pride. Soon will Krishna deliver you.' When going away Sanatan spoke a riddle: 'To be followed by a million men is not the right manner of visiting Brindaban.' At that time I did not mind the saying, and next morning reached a village named Kanai's Dancing-hall. Here at night I pondered over Sanatan's dark saying and it struck me, 'He has spoken well. With so many men following me, people will point at me as parading saint-ship. Lonely is that Brindaban, hard to win, difficult of access. I must go there alone or with only one companion. Madhavendra Puri had gone there all alone, and (hence) had Krishna appeared to him on the pretext of serving him with milk. And I,—I am going there like a travelling showman. It is not fit to visit Brindaban with a host. A pilgrimage thither accords only with solitary travelling. Instead of my going there alone (as is proper), an army is accompanying me beating drums! O Shame on me! O Shame on me!' So saying I became unsettled, gave up the journey and returned to the Ganges. Leaving my *bhaktas* at different places I have arrived here with only five or six. Favour me and give me your counsel how I may peacefully go to Brindaban. I have failed to reach Brindaban because I left Gadadhar behind here and thus pained him!" At this Gadadhar in rapture seized the Master's feet and spoke meekly, "Wherever you are, there is Brindaban, there Jamuna, Ganges and all holy places. You are going to Brindaban only to give an object-lesson to men. You will do what your heart likes. The rainy season is coming. Spend these four months at Puri. Thereafter do as you list. Go or stay as you like. Who can prevent you?" The other *bhaktas* joined in and said, "Gadadhar has voiced our thoughts." Yielding to their wishes, the Master stayed there four months. Pratap Rudra was glad to hear of it. That day Gadadhar feasted the Master and His *bhaktas*. [Text, canto 16.]

CHAPTER XV

The Pilgrimage to Brindaban

With the coming of early autumn the Master's mind turned to His pilgrimage. He secretly took counsel with Ramananda and Swarup, saying, "If you two help me, I can visit Brindaban. At night I shall quit my bed and escape by the forest path without taking a single attendant. If any one afterwards seeks to follow me, do you detain him, letting none depart. Mind not the sorrow. Be of good cheer and give me leave. If I leave you pleased, my way-faring will be happy."

The two replied, "You are God and a free agent; you act your will, subject to none. But listen to one request of ours. You have just now said that our happiness would make you happy. Well, then, Sir, grant this our prayer. You must take a good Brahman with you. He will cook your food and carry your pots. In the forest path you will not meet with any Brahman whose cooking is fit to be eaten. Give us leave to send a Brahman along with you."

The Master replied, "No, I shall take none of my own comrades with me. If I take one, the others will be grieved. Some sweet-souled stranger may be my companion. I can take one such if I can get him." Swarup suggested, "Here is Balabhadra Bhattacharya,—tender to you, a scholar, a pious man and a gentleman. He had come from Bengal with you during your first advent. He wishes to visit all the *tirthas*. He has a Brahman servant;

he will do your cooking on the way. We shall all be happy if you take him with you, as then you will feel no hardship in making your way through the forest. The Brahman servant will carry your cloth, water, and pots, while Bhattacharya will cook your food." The Master agreed to it and took Balabhadra Bhattacharya with Him.

The night before, He visited Jagannath and took the god's leave, and before sunrise He slipped away unperceived. In the morning the *bhaktas* missed Him and ran about anxiously seeking Him. Swarup stopped them, and they stayed, knowing such to be the Master's wish. Leaving the beaten track the Master took to by-paths, and passing by the left of Katak entered the jungle. In the lonely forest He fared forth, chanting Krishna's name,—elephants and tigers moved away from the path at the sight of Him. In an ecstatic mood He passed through herds of tigers, elephants, rhinoceroses and boars. Bhattacharya shrank in terror, but they stepped aside cowed by the Master's power.

One day a tiger was lying across the path. The Master in abstraction trod on it and cried, "Speak Krishna's name!" And lo! the tiger stood up and began to dance, while chanting *Krishna! Krishna!* Another day He was bathing in the river, when a herd of wild elephants came there to drink. They arrived before Him as He was offering the oblation of water. Bidding them repeat Krishna's name He rushed sprinkling the water on them. Every elephant touched by that water shouted *Krishna* and danced and ran about in love. Some rolled on the ground, some bellowed,—to the marvel of Bhattacharya.

On the way the Master sang *kirtan* aloud. The deer flocked thither, drawn by His sweet voice, and marched with Him on two sides, while He patted their backs and playfully recited the verses, *Bhagabat,* X. xxi. 11. Just then six or seven tigers came up and joined the deer in accompanying the Master. The sight reminded the Master of Brindaban and He recited the verses descriptive of the virtues of Brindaban. *Bhagabat,* X. xiii. 55.

When the Master shouted "Chant Krishna's name," the deer and the tigers danced together (peacefully) shouting *Krishna! Krishna!*—a wonderful sight to Balabhadra Bhattacharya. The tigers and deer embraced and kissed each other, the Master smiling at the fun of it. Leaving them there He went on. The peacock and other birds, on seeing Him, proceeded in His company singing *Krishna!* and dancing like mad. The Master shouted, 'Say *Hari!*' Trees and creepers rejoiced at the sound. To all the animate and inanimate things in the jungle of Chota Nagpur (*Jhárikhand*) He communicated the name of Krishna and maddened them with love. In every village that He passed through or halted in, all the men were filled with devotion. If one heard the name of Krishna from His lips, he spread it to a second, the second to a third, and so on. All chanted Krishna-Hari's name, danced, wept, and laughed ; from one to another the whole land became Vaishnav. Though for fear of drawing a crowd the Master concealed His devotion and gave no outward exhibition of it, yet the very sight of Him, the hearing of His words, and His power made all the people Vaishnav. Travelling in Central Bengal, East Bengal, West Bengal, and Orissa, He had delivered the people there. Now, on the pretext of a pilgrimage to Mathura, He came to Jharikhand and saved the ruffianly bearish people by teaching them the faith that springs from Krishna's name. The wood suggested Brindaban, every hill looked like Govardhan, every river seemed to Him a Jamuna. There He danced in ecstasy, and fell down weeping.

Bhattacharya gathered all green leaves, roots and fruits wherever he found them on the way. When they halted at a, village, six or seven Brahmans would invite Him ; one supplied Bhattacharya with rice, another with milk, curds, *ghee,* or sugar. Where there was no Brahman inhabitant, all the Shudra merchants invited Bhattacharya. He cooked the wild vegetables, which delighted the Master. He kept a store of rice to last for three or four days. In the lonely parts of the jungle, where there was no human habitation, Bhattacharya cooked that rice with soup of wild vegetables. The picnic delighted the Master exceedingly and the solitude gratified Him. Bhattacharya served Him as tenderly as a slave, his Brahman carrying the water-pot and clothing. Thrice daily He bathed in the hot springs, twice He warmed Himself by the fire, as fuel was abundant ; ever did He move in solitude rapt in love. Feeling the bliss (of such a life) He said, "Much have I travelled, but nowhere have I found any trace of the (alleged) hardships of journeying in forests. Passing gracious has Krishna been to me : He has directed me to this forest path to give me varied delight. Previously when I had resolved to visit Brindaban after seeing my mother, the Ganges and my *bhaktas,* and taking a party of my followers with me, and with that aim went to Bengal, and after delighting myself with the sight of those dear ones, I set out joyfully with my followers,—a million people joined me. Then Krishna instructed me through the mouth of Sanatan ; He hindered that journey and brought me to this forest path. O Ocean of Mercy!

gracious unto this humble wretch! There can be no pleasure without thy grace!" Then embracing Bhattacharya He said, "All this pleasure have I through thy help." But Bhattacharya replied, "You are Krishna, you are the gracious one! I am a despicable being; you have taken pity on me; you have (deigned to) take me with you, and to eat food cooked by me. I am a wretch. But you have ennobled this crow to the rank of *Garuda*. You are God Himself, a free being!"

Thus did Balabhadra hymn the Master and please His mind by his loving service. Thus enjoying much bliss He reached Benares and bathed at noon at the Mani-Karnika ghat. Tapan Mishra was then bathing there, and felt some surprise on seeing the Master, as he had previously (only) heard of Chaitanya having turned hermit. When the recognition became certain, he was filled with rapture, and wept clasping the Master's feet, but He raised and embraced him. The Mishra guided the Master to the temple of Vishweshwar and Bindu Madhav, and at last brought Him to his own house, where he served Him, danced (in ecstasy) with his garment fluttering, drank with his whole family the washings of the Master's feet, fed Him, honoured Balabhadra Bhattacharya, and arranged for his cooking.

After taking His meal the Master lay down, the Mishra's son, Raghu, shampooing His feet. The Mishra family ate the leavings of the Master's plate. Chandra Shekhar, a scribe of the Vaidya caste, resident in Benares, a friend of the Mishra and a devotee of the Master, came there on hearing of His arrival. As he wept at His feet, Chaitanya lifted up and graciously embraced him. Chandra Shekhar said, "Great is thy grace, Master that thou hast appeared to thy servant! At my first coming to Benares

I used to hear nothing but the words 'illusion' (*máyá*) and 'Brahma'. Here nothing was preached except expositions of the six systems of philosophy. Then the Mishra kindly told me of Krishna, and we two meditated ceaselessly on thy feet. Omniscient God! thou hast appeared to us. Let us both serve thee for some days before thou goest to Brindaban, as we hear." The Mishra added, "Master, during your stay at Kashi do not consent to dine anywhere except in my house." Thus the Master, compelled by His two devotees, stayed there for some ten days against His will. A Maratha Brahman came to see Him, marvelled at His beauty and devotion, and invited Him, but He declined saying that He was already engaged for the day. With the same plea He put him off day after day in fear of some *sannyasis* joining His company.

Prakashánanda used to deliver public lectures on Vedanta to his many pupils. The Maratha Brahman, after having viewed the Master, described Him to Prakashánanda thus, "A *sannyasi* has come here from Jagannath, whose glory and power I cannot adequately describe. Big of limbs, fair as the purest gold, long-armed, lotus-eyed, clad in all the marks of God-head, as one can see. O, marvel! The sight of Him convinces one that He is Narayan. Whosoever beholds Him chants Krishna's *sankirtan*. All the marks of a great *bhágabat* as described in the *Bhágabat* are evident in Him. Ever does His tongue sing Krishna's name, His eyes run tears like the Ganges stream. Now He dances, now laughs, now sings and now weeps, or at times roars like the lion. The world's benefactor is He, named Krishna-Chaitanya. His name, appearance, and virtues,—all are matchless. To see Him is to know Him as fashioned in God's mould. Hearing will not make one credit this marvellous tale."

The philosopher laughed much and scoffed at the Brahman, saying, "I have heard tLat there is a *sannyasi* in Bengal, an emotionalist, a disciple of Keshav Bhárati and a fraud on the public. He is named Chaitanya, and with his emotional band he roams over the country dancing. Everyone who sees him calls him God. Such is his spell, all beholders are bewitched. I hear that the great scholar Sarvabhauma Bhattacharya has turned mad in this Chaitanya's company. He is a *sannyasi* in name only, but really a great wizard. But his stock in trade of sentimentality will not sell at Kashi! Attend to Vedánta ; do not resort to him! The companionship of the wild man will ruin you in life and death." Grieved at these words, the Maratha Brahman left the place appealing to Krishna. His mind having been purged by the Master's sight, he came to Him and unfolded the tale of his sorrow. The Master smiled. The Brahman continued, "When I first mentioned you to him, he said that he knew you. When he uttered your name in the course of his abuse of you, he thrice used the form *Chaitanya* without adding *Krishna!* It grieved me to hear him speak your name in such a contemptuous manner. Tell me the reason of his conduct, for *my* lips uttered Krishna's name as soon as I saw you." The Master replied, "The philosophers who hold the doctrine of illusion sin against Krishna. They constantly prate about *Brahma, Atma* and *Chaitanya,* and cannot utter the name of Krishna, because that is equivalent to Krishna's self. The name, the image, and the self of a god are all one ; there is no distinction between them ; the three are of the form of soul's bliss (*chidánanda*). Between Krishna's body and personality, between his name and Krishna himself there is no difference. In the case of creatures, no doubt, name, body, and personality are different from one another. *Vide Hari-bhakti-vilas,* xi. 269.

"Therefore Krishna's name, body, and action (*vilás*) cannot be comprehended by the natural senses ; they manifest themselves. His name, qualities, and antics are the soul's bliss (*chidánanda*) like Krishna's own form......From delight in God comes the fuller pleasure of appreciating Krishna's actions (*lilá*), which attract and conquer the spiritual man. *Vide Bhagabat,* XII. xii. 52.

"From delight in God comes the fuller pleasure (of relishing) Krishna's merits, which attract the inmost spirit of the soul. *Vide Bhagabat,* I. Vi. 10. Not to speak of Krishna's feet, even the odour of the *Tulsi* plant captivates the inmost sense of the soul. *Vide Bhagabat,* III. xv. 43.

"Therefore does Krishna's name fail to rise to his lips ; the Illusionists are mere Phenomenalists. He has said that I have come to Kashi with a parcel of sentiments for which there is no customer here, and I must take it all back! Well, how shall I carry away this heavy load? I will sell it here even for a trifle!" So saying and making that Brahman His own, next morning He set out for Mathura. The three followed Him, but He sent them home from a distance. In His absence they used to meet together and sing His praise, mad with love. At Allahabad He bathed in the Triveni, and danced and sang in devotion before the image of Madhav. In rapture at the sight of the Jamuna, He jumped into it, but was hurriedly dragged out by Bhattacharya. Three days He spent thus at Allahabad saving men by imparting to them the love and name of Krishna. On the way to Mathura wherever He halted, He made the people dance to Krishna's loved name. He now made the people of the West Vaishnavs, as He had formerly done those of the South. Wherever He came to the Jamuna on the way, He leapt into it, senseless with love.

On approaching Mathura, He prostrated Himself in an ecstasy of devotion at the sight of the city. Here He bathed in the Vishrám ghat, and bowed to Kesav's image at the place of his nativity. He danced, sang, and shouted in rapture,—men marvelling at his fervour. One Brahman clasped His feet and then began to dance with Him overcome with love. Both danced in rapture, embraced each other, and cried *Hari! Krishna!* with uplifted arms. The spectators shouted *Hari! Hari!*—there was a tumult; the attendant of the image garlanded the Master. Marvelling at the sight of the Master, the people said, "Such beauty and such devotion can never be human. Verily, He is the incarnation of Krishna, come to Mathura to save mankind,—because at the sight of Him men are intoxicated with love and laugh weep dance and sing Krishna's name!"

Then the Master took the Brahman apart and asked him secretly, "You are a Brahman, noble-minded, simple and old. Whence did you acquire such wealth of love?" The man replied, "When Madhavendra Puri came here on his travels, he was pleased to be my guest; he made me his disciple and ate of my cooking. That great soul revealed the (concealed) Gopal, who is worshipped at Govardhan to this day." At this the Master touched his feet, but the Brahman in alarm fell down at the Master's feet. The Master explained, " You are my *guru,* and I am almost a disciple to you. The *guru* should not bow to the disciple." The Brahman in fear and surprise asked, "Why do you, a *sannyasi,* use such language? But stay! Your fervour makes me infer that you are connected with Madhavendra Puri [by the tie of initiation]. He was filled with love of Krishna : nowhere do we find even the savour of such love except among those connected with him." Then Bhattacharya explained the Master's relation to the Puri, at which the Brahman began to dance in rapture. He conducted the Master to his own house, and of his own will served Him in many ways. He made Bhattacharya cook (the Master's meal), but He smilingly said, "The Puri has dined with you. Do thou feed me. This is an instruction for me. *Vide Gita*, iii. 21."

Though the Brahman was a *Sanoria*, at whose house *sannyasis* do not dine, yet the Puri, drawn by his truly Vaishnav behaviour, had initiated and dined with him. Now that the Master begged to eat of his cooking, the Brahman humbly said, "Great is my fortune that I shall feast you. You are God, unfettered by rule and practice. But the ignorant will blame you, which I cannot bear to hear." The Master answered, "The *Shruti*, the *Smriti* and all the sages are not of one opinion, but at variance with one another. The actions of good men are for confirming religion. The Puri's action is the essence of that religion. *Vide Ekádashi-tattwa*, Vyás's words :

Logical reasoning cannot establish our duty. The Shrutis are conflicting. Not a rishi whose views do not differ from those of others. The truth of religion is hidden in a cave. Follow therefore the path trodden by good men."

Then the Brahman feasted the Master, to see whom the citizens of Mathura came in *lakhs*. The Master appeared to them outside the house, and with uplifted arms cried "Chant *Hari! Hari!*" The men raised a shout of *Hari!* and danced mad with love. He bathed at the 24 ghats of the Jamuna, and was shown by that Brahman all the holy sites: Swayambhu, Vishram, Dirgha-Vishnu, Bhuteshwar, Mahavidya, Gokarna, &c.

Wishing to see the woods, He took the Brahman with Him and visited the Madhu-ban, the Tál-ban, Kumud and Bahulá, in all of which He sang in a fervour of love. The cows grazing by the way surrounded the Master with loud bellowings, but grew still at the sight of His overflowing devotion, and licked His limbs tenderly. When He became quiet, He rubbed their backs, and they would not leave Him as He advanced. The cowherds stopped them with great difficulty.

His voice drew to Him herds of deer, which gazed at His face, licked His body, and followed Him on the way without fear. The black-bird and the bee sang sweetly on seeing Him; the peacocks strutted dancing before Him. At His coming the trees and creepers of Brindaban put forth sprouts (as if they were thrilled) and shed honey like tears. Branches laden with flowers and fruits, bowed to His feet, as friend hastens to greet friend with a present. At the sight of Him, the animate and inanimate things of Brindaban rejoiced, as on meeting with their friend. Seeing their affection the rapt Master played with them all, overcome by their influence. Each tree and creeper He embraced; in thought He offered every flower and fruit to Krishna. Weeping, trembling, shaken with love, He shouted, 'Say *Krishna! Krishna!*' The living and the inert shouted *Krishna* as if echoing His deep voice. Clasping the necks of the deer He wept, while the deer trembled and shed tears. The green parrot with its mate appeared on the branches, and on His wishing to hear their speech they flew on to His hand and recited verses in praise of Krishna. *Vide Govinda-lilámrita,* xiii. 29 &c.

Wonder and enthusiasm seized the Master at these words, and the birds flew back to the branch. Delighted He gazed at the dance of the peacocks, the neck of the bird reminding Him of Krishna, and He swooned away in rapture. The (local) Brahman and Bhattacharya nursed Him, sprinkled Him with water and fanned Him with His cloth. Loudly they poured Krishna's name into His ears, (at which) He awoke and rolled on the ground. The brambles of the rough jungle path scratched His limbs, but Bhattacharya took Him in his lap to soothe Him. Krishna's love had filled His mind, so He sprang up with the cry of "Chant! Chant!" and began to dance. Bhattacharya and the (Mathura) Brahman sang Krishna's name, while the Master wended His way dancing. The Brahman marvelled at the fervour of His love and grew concerned about His safety. His passion of devotion on the way to Brindaban grew tenfold of what it had been at Puri; it increased a thousandfold on seeing Mathura, and a hundred thousand times when He roamed the woods of Brindaban. When He was in other lands the mention of Brindaban had caused His love to well out; and now He had actually come to that Brindaban! His soul was steeped in love day and night, and He bathed and dined (unconsciously) as a matter of habit. [Text, canto 17.]

CHAPTER XVI

The Master's doings at Brindaban

Dancing thus the Master reached the village of Arith, where He suddenly recovered His senses. He asked the people about the Rádhá pool (*kunda*) ; but they knew it not, nor did the Brahman guide. But the omniscient discovered the hidden *tirthas* and bathed in shallow pools in two rice-fields. The villagers wondered at the spectacle. The Master began to praise the Radha pool in love: "Radha is dearest to Krishna among all the milk-maids. So is the Radha-*kunda* dear (to him) as the bathing-place of his darling. In this pool Krishna ever sported in the water with Radha and on the bank he dallied in the *rása* dance. Whosoever bathes once here gets from Krishna a love rivalling that of Radha. The pool is charming like Radha's self ; its glory is great like Radha's."

Recollecting Krishna's acts in the pool, He danced in rapture on the bank, and painted His forehead with its mud. Bhattacharya took a little of the mud. Next, the Master went to the Suman tank. At the sight of the Govardhan hill He was affected, prostrated Himself before it, and madly embraced a rock. In a frenzy of devotion He proceeded to the village of Govardhan, where he bowed to the god Hari-dev, the first incarnation of Narayan, who dwelt on the western edge of Mathura. Before the god He danced in rapture, the people at the wondrous news flocking to see Him, and admiring His beauty and devotion. The attendant of the image entertained Him. Bhattacharya cooked in the Brahma-*kunda* and the Master bathed, dined, and passed the night in the temple. At night He cogitated, 'No, I must not ascend Govardhan. How then can I get the sight of Gopal?" He remained silent over the matter, but Gopal knowing His mind, played a trick. The god Gopal was installed at Anna-kut, a village of the Rajputs. Some one informed the headman at night that the Turks were arming to sack the village, and so they should all flee at night with their god. The villagers in alarm first transferred Gopal to the Ganthuli village, where the god was worshipped in secret in a Brahman's house. Then they all fled, leaving the village empty. Thus did Gopal migrate repeatedly in fear of the Muslims, being removed from temple to bower or to another village.

In the morning the Master after bathing in the Mánas Gangá, set out to walk round Govardhan. Moved to rapture at the sight of the hill, He advanced dancing and chanting the verses, *Bhagabat,* X. xxi. 18.

Bathing at the Govinda-*kunda* and other holy spots, He learnt that Gopal had gone to Ganthuli, whither He proceeded to see the god, before whom He danced and sang in a transport of devotion. Moved by Gopal's beauty He recited a *shloka* and danced till the close of the day.

For three days did He view Gopal; on the fourth day Gopal came away with Him, as He walked singing and dancing, and went back to his former temple [on the hill], while the Master stayed at the foot of it. The people in delight cheered aloud *Hari! Hari!* Thus does the tender Gopal descend from the hill on some pretext, in order to show himself to the devotee who passionately longs to see him and yet declines to set foot upon Govardhan. Thus did he appear to Rup and Sanátan. When Rup was too old to walk and yet longed to see Gopal's charms, the god took refuge for a month in the Vithaleshwar temple at Mathura in fear of the Muslims. Then Rup with his disciples saw him there for a month. [Rup's disciples named]. After a month Gopal went back to his temple, while Rup returned to Brindaban.

Then the Master visited the Kámya forest, and all other places in Brindaban in the manner described before. Thence to Nandishwar, at the sight of whom He fell into an ecstasy. After bathing in the Pában and other pools, He climbed the hill and asked if there was any temple on the top. Being directed by the local people, He entered the cave and there beheld the image of the fair dancing Child between his robust parents. He bowed at the feet of Nanda and Yashodá, and in rapture touched all the limbs of the child Krishna. After dancing and singing there all day, He visited the Khadir wood, the Vishnu reposing on the Sesha Snake, Khelá-*tirtha,* the Bhándir wood, the Bhadra wood (across the Jamuna), the Shri-ban, the Lauha-ban, the Mahá-ban, (the birth-place of Radha), where He beheld the site of the killing of Yamalárjun, to the overflowing of His love. After visiting Gokul He returned to Mathura. Here He stayed at that Brahman's house, visiting Krishna's birth-shrine ; but He left Mathura on account of its press of people and dwelt in seclusion at Akrur-*tirtha.*

Another day He visited Brindaban, bathed in the Káliya lake and Praskandan. From the Twelve Suns (*Dwádash Aditya*) He went to the Kashi *tirtha.* At the place of *rása* He fainted away in love, and on recovering rolled on the ground,—laughed, wept, danced, recited verses, and sang. In such deeds was the day spent there ; in the evening He returned to Akrur for breakfast.

Next morning He bathed at the Chiraghat of Brindaban, and rested under a very ancient tamarind tree of the age of Krishna's exploits, with a smooth platform built round its trunk. Close by flowed the Jamuna ; cool breezes blew ; the water of the Jamuna gazed at the beauty of Brindaban. After singing the holy names under the tamarind tree, the Master performed His noonday prayer and breakfasted at Akrur. The people of the village crowded in such numbers to see Him that He could not dance freely. So He came back to Brindaban, and sitting apart sang the holy names till noon. In the third quarter of the day He appeared to the people and advised them all to make *sankirtan* of Krishna's name.

Then arrived a Vaishnav, of the Rajput race, named Krishna-das, a householder living in a village on the other side of the Jamuna. After bathing in the Keshighat he was going to the Káli lake when he suddenly beheld a holy man sitting under the tamarind tree. Admiring the beauty and fervour of the Master, he bowed to Him in devotion. To the Master's query as to who he was, he replied, "I am a miserable householder, a Rajput from across the river. I long to be servant to a Vaishnav. Last night in sleep I saw a vision which exactly agrees with you." As the Master graciously embraced him, the Rajput mad with love danced crying *Hari! Hari!* He followed the Master at noon to the Akrur-*tirtha,* and ate His leavings. Next morning he bore the Master's water-pot [to Brindaban] and kept His company, leaving his wife, children and home.

Everywhere men began to say that Krishna had again appeared at Brindaban. One morning the citizens of

Mathura were returning from Brindaban with a great noise, when the Master met them and asked them whence they were coming. They replied, "Krishna has appeared in the water of the Káli-daha lake. He is dancing on the hood of the snake Káliya, whose jewel is flashing in the water. We have seen it with our own eyes. It is beyond doubt." The Master smiled and remarked, "It is all very true." Thus for three nights people flocked there, all saying on their return that they had beheld Krishna. When they said in the Master's presence that they had seen Krishna, Saraswati indeed moved them to speak the truth, for in seeing *Him* they were beholding the true Krishna ; while they were neglecting the real before their eyes in order to behold the unreal [apparition of Krishna in the lake]. When Bhattacharya begged leave to behold Krishna there, the Master slapped him and said, "You are a learned man, and yet you have turned a fool, believing the story of fools! Why should Krishna appear in that lake? Fools in their delusion are making a fuss [about nothing]. Don't lose your senses. Stay at home. To-morrow at night go and see Krishna."

In the morning a quiet man came to the Master, and He asked him if he had seen Krishna. The man replied, "A fisherman was catching fish in the lake with a lamp in his boat. People seeing him from a distance mistook him for Krishna dancing on the snake ; the boat was regarded as the snake's hood, and the lamp as its crown-jewel! True, Krishna *has* come to Brindaban, but it is not true that the people have seen him. Far from seeing him they are holding a false notion, just as an imbecile (*sthánu*) man takes things in a contrary light." The Master asked, "Where have *you* seen Krishna?" The man replied, "You are a *sannyasi*—a walking Narayan. You have come to Brindaban, as the incarnation of Krishna, to deliver all men by your appearance." The Master invoked God in horror and cried, "Say not so! Never regard this, the humblest of creatures, as Krishna. A *sannyasi* is a particle of *chit*, a creature is like a single ray of light; but Krishna, full of all the six powers, is like the Sun. A creature and the Creator can never be equal, any more than a blazing fire and a solitary spark can be.........The fool who speaks of a creature as equal to God is a sinner, destined to be punished by Yama........."

The man replied, "You have not the human mind. Your appearance and character are like Krishna's. In form you resemble the Son of Braja's lord; your bright complexion eclipses your yellow robe. The musk's fragrance cannot be concealed even if it is tied up in a cloth; so too your Godly nature cannot be kept hidden. Supernatural is your character, your wisdom unfathomable, the sight of you has driven the world mad with the love of Krishna. Woman, child, old man, a Chandâl, or even a Muslim,—whosoever once beholds you, dances madly, chanting Krishna's name. He becomes a teacher unto others and converts the world. Not to speak of seeing you, the mere hearing of your name throws a man into a frenzy of devotion to Krishna and makes him a spiritual deliverer to all others. Your name sanctifies even Chandâls. Superhuman are your powers,—beyond description. *Vide Bhagabat*, III. xxxiii. 6. Such is your glory, you have the attributes of detachment. Your form and attributes prove you to be Krishna!"

The Master favoured these men, and they returned home wild with love. Thus did He stay a few days at

Akrur, saving men by imparting to them the love of Krishna's name. That disciple of Madhav Puri invited every householder in Mathura. The people of Mathura, Brahmans and good men, in parties of ten or twenty every day invited Bhattacharya, who could accept only one of the invitations. The people, getting no opportunity of giving dinners, pressed that Brahman to accept their hospitality. Kanauji, Deccani, and Vaidik Brahmans all humbly asked the Master to dinner. They came to Akrur in the morning, cooked, offered the food to the *Shálgrám*, and fed the Master on it. One day, sitting on the Akrur ghat, the Master reflected, "Here did Akrur see Vaikuntha, and the people of Brindaban got a view of heaven." So saying He jumped into the water; Krishnadas set up a loud lamentation; Bhattacharya hurried there and dragged the Master out. Then he took secret counsel with the (local) Brahman, saying, "The Master was rescued only because I was at hand. But if He is drowned at Brindaban who will save Him? Here we have crowds of visitors and the plague of invitation every day. It is not good for Him to be constantly in an ecstasy. The best plan would be to remove Him from Brindaban." The Brahman (host) replied, "Let us take Him to Prayág; we shall enjoy the journey along the bank of the Ganges. You should ask His consent to bathe in the Ganges at Soron and then start with Him by the same route. It is now the month of Mágh; if we start now we shall reach Prayág in time for bathing during Capricorn. After saying something of your own sorrows, broach to him the request to lead you to Prayág during Capricorn. Tell Him also of the joy of following the bank of the Ganges."

Then Bhattacharya besought the Master thus "I

cannot bear this disturbance by the people. They worry me to accept their invitations. When people come in the morning and fail to find you, they plague me to death. I shall be happy if I follow the bank of the Ganges, and starting now reach Prayág in time for bathing in Capricorn. My mind is restless. I cannot bear [our life here]. I submit to whatever the Master may be pleased to command." Though unwilling to leave Brindaban, the Master, to gratify His *bhakta,* said sweetly, "Never shall I be able to repay my debt to you for your having escorted me to Brindaban. I shall do your wish. Take me wherever you desire."

In the morning He bathed and became overcome with devotion at the thought of leaving Brindaban. Unconscious of the things outside, He fell into a trance of love. Bhattacharya took Him in a boat across the river to Maha-ban. The devoted Krishna-das and that Brahman knew the route along the Ganges. On the way He sat down under a tree with His party, in order to refresh them from fatigue. Many cows were grazing there, and the sight filled Him with delight. Suddenly a cowherd played on his flute, and at once rapture seized the Master ; He fell down in a swoon, foaming at the mouth and His breathing stopped.

Just then ten Pathan cavalrymen arrived there, dismounted, and gazing at the Master jumped to the conclusion that His five companions were sharpers who had poisoned Him with *dhuturá* in order to rob Him of His gold. So they tied up the five and threatened to behead them. The Bengalis began to tremble ; only the Rajput Krishna-das was fearless and that Brahman bold of speech. The Brahman cried out, "Pathan ! I appeal to your Padshah! Take me with you to the *shikdar*. This hermit is my *guru*; I am a Brahman of Mathura. I have a hundred acquaintances at the royal Court. This hermit has a disease which makes Him fall down in a fit. He will soon recover consciousness. Wait a little here. Keep us tied up. After inquiring of Him, slay us if [we deserve it]". The Pathan replied, "You two are up-country men; here are three Bengali *thugs* quaking in fear." Krishnadas said, "I live in this village, with 100 troopers and 200 bowmen under me. If I raise a shout they will come here, kill you, and take away your horses and accoutrement. The Bengalis are not sharpers. You are rogues, as you want to rob pilgrims and to kill them!" At this the Pathan hesitated. Just then the Master came to His senses, rose up with a shout of *Hari! Hari!* and danced in rapture with uplifted arms.

His devotional cry pierced the heart of the Muslim, who in fear released the five, so that the Master saw not the captivity of His followers. Bhattacharya held and seated the Master, who became aware of the things around Him when He saw the Muslims. The Pathans bowed at His feat and charged the five with having poisoned Him with *dhuturá*. But He replied, "They are not *thugs*, but my companions. I am a begging hermit, with no wealth to be robbed. Occasionally I fall into epileptic fits, when these five kindly nurse me." One of the Muslims, a grave man clad in black and called a Pir, was melted at heart on seeing the Master. He propounded monotheism and one common God, on the basis of his holy book (*viz.*, the *Quran*). But the Master refuted all his propositions by arguments based on the Muslim scripture, till the man was silenced. The Master continued, "Your scripture establishes one common God [in the beginning] and refuting that theory sets up in the end a particular God, who is full of all powers, dark of hue, the embodiment of *sat chit* and *ananda,* the perfect Spirit, the soul of all, all-pervading, eternal, the self of every thing, the source of creation life and destruction, the refuge of all universes whether gross or fine, the most excellent, adorable by all, the first cause of everything. Men are saved by faith in Him, and freed from the bondage of the world only by serving Him. Delight in Him is the supreme human attainment, while salvation can give only a particle of that bliss. The highest beatitude comes only from serving His feet. After first insisting on work, knowledge and mental abstraction, these are then set aside and the service of God is laid down as the final duty. Your theologians have no knowledge of their own scriptures; they forget that where there are two injunctions, the latter is sronger. Decide after studying your own holy books, and see what is laid down as the final conclusion."

The Muslim replied, "True are your words. Men cannot realize God as described in the scriptures. They discourse on the abstract God (*Gosáin*); nobody thinks of adoring the incarnate God. You are such, God's own self. Have mercy on me, unworthy sinner! Much have I read, but cannot ascertain the *sádhya* and *sádhan* from the Muslim scriptures. At the sight of vou my tongue utters Krishna's name, and I have been cured of my proud confidence in my own knowledge. Tell me graciously what are *sádhya* and *sádhan.*" So saying he fell at the Master's feet, who said, "Rise! In repeating Krishna's name you have been washed pure from the sins of million births. Say *Krishna! Krishna!*" They chanted the name and were filled with rapture. The Master renamed him Rámdás.

There was another Pathan named Bijuli Khan, a young Prince and the master of Rámdas and other Pathan troopers. He too fell down at the Master's feet, with the cry of *Krishna!* The Master touched his head with His toe, and went on His way. All the Pathans turned *bairágis* and were famous as "Pathan Vaishnavs." They roamed everywhere singing the Master's praise, The Bijuli Khan became a very spiritual person honoured in every *tirtha*.

At Soron He bathed in the Ganges and walked along the river bank to Prayág. Wheh He dismissed the Mathura Brahman and Krishna-das, they begged with folded palms, "Let us follow you to Prayág. Where again shall we see your feet? It is a Muslim country, you may be oppressed anywhere. Your companion, Bhatta-charya, is a mere pandit and does not know how to address people." The Master smilingly consented and they followed Him. Everyone who beheld Him turned frantic with love and sang *sankirtan* aloud. They communicated their faith to others, and these to others again, so that the whole land became Vaishnav, just as the Master had previously converted the South during His pilgrimage.

So walking He reached Prayág, where He bathed for ten days at the junction of the three rivers during the sun's progress through Capricorn. [Text, canto 18.]

CHAPTER XVII

How the Master favoured Rup

Rup and Sanátan, after meeting the Master at the village of Rámkeli, went back to their own quarters. The two brothers devised how to get rid of their worldly ties. They secured two priests with costly gifts, and performed two ceremonies preparatory to a journey (*purashcharan*) in the *mantra* of Krishna,—hoping thereby to attain speedily to Chaitanya's feet. Then Rup came to his own house by boat with much wealth, of which he distributed one half to Brahmans and Vaishnavs, one quarter to his kinsmen for their support, and laid by the other quarter for paying the fine. The money was lodged with good Brahmans, and ten thousand Rupees were deposited with a grocer at Gaur, subject to expenditure by Sanatan. When Rup heard of the Master's journey to Puri and of His intention to go to Brindaban by the forest route, he sent two agents to Puri to bring quickly word about the date of the Master's starting for Brindaban, as he wanted to shape his own course accordingly.

At Gaur Sanatan thought within himself, "The Sultan's love for me is a tie (keeping me here). If he were only to turn angry, it will be my deliverance." On the plea of illness he stayed at home, gave up his official work, and discontinued his visits to the Court. The greedy writers (*Káyastha*) transacted the business of state (in his absence), while he at home discussed the *Shástras*. With twenty or thirty Bhattacharya pandits he discussed the *Bhágabat* in assembly. One day the Sultan with only one attendant suddenly entered Sanatan's meeting. At the sight of the king, all hurriedly stood up, and seated him with due honour. The Sultan said, "I sent a physician to you, who reported that you were in perfect health. All my affairs depend on you, and yet you are staying at home neglecting them! You have ruined all my business. Tell me what you really mean by it?" Sanatan replied, "I am unable to do the work. Get some one else for the purpose." The Sultan in anger cried out again and again, "Your elder brother is acting like a robber. He has desolated the districts (*chákla*) under him by killing men and cattle. And here you are ruining all my affairs!" Sanatan pleaded, "You are the free king of Bengal; punish all offenders."

At this the Sultan returned to his palace and imprisoned Sanatan lest he should escape. When the king set out to invade Orissa, he asked Sanatan to accompany him. The minister replied, "I cannot bear you company, as you are going to molest my gods." Then the Sultan set out, leaving Sanatan in prison.

When the Master set out for Brindaban, the two messengers brought news of it to Rup. At this Rup wrote to Sanatan, "Chaitanya has started for Brindaban. We two brothers are going to join him. Do you run away from Gaur by hook or crook. I have left ten thousand Rupees with a grocer there. Spend it to secure your release soon, and fly to Brindaban by any way that you can find." Then Rup went to Prayag with his youngest brother, Anupam Mallik (surnamed?) Shri-Vallabh, devout Vaishnav.

The Master delighted at the news. As He was going

to visit Bindu Madhav, *lakhs* of men came to meet Him,—some weeping, some laughing, some singing and dancing, others rolling on the ground while shouting *Krishna! Krishna!* The Master drowned Prayág in the flood of Krishna's love, while the Ganges and the Jamuna between them had failed to submerge the land! Seeing the crowd, Rup and his brother stood apart. The Master was thrown into ecstasy when beholding Madhav, and danced with uplifted arms shouting 'Say *Hari! Hari!*' Men marvelled at His greatness. His feats at Prayág baffle description. A Deccani Brahman who knew Him, took Him to his house, where the Master was sitting down in seclusion when Rup and Vallabh came to Him. With two blades of grass between their teeth, they fell down prone on seeing Him from afar. Again and again they rose up and fell down, reciting many verses, overcome with love at the sight of Him. Graciously did the Master speak, "Rise, rise! Rup, come to me! Krishna's grace passes all speech: He has plucked you from the well of worldliness in which you were sunk. Witness the *Hari-bhakti-vilas*, x. 91; the words of God:

'It is not by studying the four Vedas that one can become my bhakta. Even low-caste Chandals can win my love by their faith. To such bhaktas I grant my love and accept their love, and they are worthy of adoration like myself'."

Repeating the above verse He embraced both and placed His feet on their heads as a favour. At this they praised Him humbly with folded palms. [Verses].

Then the Master seated them by Himself and asked for the news of Sanatan. Rup answered, "He is in the king's prison. If you save him then only can he be released." The Master said, "Sanatan has been set free and will soon join us all." The Brahman invited the Master to dinner. Rup passed the day there. Balabhadra Bhattacharya bade both the brotherr to dinner, and the two ate the leavings of the Master's plate. The Master lodged in a house on the junction of the rivers ; Rup and Vallabh took a house near it.

There was then one Vallabh Bhatta* at the village of Ambuli. He came on hearing of the Master's arrival, bowed to Him, received His embrace, and the two discoursed long on Krishna, at which the Master's devotion surged up, but He checked Himself in the presence of the Bhatta, who detected the uncontrollable fervour within Him and marvelled exceedingly. Then the Bhatta invited the Master, who introduced to him the two brothers. They very humbly bowed to the Bhatta from a distance, and as he ran to meet them they receded further crying, "Touch not untouchable sinners like us!" The Bhatta marvelled ; the Master was delighted and told their story to the Bhatta, adding, "Touch not these ; they are of a low caste, while you are a Vaidic sacrificial Brahman, old and a *kulin*." Hearing Krishna's name incessantly on their lips, the Bhatta, taking hint from the Master's winking, remarked, "Krishna's name is dancing on their tongue. They cannot be low ; they are the best of men. Witness the *Bhagabat* III. xxxiii. 7."

The Master, pleased to hear it, praised him much and in rapture recited these verses :

* The celebrated Vallabh-acharya (born in 1479), the founder of the Pushtimarga school of Vaishnavism. *Ambuli* is evidently *Arail*, a village on the Jamuna opposite Allahabad, which contains a temple of the Vallabh-acharya sect.

"Wise men will honour even a Chandál who has been purified in consequence of the sins of his low birth having been burnt away by the blazing fire of pure faith; while an atheist is not to be honoured even though learned in the Vedas. Vain are high pedigree, scholarship, repetition of the holy name, and austerities, in a man who lacks faith in God. As a lifeless doll is dressed up only for show to people, so are the virtues of a faithless man futile. (Hari-bhakti-sudhodaya, iii. 12 and 11.)"

The Bhatta wondered as he gazed at the Master's passion of devotion, power, true faith, and beauty. He took Him with His followers in a boat to his own house for dinner. Beholding the sparkling blue waters of the Jamuna, the Master was overcome by love, and leaped into the river with a roar. They were all seized with concern at it and hurriedly pulled Him out of the water. He began to dance on the boat, which rolled right and left under His weight and shipped a good deal of water, being ready to sink. His love was uncontrollable; still in the presence of the Bhatta the Master checked Himself, as His transport was inopportune, and disembarked at the Ambuli ghat. The anxious Bhatta, after keeping His company at bath, brought Him to his own house, gave Him a fine garment, washed His feet and poured the water on the heads of himself and his family. He clothed the Master in a new waist-band and *dhuti,* and adored Him with scents, flowers, incense and lights. Bhattacharya cooked and the Master dined; so did Rup and his brother; Rup and Krishna-das were given the leavings of His dinner. After chewing spices the Master lay down to repose, the Bhatta rubbing His feet. Sent away by the

Master, the Bhatta despatched his own dinner and came back to His feet.

Now came there Raghupati Upádhyáya, a great scholar and Vaishnav of north Bihar (Tirhut). As he bowed, the Master greeted him with "Be thy mind fixed on Krishna,"—to the great delight of the Upadhyaya. At the Master's request he recited verses of his own composition describing Krishna's deeds. [Verses.]

The Master had a transport of love as He listened and urged the poet to proceed further. The Upadhyaya marvelled at such fervour, and knew Him to be Krishna himself and not a mortal. The Master asked, "Upadhyaya! what do you consider most excellent?" The poet replied, "Black in the best of colours." "Where is the best abode of the black complexion?" The poet answered, "Mathura is the best of cities." "Which is the best age—boyhood, maturity, or adolescence?" The Upadhyaya replied, "Adolescence is the only age fit for our meditation." "Which do you think is the best among emotions?" "Love is the highest of all emotions (*ras*)." The Master remarked, "Thou hast taught me the true lore", and then in a tremulous voice recited Madhavendra Puri's verses (embodying the above answers). In rapture He embraced the Upadhyaya, who began to dance in a frenzy of love.

Vallabh Bhatta marvelled at the sight. With his two sons he fell down at the Master's feet. The villagers flocked thither to see Him, and at His sight became worshippers of Krishna. Vallabh Bhatta stopped the Brahmans who were inviting the Master, saying, "This holy man jumped into mid-Jamuna in ecstasy. I must not detain Him here, but convey Him back to Prayag.

Invite Him there, if you list." So saying he carried the Master across in the boat.

Avoiding the press of the people, the Master went to the Dasháshwamedh ghat and there taught Rup about Krishna's essence, the path of *bhakti,* the lore of emotions, the conclusions of the *Bhágabat.* He imparted to Rup all the doctrines He had learnt from Rámánanda, and infused (His own) force into Rup's heart, in order to make him a perfect doctor of Vaishnav theology. (Verses quoted from the *Chaitanya-chandrodaya.*)

Thanks to the Master's grace on them, Rup and Sanatan became objects of favour and pride to all His leading devotees and associates. Chaitanya's attendants used to ask every one who returned to Bengal from Brindaban, "Tell us how Rup and Sanatan are living there. Tell us of their asceticism, their meals, their adoration of Krishna all day." Then praising the two, the returned pilgrims would answer, "The two are living homeless, sleeping every night under a different tree. In the Brahman houses they get coarse food, in contrast with the sweetmeats they formerly fed upon. They chew dry bread or gram, leaving all enjoyments. In their hands is the beggar's gourd, they are wrapped in tattered quilts; they speak of Krishna, chant his name, dance, and exult. Throughout the day and night they recite Krishna's praise, and sleep for two hours, and sometimes, absorbed in the passion of chanting the name, they deny themselves even that short sleep. At times they compose works on *bhakti,* hear discourses about Chaitanya, and meditate on Him." These words greatly pleased the Fathers of the Church. What wonder [that such should be their life], when Chaitanya's grace was on them?

Thus passing ten days at Prayág, the Master taught Rup and inspired him with strength, adding, "Listen, Rup! to the signs of a *bhakta,* which I shall describe in brief sentences, without going into detail. I speak to you only of one drop of the shoreless profound ocean of *bhakti,* in order to give you a smack of it. Behold in the universe countless beings that pass through 84 *lakhs* of births. The nature of a creature is as minute as a hundredth part of a hundredth part of the point of a hair. [Verses from the *Shruti-byákhyá,* and the *Panchadashi,* 83.]

O, immutable God! if we admit that bodied beings are limitless, eternal and omnipresent, then we cannot maintain the law that they are subject to you. Then the creatures, though subject to birth, will be law-givers unto themselves, even though they have not risen above their mortal nature. Those who say that God and beings are equal, know not thy true nature and their doctrines are false. (*Bhagabat,* X. lxxxvii. 26.)

"Among creatures we must distinguish between the animate and the inanimate. Among the animate are many classes, such as sky-dwellers, land animals, water animals &c., men being only a minority of them. [Eliminate from] men the Mlechchhas, Pulindas, Bauddhas, and Shabars; and from the followers of the Vedas one-half who follow the Vedas in lips only, doing sins condemned by the Vedas and disregarding piety. Among religious people many are devoted to work [as the means of salvation]. For ten million men devoted to work we have one devoted to knowledge, and therefore superior to the former. Among ten million men devoted to knowledge we have only one liberated soul. And among ten million liberated souls hardly one devotee of Krishna is found. The *bhakta* of Krishna is passionless and tranquil,—while those who covet enjoyment, salvation or *siddhi* are perturbed. Witness the *Bhagabat,* VI. xiv 4.

"In roving through the universe, lucky is the man who gets the seed of the creeper of faith (*bhakti*) through the grace of his *guru* and Krishna. He sows the seed like a gardener, waters it with hearing and chanting [the holy name]. As the creeper grows it pierces through the universe, passes beyond the *Birajá Brahma* world to the *Para-byom,* and above that to the heavenly Brindaban, where it creeps up the wishing-tree of Krishna's feet, spreads and bears fruit in the form of love (*prem*)......If any sin against Vaishnavism is done, it uproots or tears the creeper like a wild elephant, its leaves wither. Then the gardener on earth carefully covers it, to save it from the elephant of sin. But if parasites, like love of enjoyment or salvation and countless other things,—or forbidden practices like rubbish,—slaughter of living beings,—thirst of gain or fame, adhere to the creeper,—then these parasites flourish from the watering, while the main creeper's growth is arrested. Cut off the parasites first ; then will the main branch reach the heavenly Brindaban. When the mature fruit of love drops down, the gardener tastes it, and proceeding up the creeper he reaches the wishing-tree. There (in Vishnu's heaven) he tends the wishing-tree, and blissfully tastes the juice of the fruit of love. That is the highest fruit, the supreme human bliss, in comparison with which the four human attainments are as straw...........From pure faith is born love. Therefore I tell you of the signs of pure faith : Leaving desire for others, worship of others, knowledge and work, devote all your senses to the cultivation of Krishna. This is pure faith, the source of love. Its signs are described in the *Narada-pancha-ratra* and the *Bhagabat,* III. xxix. 10—12 &c.

"If one desires enjoyment, salvation, &c., he cannot kindle love, even by means of devotion (*sádhan*). From the culture of *bhakti* ardour is born ; when ardour deepens it is called love (*prem*). As love grows it is successively called *sneha, mán, pranaya, rág, anurág, bháb, mahá-bháb,*—just as we have successively cane-seed, sugarcane juice, molasses, sugar, and fine sugarcandy. All these are the enduring forms of *bhakti* in Krishna, if they are joined by provocation and addiction of mind. When the spiritual (*sátwik*) and extensive (*byabhichári*) emotions mingle together, *bhakti* in Krishna becomes a veritable nectar in taste,—just as curd, when mixed with sugar, ghee, pepper, and camphor, becomes deliciously sweet. In different *bhaktas* the inclination (*rati*) assumes different forms, *viz.*, the *shánta,* the *dásya,* the *sakhya,* the *bátsalya,* and the *madhur.* From these differences in the nature of the passion, the mood (*ras*) of Krishna's love assumes five forms of the same name, which are called the chief *rasas,* while there are seven minor *rasas, viz.*, the comic, the grotesque, the heroic, the pathetic, the rude, the horrible, and the timid. The five former moods permanently occupy the minds of *bhaktas* ; while the seven minor moods rise fitfully when they get a favourable occasion. The nine sages [who instructed king Nimi] and Sanak and others are examples of *bhaktas* of the *shánta* mood. Countless are the *bhaktas* everywhere who illustrate the *dásya* mood. The *sakhya* mood is typified in Shridám and other [cow-boys] and in Bhim and Arjun of Hastinapur.

The *bhaktas* of the *bátsalya* mood are father, mother and other elders. Of the *madhur* mood of *bhakti*, the examples are chiefly the milkmaids of Brindaban, Krishna's queens, Lakshmi and countless others.

"Again, ardour (*rati*) for Krishna is of two kinds: (1) accompanied by a sense of his Godhead, and (2) pure and simple. At Gokul the latter was displayed, free from any consciousness of his Godhead, while at Mathura, Dwaraka, Vaikuntha and other places the former prevailed. Where the sense of his Godhead is predominant, love [for him] is contracted; whereas the way of pure ardour is to disregard his Godhead even when it is openly shown. In the *shánta* and *dásya* emotions this consciousness of his Godhead is a little kindled, but in the *batsalya, sakhya* and *madhur* it is shrunk up. When Krishna bowed at the feet of Vasudev and Devaki, they were frightened by the sense of his Godhead. Witness the *Bhagabat*, X. xliv. 35.

"Arjun was awe-struck at beholding the vision of Krishna as God, and begged his pardon for having treated him familiarly under the notion of a friend. *Vide* the *Gitá*, xi. 41. When Krishna jested with Rukmini, she became mortally afraid lest he should quit her. *Vide* the *Bhagabat*, X. lx. 23.

"The pure love called *kebalá* (unmixed) ignores his divinity, and in case it does recognize him as God, it disavows its loving connection with him. *Vide* the *Bhagabat*, X. viii. 35, ix. 12, xviii. 14, xxx. 32, xxxi. 16.

"The *shánta ras* consists in recognizing the true nature of Krishna and fixing the mind on him only. Krishna has himself said, 'Devoting the mind exclusively to me is the virtue of *shama*.' *Vide* the *Bhagabat*, XI. xix. 33:

'Shama consists in fixing the mind on me; dama is control of the organs of the senses; titikshá is endurance of sorrow: and dhriti is checking what rises on the tongue.'

"It is the duty of a *shánta* votary to give up thirst for everything except Krishna; hence a *shánta* and a *bhakta* of Krishna are identical terms. Krishna's devotee regards heaven and even salvation as no better than hell. *Vide* the *Bhagabat,* VI. xvii. 23.

"Devotion to Krishna and conquest of desire are the two marks of a *shánta bhakta.* All the five kinds of *bhaktas* are necessarily marked by these qualities, just as sound, the attribute of the sky, is possessed by the other four elements also. A *shánta* votary's attachment to Krishna is like an odourless flower; he has *only* acquired a true sense of God's nature, as the supreme spirit and divinity. The *dásya* mood better developes the cognition of Krishna as the Lord of full powers. A *dás bhakta* constantly gratifies Krishna bv serving him with a sense of his divinity, honour, and great glorification; *dásya ras* has the merit of the *shánta ras* plus service, *i.e.,* it has *two* merits. The *sakhya ras* possesses these two merits [plus absolute trust in Krishna]. In *dásya* Krishna's service is marked by honour and glorification; in *sakhya* by reliance.

"A *sakhá bhakta* sits on Krishna's back, or carries him on his shoulders, or has a mock fight with him; he serves Krishna and at times makes Krishna serve *him!* The chief characteristic of the *sakhya ras* is free comradery, without any feeling of respect or awe. So this *ras* has *three* qualities; in it Krishna is loved more ardently, as he is held equal to the *bhakta's* self; hence this *ras* captivates the good. In the *batsalya ras* there are the above three qualities, plus tenderness, which in its excess leads to chiding and chastisement. Such a devotee regards himself as the patron and Krishna as the *protégé* ; his service takes the form of paternal care. This *ras,* therefore has *four* qualities, and is like nectar.........

"In the *madhur ras* all the above four qualities are present in a heightened form, and in addition to them the votary serves Krishna as a lover offering him his or her own person. Here *five* qualities are present. All the [four] emotions find their synthesis in the *madhur,* just as in the case of the five elements (sky, air, light, water and earth) the attributes of the first four are all united in the fifth. Hence is the *madhur ras* of wondrous deliciousness. This emotion has been fully described. Reflect how to spread it. While meditating, Krishna will illuminate your heart. Through Krishna's grace, even an ignorant man reaches the farthest shore of the emotions."

So saying the Master embraced Rup and started for Benares next morning. Rup begged leave to accompany Him as he could not bear the pang of parting. But the Master objected, "Let me lay down your duty. You are now within easy reach of Brindaban ; go there. Thence return to Bengal and join me at Puri." After giving him a (parting) embrace the Master embarked. Rup fell down there in a swoon. The Deccani Brahman took him to his house.

Then Rup and his brother went to Brindaban. When the Master reached Benares, Chandra Sekhar met Him outside the village, as he had dreamt the previous night that the Master had come to his house and so he had come out of the village to wait for Him. Delighted to see the Master, he bowed at His feet and took Him home with him. At the news, Tapan Mishra came to the Master; forming a select assembly he invited Him and made Him dine at his house. Chandra Shekhar invited Bhattacharya. After the feast Tapan Mishra begged Him, "Grant me kindly one favour that I beg of thee. So long as thou stayest at Kashi do not dine anywhere except in my house." The Master accepted his invitation as He knew that He would stay for a week only and would not dine with hermits. He lodged with Chandra Shekhar. The Maratha Brahman and many good men of the Brahman and Kshatriya castes visited the Master. [Text, canto 19.]

CHAPTER XVIII

Sanatan meets the Master and is taught of God's forms

At Gaur, Sanatan lay in prison, when to his delight he received Rup's letter. Then he spoke to his Muslim jailor: "You are a living saint, a very pious man, well-read in the *Quran*. [There it is written that] if a man ransoms a captive with his wealth, God gives him salvation. Formerly I had done you good turns; now show your gratitude by releasing me. I offer you five thousand Rupees. Accept the sum, and by setting me free gain both money and religious merit."

The Muslim replied, "Hark you, Sir, I can let you off, but I fear the Sultan." Sanatan rejoined, "Fear not the Sultan. He has gone to Orissa. If he comes back, tell him that when Sanatan was sent to the bank of the Ganges to ease himself, he jumped into the river, sank down with his fetters, and could not be traced after much search. Fear not, I shall not live in this country, but turn *darvesh* and go to Mecca." The Muhammadan was still reluctant. So Sanatan heaped up seven thousand Rupees before him, at the sight of which his greed was roused. At night he sent Sanatan across the river after filing off his fetters. Sanatan avoided the road by Telia Garhi, the gate of Bengal, and travelling day and night entered the Pátrá hills. There he besought a rustic landowner to guide him over the hill. A palmist present with the landowner whispered to him that Sanatan had eight gold coins with himself. At this the man gladly promised to convey Sanatan over the hill by his own servants at night and asked to prepare his meal in the meantime. With marks of honour he gave him rice. Sanatan bathed in the river, broke his two days' fast, and reflected, "Why does this land-owner show respect to me?" Then he asked [his attendant] Ishán if he had any property with himself. Ishán replied, "Seven gold coins." At this Sanatan rebuked him saying, "Why have you brought this deadly thing with yourself?" Then he gave the seven pieces to the land-owner and sweetly said, "Take these from me and honestly conduct me over the hill. I am a run-away from the king's prison and cannot take the Telia Garhi road. You will acquire merit if you help me to cross the hill." The land-owner replied, "I knew before that your servant had eight gold pieces with him, and I had determined to murder you at night for the money. It is well that you have told me of the money, and so I have been saved from the sin of murder. I am so pleased that I shall not take the coins, but guide you gratis for the sake of merit."

But Sanatan urged, "Some one else will murder me for the money. Accept it and save my life." Then the land-owner sent four footmen of his own, who led Sanatan across the hill by the forest paths at night. Emerging from the hill Sanatan asked Ishan, "I know you have still something left." "Yes, one gold coin," answered Ishan. Sanatan said, "Return home with it." So, leaving him, the holy man set out alone, a bowl in his hand, a tattered quilt on his back, and (therefore) fearless (of robbers).

In course of time he reached Hajipur,* and in the

* The town of Hajipur on the north bank of the Ganges, opposite

evening sat down in a garden. His brother-in-law, Shrikánta, a royal officer, lived here, entrusted by the Sultan with three *lakhs* of Rupees to buy and despatch horses. From a height he discerned Sanatan, and at night came to him with only one attendant. The two had a friendly meeting, and Sanatan told the tale of his escape. Shrikanta said, "Stay here a day or two. Put on decent robes and cast off your rags." Sanatan replied, "No, I shall not linger a minute here. Help me to cross the Ganges, I shall go away at once." Shrikanta with care gave him a Bhutiá blanket and ferried him over.

Sanatan in time reached Benares, where he was glad to hear of the Master's arrival. Going to Chandra Shekhar's house, he sat down at the gate. The Master, knowing it, told Chandra Shekhar, "There is a Vaishnav at the gate. Bring him in." Chandra Shekhar reported to the Master that there was no Vaishnav but only a *darvesh* at the gate. The Master replied, "Well, bring him in." Glad to be called, Sanatan entered. When he was in the court-yard, the Master rushed out and embraced him in rapture. At His touch Sanatan was overcome by love and cried out in a faltering voice, "Touch me not! touch me not!" The two wept ceaselessly, clasping each other's necks, to the wonder of Chandra Shekhar. Then the Master took him by the hand and seated him by His side on the *veranda* of the house, stroking Sanatan's body with His own hands. Sanatan cried, "Touch me not, Master!" but the Master answered, "I touch you to purify myself. Through the strength of

---

Patna, was the seat of the governor of Bihar on behalf of the Sultans of Bengal. (*Riyaz-us-salatin*, Eng. tr., 134 *n.*)

your faith you can cleanse the whole universe. Witness the *Bhagabat,* I. xiii. 8, VII. ix. 9. By seeing, touching, and praising a *bhakta* like you, all my senses are gratified, as the scripture asserts. *Vide* the *Hari-bhakti-sudhodaya,* xiii. 2."

The Master continued, "Listen, Sanatan! Krishna is very kind, the saviour of the fallen. He has delivered you from the worst hell (*rauraba*). Limitless and profound is the ocean of his mercy." Sanatan objected, "I know not Krishna. I recognize your grace as having effected my deliverance." Then at the Master's request he told the whole story of his flight. The Master told him, "I met both your brothers, Rup and Anupam, at Prayag. They have gone to Brindaban." Then He introduced Sanatan to Tapan Mishra and Chandra Shekhar. Tapan Mishra invited him, the Master adding, "Go, Sanatan, shave yourself," and telling Chandra Shekhar to take away the rags of Sanatan. They made him bathe in the Ganges, and Chandra Shekhar gave him a new garment, which he refused to accept. At this the Master was delighted exceedingly.

After His noon-day prayer, the Master went with Sanatan to dine at Tapan Mishra's house. As He sat down to His meal He ordered the Mishra to serve Sanatan also, but he replied, "Sanatan has some rites to perform. You dine first. I shall give him your *prasád.*" After dinner the Master rested. The Mishra gave Sanatan His leavings and offered him a new cloth, which Sanatan declined to accept, asking instead for one of the Mishra's old clothes. So the Mishra gave him an old cloth, which he cut into a waist-band and wrapper.

Sanatan was introduced by the Master to the Maratha

Brahman, who gave him a general invitation to dinner during the whole of his stay at Kashi. But Sanatan declined saying, "I shall rove (begging alms) like the bee. Why should I procure all my food from one Brahman's house."

Exceedingly pleased was the Master at Sanatan's detachment from the world, and He often cast glances at the Bhutia blanket, from which Sanatan guessed that He disapproved of it. So Sanatan planned to get rid of the blanket. When he went to the Ganges to perform his noon-day rites, he met a Bengali drying his quilt, and asked him to exchange it for his blanket, as a favour. The man retorted, "Why are you, a venerable man, mocking me? Why should you exchange your costly blanket for a quilt?" Sanatan replied, "I am not joking but am in earnest. Do make the exchange." So saying he gave up the blanket, placed the quilt on his shoulders and came to Chaitanya. At the Master's query he told the whole tale. The Master remarked, "I have thought of it. Krishna, who has delivered you from attachment to earthly goods, cannot have left a remnant of that attachment in you. No good physician leaves even a trace of the disease unremoved. You were living on alms from door to door, and yet there was a three Rupee blanket on your back! It spoiled your virtue and made you a mock unto the beholders." Sanatan replied, "He who has released me from worldly ties has also cured this last remnant of worldliness in me."

The pleased Master showed grace to him, and thus emboldened him to put questions. Formerly the Master had put questions to Ramananda Ray, which the latter had answered under His inspiration. So, now, inspired

16

by the Master, Sanatan put questions, while He established spiritual truths.

Then Sanatan, biting a blade of grass as a token of abjectness, clasped the Master's feet and said, "Low-born, with low comrades, a fallen wretch, I have wasted my life, plunged in the well of vile worldliness. I know nothing of my own good or evil, but I have held as truth whatever was approved in vulgar practice. As you have graciously saved me, tell me of your grace what my duties are. Who am I? Why are the three afflictions (*tápa*) oppressing me? I know not what will do me good. I know not even how to ask about the truth of *sádhya* and *sádhan.* Do you of your own accord, unfold all these truths to me." The Master replied, "Full is Krishna's grace to you. You know all the truths and are not subject to the three afflictions. You are strong in Krishna's strength, you know the truths already. It is the nature of *sádhus* to inquire about what they know, only to confirm it.

"You are a proper agent for preaching *bhakti*. Listen to all the truths as I tell them in due order:

"The soul of man is the eternal servant of Krishna. The *tatasthá* power of Krishna manifests differences [between the Creator and His creatures],—just as a ray of the sun transforms itself into a flame of fire. Krishna has by nature three powers: *viz.*, the *chit,* the life, and the illusion powers. *Vide* the *Vishnu Puran* I. xxix. 50, VI. vii. 60 and 61, I. iii. 2, the *Gita* vii. 5 and 14, and the *Bhagabat,* XI. ii. 35.

"When a creature forgets Krishna, his face is ever turned to external things, and therefore under the influence of illusion he undergoes the misery of being born in the world, now rising to heaven, now sinking to hell, just as a criminal is ducked in water by royal command.

"If under the teaching of true scripture, a man turns to Krishna, he is saved, he gets rid of illusion. A creature labouring under illusion remembers not Krishna. So Krishna kindly created the Vedas and Purans. He makes himself known through scripture, *guru*, and the soul ; and man comes to realize 'Krishna is my lord and saviour.' The Vedas treat of Relation, Epithet, and Needs ; that Relation is the attaining of Krishna, faith is the means of this attainment, the epithets are his names ; love is the (supreme) need, the most precious treasure and the highest achievement of humanity. *Madhur* service is the means of gaining Krishna ; by serving him we can enjoy the relish of him. The following parable will illustrate it: An all-knowing seer visited a poor man and seeing his misery said, 'Why are you so poor? Your father has left you a large legacy. He died elsewhere and therefore could not inform you of it.' At these words the man began to hunt for his treasure. In the same manner the *Vedas* and *Purans* instruct men about Krishna......The counsel of the seer is the source, the treasure is the consequence. By his own knowledge the man could not attain to his father's treasure—the seer had to tell him the method of discovering it: 'Here lies the treasure. If you dig in the south, hornets will rise and not money. If you dig west a gnome will show itself and hinder you. In the north your diggings will discover a dark serpent, which will swallow you up. But by digging a little on the east side you will get the pots of treasure.' Similarly the *Shastras* assert that leaving work, knowledge and abstraction (*yog*), one can influence Krishna by faith alone. *Vide* the *Bhagabat*, XI. xiv. 19 & 20.

Therefore is faith the only means of gaining Krishna, and it is described in all *Shastras* as *abhidheya.* As wealth gives pleasure and drives away sorrow of itself, so *bhakti* kindles love of Krishna, and when love is turned to Krishna man is freed from bondage to the world. The fruit of love is not riches or the cessation of re-birth, but its chief object is the enjoyment of the beatitude of loving ......[A long discourse on Krishna's forms, omitted in the second edition.] [Text, canto 20.]

CHAPTER XIX

On the sweetness of Krishna's attributes

[The Master continued His teaching of Sanatan thus:]

"God in His all-embracing form dwells in the highest Space (*para-byom*). The diverse Vaikunthas are beyond count. The extent of each Vaikuntha is millions and millions of miles. *Ananda* inspired by *chit* fills all the Vaikunthas. All of [His] attendants are filled with the six attributes (*aishwaryya*). The endless Vaikunthas and Space are His retinue; above all of them is Krishna's Heaven, like the seed-pod of the lotus. Thus, [Krishna's] six attributes are [only] places of [His] incarnation. Even Brahma and Shiva cannot count them, what to speak of men? *Vide* the *Bhagabat*, X. xiv. 21, Brahma's hymn to Krishna.

"Thus Krishna's celestial attributes are endless; Brahmá, Shiva, Sanak and others cannot see their end. *Vide* the *Bhagabat*, X. xiv. 7.

"Not to speak of Brahmá and others, even Ananta with his thousand tongues, is eternally singing [of His attributes] without being able to finish them. *Vide* *Bhagabat*, II. vii. 40.

"Even Krishna, the omniscient and supreme being, cannot find the end of His own attributes, but remains eagerly longing [to know of them]. *Vide Bhagabat*, X. lxxxvii. 37.

"The mind fails to comprehend His exploits, even

of the time when He incarnated himself in Brindaban. At one and the same time He created the natural and the supernatural groups of cow-herds and kine, as described in *Bhagabat,* [X. xiii and xiv], countless Vaikuntha-born embryos, with their respective Lords. Such a marvel is heard of no other [god]. The hearing of it makes the heart overcome [with rapture]. In that miracle of His every one of the millions and millions of calves, cowboys, their rods, pipes, horns, clothes and ornaments,—all assumed the form of the four-armed Lord of Vaikuntha, each with a separate universe, and Brahma adored him. From the body of *one* Krishna *all* these appeared! And after a moment they all disappeared in that body! The sight amazed and fascinated Brahmá, and after hymning [to Krishna], he declared this, 'Let him who says that he knows the full extent of Krishna's power, know it. But as for me, I admit with all my body and mind that not a drop of this endless ocean of your power is cognizable by my speech or intellect!' *Vide Bhagabat,* X. xiv. 36.

"Many are the glories of Krishna; who can know them? Think of the wondrous quality of the place Brindaban: the *Shastras* speak of it as 32 miles in extent, and yet in one corner of it the embryos of the universe floated! Krishna's divine power is boundless beyond calculation."

The Master, Himself the ocean of divine attributes, was seized with ecstasy in speaking of Krishna's divine attributes; His mind became absorbed in the subject and He lost consciousness. He (then) recited *Bhagabat,* III. ii. 21, and expounded it, relishing with delight its sense. "Krishna is the Supreme Deity, God Himself. None else is greater than He or even equal to Him. *Vide Brahma*

Samhita, v. 1. Brahmá, Vishnu, and Shiva,—the lords of creation, [preservation, and destruction],—all obey Krishna ; He is their suzerain. *Vide Bhagabat,* II. vi. 30.

"Hear the meaning of the phrase *unequalled Supreme Lord*: Three *purush* incarnations are the causes of the universe, *viz.,* Mahá-Vishnu, Padmanáva, Kshirodak Swámi. These three occupy the souls of everything, gross or subtle. These three are the refuge of all, and the lords of the universe. And yet they are mere particles of Krishna, who is supreme [over them]. *Vide Brahma Samhita,* v. 54.

"This interpretation is only external. Listen to the esoteric sense. The *Shastras* speak of three abodes of Krishna, *viz.,* Antahpur, Golok, and Brindaban, in which [last] ever dwell [His] parents and friends ; where He manifested His sweet attributes, tenderness, mercy, &c ; where the illusion of *yog* was His bondmaid, and where *rása* and other exploits took place.

"Below it the Supreme Space named Vishnu's Heaven, where dwell Narayan and other eternal forms of Him, is situated. The middle abode of Krishna is the store-house of the six attributes, where He dwells in His eternal form (*ananta*). The Vaikunthas are endless, and there the rooms and attendants (even) are full of the six attributes. *Vide Brahma Samhita,* v. 49, [and other Sanskrit verses].

"Below it is His external abode, beyond the *Birajá,* where the universes are endless, and the rooms are illimitable. It is named Devidhám, where creatures dwell. The Lakshmi of the Universe nourishes it ; illusion dwells there as His slave.

"In these three places does Krishna dwell as the Supreme Lord, *viz.,* Golok, the Supreme Space, and

Nature. The region where He manifests His *chit* power is called the Three-fold Divinity (*tripád aishwaryya*), whereas the places of the display of His power of illusion are called One-fold (*ekapád*).

"The Three-fold Divinity of Krishna is beyond speech. Hear, therefore, of the One-fold Divinity. All the Brahmás and Shivas of the eternal universe are embraced by the term 'eternal rulers of spheres' (*chira-loka-pála*). One day Brahmá came to Dwáraká to see Krishna; the porter took the message to Krishna, who asked 'Which Brahmá? What is his name?' The porter returned and asked Brahmá, who replied in amazement, 'Go, tell him, it is the four-headed father of Sanak'. After taking Krishna's permission, the porter introduced him. Brahma prostrated himself at Krishna's feet, who showed him honour and reverence and asked for the reason of his visit. Brahma replied, 'I shall tell you of that afterwards. First solve one problem of my mind. What did you mean by asking 'Which Brahma?' What Brahma other than I can there be in the universe?' At this Krishna smiled and plunged into meditation, and immediately innumerable troops of Brahmás came there,—some with ten heads, some with twenty, hundred, thousand, million, even a milliard, beyond the power of counting. Rudras came with millions of millions of heads. Indras appeared with millions of eyes. At the sight the four-headed Brahmá became senseless, like a hare surrounded by a herd of elephants. All these Brahmas prostrated themselves before Krishna's seat, which was touched by their crowns. None can [adequately] describe the unimaginable power of Krishna. In one body there were as many images as there were Brahmás. His seat, struck with the crowns of the Brahmás, set up a sound, as if the crowns recited praises of His seat! With folded palms, Brahma Rudra and other deities hymned Krishna thus: 'Lord! Great is thy mercy to us, as thou hast shown us thy feet. Oh our good fortune! thou hast called and accepted us as thy slaves. Bid us, and we shall place thy behest on our heads.' Krishna replied, 'I longed to see you, and so called you all together. Be ye all happy! Have you anything to fear from the demons?' They said, 'Thanks to thy grace, we are everywhere triumphant. Latterly thou hast, by incarnating thyself, destroyed the load of sins which used to weigh the Earth down.' This proves the divine nature of Dwáraká and other [spheres], each of which imagines 'Krishna dwells in *my* region.' The presence of Krishna made Dwaraka feel glory (*baibhaba*); they had all met together, and yet none could see the others. Then Krishna gave leave to all the Brahmás, and they returned home after bowing to Him. The four-headed Brahmá was amazed at the sight, and again bowed at Krishna's feet, saying, 'I have to-day witnessed an example of what I had previously known for certain in my mind.' *Vide Bhagabat,* X. xiv. 36.

"Krishna replied, 'This universe, though 500 million leagues in extent, is very small; hence you have four heads only. Other universes are a thousand million, a *lakh kror,* or even a *kror kror* leagues in extent, and *their* Brahmás have heads proportioned to these sizes. Thus do I uphold the whole system of universes. Even my one-fold divinity cannot be measured. Who will measure my three-fold divinity?'......So saying Krishna dismissed Brahmá. The divine form of Krishna cannot be explained. The phrase *Supreme Lord* has another deep meaning: the term *tri* means the three regions of Krishna, *viz.*, Gokul (named Golok), Mathura, and Dwáraká. In these three He always dwells naturally. These three places are full of His inner complete divinity. Of these three Krishna Himself is the lord. The guardians of directions in all the aforesaid universes, and the eternal guardians of creation in *Ananta* and Vaikuntha,—all bow to Krishna's seat, touching it with the jewel of their crowns......In His own *chit* power Krishna dwells ever. This property of *chit*-power is called 'the six divine attributes'; it is also styled 'Lakshmi in the form of supreme bliss.' Hence, the Vedas declare Krishna to be God Himself. I cannot plunge in the boundless nectar-ocean of Krishna's divine power, but have touched only a drop of it"...The Master paused for a while, and after composing Himself continued to teach Sanatan. [Text, canto 21.]

CHAPTER XX

Discourse on Devotion as the Aim

[The Master continued His address to Sanatan thus]:—

"The Vedas teach that Krishna is the sole Essence. Now let me speak of the signs of the aim (*abhidheya*), from which one can get Krishna and the treasure of Krishna's love. All the *Shastras* speak of faith in Krishna as the aim. Hence the sages declare,

'We know for certain that thou, O Lord, art our refuge, because the mode of thy worship that Mother Shruti lays down in answer to our questions, is also indicated by Sister Smritis and Brother Purans'.

"This truth is taught by the Monist school that Krishna is God Himself; He dwells in the form of the *Swarup* power; spreading out in the forms of *swámsha* and *bibhinnámsha,* He disports Himself in Ananta, *Vaikuntha,* and Brahmanda. The four-sided incarnations are His *swámsha* extension. The created world is the example of His *bibhinnámsha* power. Such creatures are of two classes, *viz.*, one ever liberated, the other ever fettered to the world. The 'ever liberated' are ever eager for Krishna's feet; they are named Krishna's followers and they enjoy the bliss of serving Him. The 'ever fettered' are ever excluded from Krishna, and ever feel the sufferings of Hell; the Fury, Illusion, ever torments them for that reason; the three internal agonies scourge them; they are kicked at by Lust, Anger [and other deadly sins] whose slaves they are. If in the course of their life's wanderings they meet with a saint as their healer, his teaching like a charm exorcizes the demon (Illusion) out of them ; then they feel *bhakti* for Krishna and come to Him. Faith in Krishna is the supreme end (*abhidheya*). Worthless are the fruits of other kinds of devotion, such as work, *yog*, and knowledge,—in comparison with the bliss of *bhakti* ; the former cannot give us Krishna unless we have *bhakti* in Him. *Vide Bhagabat* I. v. 12 and II. iv. 16. Knowledge dissociated from *bhakti* cannot give salvation ; but a man devoted to Krishna can gain salvation without knowledge. *Vide Bhagabat*, X. xiv. 4 and the *Gita*, vii. 14.

"Creation, the eternal slave of Krishna, forgot this fact ; hence Illusion tied a rope round its neck. If a creature adores Krishna and serves his *guru*, he is released from the meshes of Illusion and attains to Krishna's feet. If, while observing the rules of his caste, a man does not adore Krishna, he will be plunged in hell in spite of his doing his caste-duties. *Vide Bhagabat*, XI. v. 2 & 3. The votary of knowledge imagines that he has attained to the condition of one 'liberated even in earthly life' ; but in truth his mind cannot be purified without faith in Krishna. *Vide Bhagabat*, X. ii. 26. Krishna is like the Sun, while Illusion is as darkness ; hence Illusion has no power to remain where Krishna is. *Vide Bhagabat*, II. v. 13. Even if a man prays once saying 'Krishna I am thine,' he is saved by Krishna from the bonds of Illusion. If the seeker after enjoyment, salvation and attainment (*siddhi*). is wise, he adores Krishna with deep *bhakti*. *Vide Bhagabat*, II. iii. 10. If a man adores Krishna in longing for other [material] gains, He gives the votary

His own feet unasked, arguing, 'In adoring me he is soliciting for material joys. What a great fool is he, in thus begging for poison instead of nectar! I am wiser, why then should I grant this fool [his coveted] earthly pleasures? Let me give him the nectar of my feet, so that he may forget earthly joys.' *Vide Bhagabat,* V. xix. 28. If a man adores Krishna even for fleshly lusts, he [soon] longs to abandon his desires and become a slave of Krishna. In going through this worldly life, some are fortunate enough to gain salvation; just as a log of wood drifting down the current now and then lands on the bank. *Vide Bhagabat,* X. xxxviii. 4. By good luck some men's bondage to the world is about to be severed, [when] they are emancipated by the society of holy men, and are inspired with devotion to Krishna. *Vide Bhagabat* X. li. 35. If Krishna favours any blessed man, He teaches him as his *guru* seated in the heart. *Vide Bhagabat,* XI. xxix. 6. If in the company of holy men a man feels inclined towards *bhakti* in Krishna, he gets love, the fruit of *bhakti,* and is freed from the world. *Vide Bhagabat,* XI. xx. 8. Save through the favour of the noble a man cannot feel *bhakti* in anything; not to speak of his gaining devotion to Krishna, he is not even freed from bondage to the world. *Vide Bhagabat,* V. xx. 12 and VII. v. 25. All *Shastras* recommend the companionship of the holy. As soon as such society is resorted to, it gives success in everything. *Vide Bhagabat,* I. xvii. 13. The gracious Krishna, in addressing Arjun [in the *Gita*], has laid down instructions for the salvation of mankind. *Vide* the *Gita,* xviii. 64 and 65.

"God had first commanded the Vedic religion, work, *yog,* and knowledge. After these had been observed,

He finally commanded *bhakti*, which must, therefore, be superior [to the former]. If, in accordance with this [latest] dispensation, a devotee feels *shraddhá*, he leaves all works and adores Krishna. *Vide Bhagabat*, XI. xx. 9. The term *shraddhá* means firm and unquestioning faith. If one adores Krishna, it is equivalent to his doing all the prescribed ceremonies [of religion]. *Vide Bhagabat*, IV. xxxi. 12.

"Men who have *shraddhá* are qualified for *bhakti*, and are ranked as superior, average, and inferior, according to the quality of their *shraddhá*. He whose *shraddhá* is confirmed by listening to the reasoning contained in the *Shástras* is a superior 'entitled to *bhakti*', and he is liberated from the world. He whose *shraddhá* is strong in spite of his ignorance of *shastric* arguments, is an average 'entitled to *bhakti*' ; he, too, is very fortunate. He whose *shraddhá* requires a visible object [of adoration] is an inferior 'entitled to *bhakti*' ; in time he will advance to the stage of a superior *bhakta*. There are different grades of *bhakti*, according to differences of ardour and passion, as has been described in the eleventh *skanda* of the *Bhágabat*, (XI. ii. 43-45).

"All the high attributes are found in the person of a Vaishnav, because Krishna's attributes spread to His *bhaktas*. (*Ibid*, V. xviii. 12). The following qualities mark a Vaishnav ; they cannot be exhaustively named, I only take a rapid view:—he is compassionate, spiteless, essentially true, saintly, innocent, charitable, gentle, pure, humble, a universal benefactor, tranquil, solely dependent on Krishna, free from desire, quiet, equable, a victor over the six passions (*sharguna*), temperate in diet, self-controlled, honouring others and yet not proud himself, grave, tender, friendly, learned, skilful and silent. *Vide Bhágabat,* III. xxv. 20, V. v. 2. The society of holy men is the root of the birth of devotion to Krishna (*Bhagabat,* X. li. 35, XI. ii. 28, III. xxv. 22). The principal limb that springs up from it is love of Krishna. It is proper conduct for a Vaishnav to abjure the society of the wicked. The man who consorts with women is one kind of sinner, while the man lacking in faith in Krishna belongs to another kind. *Bhagabat* III. xxxi. 35, 33 & 34). Leaving these [temptations] and the religious system based on caste, [the true Vaishnav] helplessly takes refuge with Krishna. *Vide* the *Gitá,* xviii. 66; *Bhagabat,* X. xlviii. 22. If a learned man happens to sing Krishna's praise, he adores Krishna to the exclusion of all other deities, as is proved by the case of Uddhav. *Vide Bhagabat,* III. ii. 23. The helpless and the refugee [among devotees] have the same characteristics. Then comes resignation in. After taking refuge in Krishna, the votary gives himself entirely up to Krishna, who then elevates him to His own nature. *Vide Hari-bhakti-vilas,* xi. 417 & 418; *Bhagabat,* XI. xxix. 32.

"Give ear, O Sanatan, while I turn to speak of the attainment (*sádhan*) of *bhakti,* which gives us the rich treasure of love for Krishna. Hearing [chant] and other acts [of the physical organs] are the *swarup* signs of it; while in the *tatastha* sign love is born. Love for Krishna is ever an end (*siddha*); it is never a means (*sádhya*). It is kindled in a pure heart by listening [to Krishna's praise], and other acts of the organs. The *sádhan* of *bhakti* is of two kinds: one following the ordinances of religion, the other following the [heart's] inclination. The man without a natural desire [for Krishna] adores

Him in obedience to the bidding of the *Shastras* ; such *bhakti* is called regular (*baidhi*).

'*King! It is the duty of the men who seeks liberation to hear, to praise, and to meditate about God, the universal Soul, the supremely Beautiful, and the Liberator from bondage.*' (*Bhagabat*, II. i. 5. and also XI. v. 2.)

"The modes of cultivating *bhakti* are many ; I shall only tell you briefly of the chief of them :—[they are] taking refuge at the feet of the *guru*, initiation, service of the *guru*, inquiry into the true religion, following the path of saints, renunciation of enjoyment out of love for Krishna, residence at holy places associated with Krishna, accepting alms no further than suffices [for one's sustenance], fasting on the 11th day of the moon, reverence to foster-mothers, fig trees, kine, Brahmans and Vaishnavs, shunning from a distance all offences against adoration and the holy name, abjuring the company of non-Vaishnavs, taking only a few disciples, avoiding the study and exposition of too many books and arts, looking at loss and gain as alike, control of grief and other passions, abstention from abusing other gods and scriptures, never listening to scandal about Vishnu or Vaishnavs nor to village gossip, giving no shock by thought or speech to any creature that lives, listening [to chant], hymn-singing, keeping God in remembrance, worship, adoration [in words], attendance [on idols], assuming the attitudes of servant and comrade [to Krishna], dedication of one's own self [to God], dancing, singing, petitioning and prostration before [Krishna's image], rising to welcome [His image], and following it as a mark of respect, visiting shrines at *tirthas*, walking round shrines, hymning, reading scriptures, reciting the holy name, *sankirtan*, enjoying incense garlands perfumed essence and the *maha-prasad*, witnessing the grand celebration of *árati* and the divine image, giving up whatever is dear to one's own self, meditation, and serving Him.

"The service of the following four is approved by Krishna:—the *Tulsi* plant, Vaishnavs, Mathura, and the book *Bhágabat*.

"Direct all your efforts to [the service of] Krishna, witness His mercies, celebrate His Nativity and other days in the company of *bhaktas*. Ever fly to him for refuge, celebrate Kártik and other *bratas*.

"These are the sixty-four modes of cultivating *bhakti*. The five chief of them are (1) the society of holy men, (2) *kirtan* of Krishna's name, (3) listening to the reading of the *Bhágabat*, (4) dwelling at Mathurá, and (5) reverential service of His image. Even a little of these five creates love for Krishna.

"Some *bhaktas* pursue only one of these modes, some many. When the mind has become steady, the wave of love surges up [in it]. Many *bhaktas* have attained to success by following one mode only. Ambarisha and other *bhaktas* cultivated many modes. (*Vide Bhagabat*, IX. iv. 15-17). The man who by renouncing desire adores Krishna in obedience to the injunctions of the *Shastras*, is not indebted to the gods the *Rishis* or the manes of his ancestors. (*Bhagabat*, XI. v. 37). He who adores Krishna's feet rejecting *shastric* rites, feels nevertheless no temptation for forbidden sins. Even if he commits a sin unwittingly, Krishna purifies him and he need not practise penance for it. (*Bhagabat*, XI. v. 38). Theological knowledge and monachism are not at all necessary means of cultivating *bhakti ;* Krishna's society gives inoffensiveness and discipline. *Vide Bhagabat,* XI. xx. 31.

"Hitherto I have held forth on the cultivation of *bhakti* in accordance with the *shastric* teaching. Now, let me tell you, Sanatan, about *bhakti* in compliance with natural inclination. This latter kind of *bhakti* is chiefly found in the people of Brindaban, and those who cultivate it are called *rágánuga* ('inclination-led'). A passionate longing for the object of desire is the *swarup* characteristic of inclination (*rág*) ; absorption in the object of desire is its *tatastha feature*......The nature of an 'inclination-led' *bhakta* pays no heed to *shastric* reasoning.

"Its two types are *external* and *internal.* In the external, the devotee through his physical organs performs listening (to chant) and chanting, while in his mind he imagines himself to be identical with his ideal [such as any *sakhi* or cowherd mate of Krishna], and thus [in fancy] serves Krishna at Brindaban day and night. Withdrawing himself into his own mind, such a votary ever remains close to his object, the dearest Krishna, and thus serves Him incessantly. In the path of inclination (*rág*), he takes Krishna as the object of his chief emotion, *viz.,* as master, comrade, child or sweetheart. (*Bhágabat,* III. xxv. 35)......

"From the sprout of love (*prem*) issue two things, *rati* (addiction) and *bháb* (emotion). These two conquer the Lord for us. Thus have I expounded *abhidheya,* from which we gain the treasure of love for Krishna." [Text, canto, 22.]

CHAPTER XXI

On Love, the fruit of Devotion

[The Master continued]—"Listen now, Sanatan, to love, the fruit of *bhakti*, the hearing of which gives knowledge of the spirit of *bhakti*. When passion (*rati*) in Krishna is deepened it is called *prem* (love), the permanent form of *bhakti* in Krishna. It also has two aspects, *viz.*, *swarup* and *tatastha*. If any man has the grace to feel *shraddhá*, he consorts with pious men, from which companionship result the hearing and chanting of Krishna's name. From the attainment of *bhakti*, all his troubles are removed, and as a consequence of the latter, his faith becomes constant, which gives him a taste for the listening and [hymning of Krishna's name]. From taste (*ruchi*) comes strong inclination (*ásakti*), which gives birth to the sprout of passion for Krishna in the soul. When this emotion is deepened, it takes the name of love (*prem*). That love is the (ultimate) fruit, the source of every bliss. *Vide Bhagabat*, III. xxv. 22. The man in whose heart this emotion sprouts up, is marked by the many qualities named in the *Shastras*. (*Bhakti-ras-amrita-sindhu*, I. Rati-bhakti, verse 11, *Bhagabat* I. xix. 13). No earthly affliction can disturb his mind. Such a man never wastes his time without communing with Krishna. He never fears [attack by] enjoyment, material success, or the objects of sensual gratification. (*Bhagabat*, V. xiv. 42). Even the noblest *bhakta* considers himself as lowly, and firmly believes that Krishna will take pity on him. He is ever expectant, ever passionately longing [for union with Krishna]. Ever does he relish the work of singing Krishna's names, and ever engages in it. At all times is he addicted to holding forth on Krishna's charms. Ever does he reside at the scenes of Krishna's exploits.

"So far I have described the marks of *rati* for Krishna. Now let me describe the characteristics of love for Krishna. Even the wise fail to comprehend the speech, acts and gestures of the man whose heart is full of love for Krishna. (*Bhagabat*, XI. ii. 38). As love developes, it takes the forms of *sneha, mán, pranaya, rág, anurág, bháb*, and *mahábháb*,—just as, from the same source of sugar-juice we have molasses, *gur* (*khanda*), black sugar, [yellow] sugar-candy, and white sugar-candy. As these grow successively purer and more delicious, so too do the above stages in the development of love. In relation to its subject, *rati* is of five kinds *viz.*, *shánta, dásya, sakhya, bátsalya*, and *madhur*. These five permanent emotions (*bháb*) have five different flavours, which delight the *bhakta* and over-power Krishna. The permanent emotions of love etc., on meeting with the proper ingredient, mature in the form of Krishna-*bhakti ras*. The permanent emotion (*bháb*) on being mingled with *ras* is changed into these four,—*bibhába, anubhába, sátwika, byabhichári* ;—just as curd, on being mixed with *gur*, black pepper, and camphor, becomes a thing of matchless deliciousness named *rasál*. *Bibhába* is of two kinds,—(i) *álamban*, which is kindled by Krishna, etc., and (ii) *uddipan*, by the notes of His flute, etc. *Anubhába* is stimulated by smile, dance and song. Stupor and other sensations are included in *sátwika anubhába*. *Byabhichári* is of 33 kinds, such as delight, rapture, &c.

"*Ras* is of five kinds,—*shánta, dásya, sakhya, bátsalya,* and *madhur.* In the *shánta ras, rati* advances to the stage of *prem ;* in the *dásya* to *rág, sakhya* and *bátsalya* attain to the limit of *ánurág* (as was the case with Subal and others' love for Krishna)......

"Krishna, the darling of Braja's lord, is the chief of lovers, while the lady Radha is at the head of mistresses. Krishna's qualities are endless, even a single one of them when unfolded can soothe the ears of a *bhakta*......

Countless are Radhiká's qualities, of which 25 are the principal ones, which have conquered Krishna......

"The lover and his mistress are the themes of two *rasas,* and the foremost of the class are Radha and Krishna. Similarly, in the *dásya ras,* the subject is a servant, in the *sakhya* a comrade, in the *bátsalya* the parents.

"This *ras* is tasted only by Krishna's *bhaktas ;* those who are not devoted to Him have not the lot to enjoy it......Before this, at Allahabad I discoursed on *ras* and inspired with my power your brother Rup Goswami. Do you preach the lore of *bhakti ;* do you discover the lost shrines of Mathura. At Brindaban teach the adoration of Krishna, the proper conduct of Vaishnavs, and the scriptures of the creed of *bhakti.*"

Thus did the Master teach Sanatan all about the temperate conquest of passions (*bairágya*) and condemned arid *bairágya* which consists of (mere) knowledge. *Vide* the *Gitá,* xii. 13 *et seq* and *Bhagabat,* II. ii. 5.

Then Sanatan asked about the metaphorical interpretations (*siddhánta*) of all the acts of Krishna's life, and the Master clearly explained them. At last Sanatan clasped His feet and biting a wisp of grass in sign of abjectness prayed to Him thus: "I am a wretch, of low caste, and the servant of the unclean. And yet thou hast taught me theological expositions which even Brahmá knows not! My despicable mind cannot contain even a single drop of this ocean of exposition that thou hast poured into it. Thou canst make even the lame dance, if so thou wishest. Lay thy feet on my head and pronounce on me the blessing that all that thou hast taught me may become bright within me. May I derive power from thy power!" And the Master blessed him accordingly. [Text, canto 23.]

Again did Sanatan clasp the Master's feet and ask Him, "I have heard that you explained to Sarvabhauma in eighteen different ways the following couplet of the *Bhágabat*, I. vii. 10:—

आत्मारामाश्च मुनयो निर्ग्रन्था अप्युरुक्रमे
कुर्वन्त्यहैतुकीं भक्तिमित्थम्भूतगुणो हरिः ।

"My mind, on hearing of it, has been seized with wonder and curiosity. If thou tellest it [again] graciously, my ears will be charmed." The Master answered, "I am a mad man; Sarvabhauma took my mad words for truth. I do not remember what ravings I uttered in his house. But should your company inspire me I may possibly recollect a little of it. My mind is not naturally enlightened as to the sense of the verses; what I shall say is only the outcome of the influence of your company."

[His 61 subtle interpretations of the above stanza and the rules of Sanskrit grammar lexicography and logic appealed to by the Master in support of them, are omitted here in the 2nd edition.]

Listening to these [sixty-one diverse] explanations,

Sanatan was filled with wonder, and praised the Great Master, clinging to His feet, "Thou art God incarnate, the darling of Braja's lord. Thy breath called into being all the *Vedas*. Thou art the speaker in the *Bhágabat*, and thou knowest its meaning, which none else can understand!" The Master objected, "Why praise *me*? Why not consider the nature of the *Bhágabat*, which is like Krishna, all-embracing, the refuge of all. Every couplet, nay every letter of it breathes a variety of senses. By means of a dialogue this fact has been established in the *Bhágabat* itself. (I. i. 23 and iii. 42). These my interpretations of the *shloka* are like the ravings of a mad man. Who will accept them? If any one be mad like me, he will understand the meaning of the *Bhágabat* from this [specimen]."

Again did Sanatan with folded palms entreat Him,—"Master, thou has bidden me write the sacred code (*smriti*) of Vaishnavs. I am a man of low caste, ignorant of ceremonial cleanness (*áchár*). How can *smriti* be taught by me? If you teach me an outline of it in the form of *sutras* (aphorisms), if you yourself enter my heart, then the sketch will inspire the mind of a low man like me. Thou art God; whatever thou makest me speak will prove true." The Master replied, "Whatever you wish to do, Krishna will inspire your mind with [knowledge of it]. I, however, give you a rapid survey of the different points [which you should deal with in compiling the Vaishnav sacred code] (*A long list, not translated here*). In every case quote as your authority the sayings of the *Puráns*...... When you will write, Krishna will inspire you." [Text, canto 24.]

CHAPTER XXII

The Master converts the people of Benares and returns to Jagannath

Thus did the Master in two months instruct Sanatan in the entire lore of the philosophy of faith. Chandra Shekhar's comrade, Paramánanda Kirtaniá, an expert artist, performed *kirtan* before the Master.

As the Master had slighted the *sannyasis*.........they everywhere spoke ill of Him. At this the Maratha [Brahman] sadly reflected, "Whosoever has a close view of the Master's character feels Him to be God indeed, and admits Him as such. If I can bring them and Him together, they will perceive this [quality] and become His followers. I have always to dwell in Káshi, and if I do not effect this, it will be a matter of everlasting regret to me."

So, he invited all the *sannyasis*, and himself went on a visit to the Master. Chandra Shekhar and Tapan Mishra, grieved to hear Him defamed, were humbly entreating Him, and His mind, too, was thinking of the conversion of the *sannyasis*, in order to remove the grief of His *bhaktas*. Just then the Maratha Brahman arrived and clasping the Master's feet by much entreaty induced Him to accept his invitation. At noon He went to His host's house, and bestowed salvation on the *sannyasis* in the manner described in Part I. of this book.

From the day on which He blessed the *sannyasis*, a sensation was created in the village ; crowds flocked to behold the Master; scholars of various schools came to discuss theology with Him, but He refuted all their philosophies and established faith as the final truth. By His reasoned speech He turned the minds of them all, and they followed His instruction and began to chant Krishna's name. All men laughed, sang, and danced. The *sannyasis* submitted to Him; quitting their studies they formed assemblies of their own [to discourse on faith].

A disciple of Prakáshánanda, equal to him in attainments, spoke reverently of the Master in open meeting thus, "Chaitanya is Narayan himself. He explains the aphorisms of Vyás most charmingly. His exposition of the root meaning of the *Upanishads* gratifies the hearing and mind of scholars even. Our teacher [Prakáshánanda] gives a fanciful explanation of the aphorisms of the *Upanishads* leaving their essential meaning out. On hearing his fanciful explanations scholars pretend to approve, but are not inwardly convinced, whereas Chaitanya's words we feel to be truth indeed. In the Kali Yug, one cannot vanquish the World by asceticism; the highest conclusion and true source of bliss is contained in the exposition which He gave of the verses '*Hari's name alone* &c'. The *Bhagabat* asserts that there cannot be salvation without faith, and that rapture in the name [of Hari] can give an easy deliverance in the Kali Yug. (*Bhagabat*, X. xiv. 4 and ii. 26).

"The term *Brahma* connotes God full of the six divine attributes. To describe Him as abstract is to impair His fulness. The *Shruti Purans* deal with the manifestations of Krishna's *chit* power. Philosophers laugh at it irreverently. They look upon Krishna's *chidánanda* images as a mere piece of illusion. In this they sin grievously. Chaitanya's view is the true one. (*Bhágabat,* III. ix. 3 and 4 ; *Gita,* ix. 11 and xvi. 19). The *aphorisms* [of Vedanta] teach the theory of *parinám* (result), but our teacher disregards it, calls Vyás ignorant, and asserts the theory of *bivarta.* This fanciful interpretation does not satisfy the mind. Fancies at variance with scripture prove a man a wretch. Engaged in vain disputation, I have hitherto forgotten to know the Supreme Essence. Oh! how shall I merit Krishna's grace? Our teacher has obscured the meaning of Vyás's aphorisms, whereas Chaitanya has revealed it. True are His words ; all other theories are false and futile."

So saying he began to sing Krishna's *sankirtan.* At this Parkashananda remarked, "The Acharya was eager to establish Monism, and he had therefore to twist the sense of the aphorisms. If you admit God's *bhagawán*-ship, you cannot establish Monism. So the Acharya had to refute all the *Shástras.* No author who wishes to set up his own theory can give the plain meaning of the scriptures. A philosopher of the *Mimánsa* school speaks of God as a part and parcel of [His] work ; the *Sánkhya* speaks of Him as the cause of Nature all over the universe. The *Nyáya* asserts that the world was composed out of atoms ; the Illusionist speaks of the abstract Brahma as the Cause. Patanjal (alone) tells us of the true nature of Krishna ; so He is the true God, according to the *Vedas.* None recognizes God as the Supreme Cause ; each school of philosophy only sets up its own theory by refuting the views of its rivals. Thus from the six schools of philosophy we cannot know the [spiritual] truth. Only the words of great men are reliable. Chaitanya's words are a stream of nectar. What He says is the essence of spiritual truth." Hearing all this, the Maratha Brahman in delight went to report it to the Master, whom he met going to visit Bindu Madhav after His bath in the five streams. At the Brahman's narration He was pleased. Beholding the beauty of Bindu Madhav He was enraptured and danced in the courtyard [of the temple] in love, while Chandra Shekhar, Paramananda, Tapan, and Sanatan joined in a *sankirtan* chanting,—

"Hail to Hari and Hara! to Krishna the Yádav, to Gopál, Govinda, Rám and Madhusudan."

Lakhs of men surrounded them shouting *Hari! Hari!* The blessed cry filled earth and heaven. Hearing it near him, Prakashananda came there with his pupils, moved by curiosity. Beholding the Master's charm of person and dancing, he with his disciples joined the cry of *Hari! Hari!* The Master trembled, spoke in a choking voice, perspired, changed colour, or at times stood rigidly inert, bathing the bystanders with His tears, His body thrilled with ecstasy like the *Kadamba* tree. He displayed every passion,—exultation, abjectness, lightness &c., to the marvel of the people of Benares.

On seeing the crowd, the Master recovered His senses, and stopped His dance before the *sannyasis*. He bowed very low to Prakashananda, who, however clasped His feet. The Master cried out, "You are the instructor of the world, and beloved [of all], while I am not worthy to be your pupil's pupil. Why should a high one like you bow to a low one like me? As you are God-like, by so doing you are destroying me [in sin]. Though everything becomes you, as it becomes God, yet, for the sake of holding up a lesson before the people, you should cease acting thus [humbly]." Prakashananda replied, "By touching your feet I have washed away all the sin of my former abuse of you!" (*Bhagabat*, I. v. 12, Chakravarti's commentary, quotation from the appendix cited in the *Básaná-váshya*, also X. xxxiv. 7).

The Master cried out, "O God! O God! I am a despicable creature. It is a sin to regard any creature as Vishnu. Even if a God-like person holds a creature to be Vishnu, then God will rank him among the infidels. (*Hari-bhakti-vilás*, i. 71)."

Prakashananda replied, "You are God himself. But even if you insist on being regarded as God's slave, you are still worthy of being honoured above us. That I once abused you will be the cause of my ruin. (*Bhagabat* VI. xvi. 4, X. iv. 31, and VII. v. 25). I now bow at your feet, that I may kindle faith in them."

So saying he sat down there with the Master, and asked Him, "The errors you have pointed out in the theory of illusion, are, I know, the fanciful interpretations of Shankar Acharya. Your exposition of the essential meaning of the aphorisms has charmed the minds of all. You are God and can do everything. Tell me then briefly, I long to hear [your interpretation of Vyas's aphorisms]." The Master protested, "I am a creature insignificant in knowledge. Vyas was God's self and his aphorisms have a deep meaning, which no creature can know. Hence he has himself explained his aphorisms. When the writer is his own commentator, men can understand his meaning. The meaning of *pranaba* in the *Gáyatri mantra* is explained at length in the four verses of the *Bhágabat*, II. ix. 30-33. First God imparted these four verses to Brahmá, who taught them to Nárad, and the latter to Vyás, who reflected, "I shall make the *Bhágabat* itself a commentary on any aphorisms." So he accumulated the teaching of the four *Vedas* and the *Upanishads*. Every *rik* which is the subject matter of a particular aphorism, is formed into a separate verse in the *Bhágabat*. The *Bhágabat* and the *Upanishads*, therefore, speak with one voice ; the former is nothing more than a commentary on the latter. *Bhágabat*, VIII. i. 8, says,—

"*Everything that exists in the world is the abode of God. Therefore enjoy what God has given you, and covet not another's possessions.*

"The above verse takes a bird's-eye view of the whole subject. Similarly every verse of the *Bhagabat* is like a *rik*. In the 'four verses' the *Bhagabat* has unfolded the characteristics of Connection, Means (*abhidheya*), and Need. Connection with 'I' is the truth ; perception of 'I' is the highest knowledge, the devotion and faith necessary to attain to 'I' is called the Means. The fruit of devotion is love, which is the radical Need. That love enables a man to enjoy 'I'. *Vide* the *Bhagabat*, II. ix. 30, God's words to Brahmá:

'*The knowledge of me is deeply mysterious. Accept as spoken by me whatever is united to supreme knowledge (bijnán), attended by mystery, and a part of tat.*' Or in other words, God says here, 'These three truths have I explained to you, because being a creature you could not have understood them,—*viz.*, my nature, my dwelling (*sthiti*), and my attributes, works, and six powers. My grace will inspire you with all these.' So saying God imparted the three truths to Brahmá: (1) *Bhagabat*, II. ix. 31,—

'*May you, through my grace, at once attain to true*

knowledge about the nature of my form (swarup), my component element (sattwa), and my attributes and acts.' (God's speech to Brahmá).

"Or in other words, God says, 'Before creation, being myself endowed with the six divine powers, and drawing into myself *Prapancha*-Nature, I create while dwelling within it. The *Prapancha* that men beholds is no other than me. In destruction my remaining attributes manifest themselves, completing me and so *Prapancha*-Nature finds absorption in me.'

"(2) Again, *Bhagabat*, II. ix. 32, God speaks to Brahmá:—

'This I alone existed before creation, and none else. Nature, the cause of the gross and subtle universes, did not then exist. This I alone exist even after creation; this universe is indeed myself. Whatever will survive the destruction (pralaya) of the world will also be this I.'

"In this verse the phrase 'This I' occurs thrice and determines the dwelling of the full-power divine incarnation (*vigraha*). He has (clearly) pronounced on this point in order to rebuke those (philosophers) who do not admit incarnations (*vigraha*). The term *'this'* indicates *jnán, vijnán,* and *vivek*. Illusion is God's work, therefore God's self (*'I'*) is different from illusion,—just as a faint glow shines in the sky where the Sun was, but it cannot appear of itself without aid of the Sun. It is only by going beyond illusion that we can perceive *'I'*. Here the truth of Connection [with God] has been unfolded.

"(3) Next in *Bhagabat*, II. ix. 33, God tells Brahmá,—

'Know that to be my illusion which being unreal appears to the (human) mind as real, or being real is not

recognized by the mind ; just as the reflection in the water of the moon of the sky, though unreal, seems to be a second moon indeed ; or as the Ráhu of darkness, though real, escapes man's perception.'

"Listen to an exposition of faith as a means of devotion. In religious rites we have to observe distinctions according to person, locality, time and condition. But in the practice of *bhakti* no such difference has to be made ; it is the duty of all in every place, condition and time. Ask a *guru* about faith, and learn its nature from him. (*Bhagabat*, II. ix. 35).

'The man who seeks spiritual truth will admit that that substance alone is the Soul (átmá) which dwells at all times and within everything by acting as the anwaya (necessary) and byatireka (non-necessary) causes [of things].'

"Attachment to '*I*' is love, the Needful thing. I shall describe its marks by means of actions. As the five spirits (*pancha-bhut*) dwell within and without all creation, similarly I inspire my *bhaktas* within and without. (*Bhagabat*, II. ix. 34),—

'As the Great Spirits (mahá-bhutáni) enter material objects after their creation, but remained outside them as causes before their creation,—so I too remain at once within and without all created things.'

'My *bhakta* has confined me to his lotus-like heart. Wherever he glances he beholds me.' (*Bhagabat*, XI. ii. 50 and 43, X. xxx. 4).

"Thus does the *Bhágabat* explain three things,—Connection, Means, and Need. (*Bhágabat*, I. ii. 1[illegible]).

"Now listen to the *abhidheya* faith, which inspires every line of the *Bhágabat* (XI. xiv. 20).

"Now hear about love, the radical Need, whose marks are joyous tears, dance and song. (XI. iii. 32 and ii. 38).

"Therefore is the *Bhagabat* the author's own commentary on the *Brahma Sutra ;* it settles the meaning of the [*Mahá*] *Bhárat,* explains the *Gáyatri,* and amplifies by gloss the meaning of the *Vedas,* as is said in the *Garuda Purán. Vide* also the two verses from the same *Purán* quoted by Shridhar Swami in his commentary on the *Bhagabat,* I. 1, also *Bhagabat,* I. 1. 1-3 and 19, the *Gitá.* xviii. 54, *Bhagabat,* II. i. 9, III. xv. 43, I. vii. 10)."

Then the Maratha Brahman told the assembled people how the Master had explained the last mentioned verse in sixty-one different ways. The men wondered and pressed the Master, who gave His interpretations again. They marvelled exceedingly and concluded that Chaitanya was Krishna incarnate.

This said, the Master left the place. Men bowed to Him and shouted *Hari! Hari!* All the people of Benares began to make *sankirtan* of Krishna's name, laughing, dancing and singing in love. The *sannyasi* philosophers took to the study of the *Bhágabat.* (In short) the Master saved the city of Benares, which became a second Navadwip [in fervour].

Returning to His quarters with His attendants, the Master said jestingly, "I had come to Benares to sell my sentimental stuff, for which there was no purchaser here. I could not carry my merchandise back to my country, as you would have been grieved to see me carrying the load. So, to please you all, I have distributed my goods freely!"

They all replied, "You have come to deliver mankind.

Before this you had carried salvation to the South and the West. Benares alone was adverse to you, and now you have redeemed it, to our delight."

The sensation at Benares spread. Millions of country people began to come to the city. They could not see the Master at the place of *sankirtan,* but formed lines on both sides of the road to watch Him going to bathe or visit Vishweshwar. With uplifted arms He ordered them to chant Hari's name; they prostrated themselves and shouted *Hari! Hari!*

Five days were thus passed in delivering the people, and then the Master grew anxious. When He started walking away at night, His five *bhaktas* followed Him,—*viz.,* Tapan Mishra, Raghunath, the Maratha Brahman, Chandra Shekhar, and the singer Paramananda,—all wishing to accompany Him to Puri. But the Master sent them back gently, giving them leave to come afterwards, as He was returning alone by the Jhárikhand route. To Sanatan He said, "Go to Brindaban, to your two brothers. If my *bhakta* beggars, clad in quilt and bowl in hand, go there, cherish them." So saying He embraced and left them, while they all fell down fainting. Recovering they sadly took the way back to home.

When Rup reached Mathura, at the Dhruba *ghat* he met Subuddhi Ray, who had once been governor of Gaur with Sayyid Husain Khan as his servant. Husain was ordered to dig a tank, and on his committing some fault, his master, the Ray, flogged him. When, afterwards, Husain Shah became Sultan of Bengal, he greatly promoted Subuddhi Ray.

But the Sultana, noticing the scar of the lash on Husain's back, pressed him to murder the Ray. The

Sultan declined saying that the Ray was his former patron, a father unto him. But the queen urged him to destroy the Ray's caste while sparing his life. Husain answered that Subuddhi would not survive the loss of his caste. The king was hard pressed by the queen, and at last forced water from his own goglet into the Ray's mouth. At this the Ray left all his possessions, fled to Benares, and asked the *pandits* there about the proper penance. They replied, "Give up your life by drinking steaming *ghee*. This is not a venial sin!" The Ray remained perplexed, but when the Master arrived there, he told Him all. Chaitanya advised him to go to Brindaban and ceaselessly chant Krishna's name, as one utterance of the name would wash away all his sins and a repetition of it would gain him Krishna's feet.

The Ray reached Mathura by way of Prayag, Ayodhyá, and the Naimish forest (where he lingered some days). In the meantime the Master returned from Brindaban to Prayag, and Subuddhi on reaching Mathura grieved to miss Him. The Ray sold dry faggots at Mathura, at five or six piece per bundle. He lived by chewing one pice worth of gram and lodged the rest of his earnings with a *bániá*. Whenever he met a poor Vaishnav, he fed him, and to Bengali pilgrims he gave curd, rice and oil for anointing the body. Rup greatly favoured him, and took him through the "Twelve Woods" in his own company.

After a month at Brindaban, Rup hurriedly left to search Sanatan out. Hearing that the Master had taken the Ganges route to Prayag, Rup and his brother Anupam followed that path. But Sanatan from Prayag went to Mathura by the king's highway, and so missed Rup, who had taken a different route, as Subuddhi Ray told Sanatan on his arrival at Mathura. Tenderly did the Ray treat Sanatan, who cared not for tender treatment; being very averse to the world, he roamed through the woods, passing a day and night under each tree and grove. Securing a copy of the holy book named *Mathurá Máhátmya,* he searched the forests to discover the forgotten shrines.

Rup with his youngest brother came to Kashi and there met the Maratha Brahman, Chandra Shekhar, and Tapan Mishra. He lived with Chandra Shekhar, dined with the Mishra, and heard from the latter how the Master had taught Sanatan. Delighted was he to hear from them about the Master's doings at Kashi and His grace to the *sannyasis,* and to see the devotion of the people to him, and hear them chanting *kirtan.* After a ten days' stay there, Rup left for Bengal.

The Master wended His way to Puri, feeling intense bliss in the lonely jungle path. Balabhadra accompanied Him, and He sported with the deer and other animals as during His first journey. Reaching Athára-nálá He sent Bhattacharya in advance to summon His followers. At the news of His return, they got a new life as it were, ran to Him in rapture and met Him at the Narendra tank. The Master touched the feet of the Puri and the Bhárati, who embraced Him lovingly. Damodar Swarup, Gadadhar Pandit, Jagadananda, Kashishwar, Govinda, Vakreshwar, Kashi Mishra, Pradyumna Mishra, Damodar Pandit, Haridas Thakur, Shankar Pandit, and all other *bhaktas* fell down at His feet. He embraced each and was overcome with love. The faithful swam in the ocean of bliss. With them He went to visit Jagannath, before whom He with His party danced and sang long in rapture. The servitor of the god presented Him with a garland and *prasád,* while Tulsi Parichhá bowed at His feet.

The Master's arrival was [soon] noised abroad in the village. Sarvabhauma, Rámánanda, and Vánináth joined Him. With them all He repaired to Kashi Mishra's house. Sarvabhauma bade Him to dinner, but He declined, and ordering some *maha-prasad* to be brought, feasted there with all His followers. [Text, canto 25.]

CHAPTER XXIII

The Master teaches His disciples at Puri; the meeting with Sanatan*

Author's words in commencing the Last Acts (*Antya Lila*) :—"I bow to the Lord God Krishna-Chaitanya, whose grace enables a cripple to cross mountains and a dumb man to recite the scriptures. I am blind; this path is difficult, and I am again and again stumbling on it. May the saints be my support by lending me the staff of their compassion!

"I adore the feet of my six *gurus*,—Rup, Sanatan, Raghunath Bhatta, Jiv, Gopal Bhatta, and Raghunath-das,—who will remove evil (from my path) and fulfil my desire. In the *Madhya Lila* I have given a brief outline of the *Antya Lila*. I am now stricken with the decrepitude of age, and know death to be near. Therefore, I write in detail such acts of the *Antya Lila* as have not been described before."

When the Master returned from Brindaban to Nilachal, Swarup Goswami sent word of it to Bengal. Shachi rejoiced to hear of it; all the *bhaktas* rejoiced. They all set off for Nilachal. The men of Kulin village and the men of Khand all joined Acharya Shivananda. Shivananda Sen undertook to pass them through the police outposts (*ghati*) on the road, looked after them, and secured lodgings for them......When they arrived at Nilachal, they all met the Master, as in past years......At the end of four months, the Master sent the *bhaktas* back to Bengal.

* Chapters XXIII—XXVII are taken from the *Antya Lila* or Third Book of the text.

Every year the Bengali adorers used to come, meet the Master, and then return home. From other provinces, too, people used to come to Jagannath-Puri and attain the bliss of gazing at the feet of Chaitanya......But there were many householders who could not come. For their salvation the Master inspired worthy disciples in those countries with His own force, and thus all countries were made Vaishnav.

Bhagabán Acharya, a great Vaishnav, very learned and high-born (*árya*), lived at Jagannath-Puri, seeking the Master's company, as the cow-boys [of Mathura did Krishna's]. He was a comrade of Swarup Goswami, and took absolute refuge at the feet of Chaitanya. At times he used to invite the Master and make Him dine alone in his house.

One day, when the Acharya had bidden the Master to dinner at his house, he called the Master's chanter, the Lesser Haridas, and told him to bring on his behalf a *maund* of white rice from the sister of Shikhi Mahiti. She was named Madhavi Devi, an old anchorite and devout Vaishnav. At his meal the Master praised the rice and learnt that it had been supplied by Madhavi through the Lesser Haridas. When He returned to His lodgings, he ordered Givinda to exclude Haridas from the place from that day onwards.

Haridas grieved at the Master's doors being closed to him. For three days he fasted. None knew the reason of his exclusion. Then Swarup and others asked the Master, who replied, "I cannot look at the face of a bairagi who speaks to a woman. Our passions are hard to control and take hold of their natural objects of gratification. Even the wooden statue of a woman can steal the heart of an ascetic." (They prayed for His pardon, but in vain.

When even Puri Goswami interceded for Haridas, the Master in anger threatened to leave His disciples there and migrate alone to Alalnath). At the sight of Haridas's punishment, terror seized all the *bhaktas*. They gave up conversing with women even in dreams.

Thus did Haridas pass a year, and yet the Master did not feel any grace for him. So, one night Haridas bowed to the Master [from a distance] and went away to Allahabad without telling anybody. He concentrated his mind on attaining to the Master's feet [in the next life] and gave up his life by plunging into the junction of the three rivers, (*Triveni* at Allahabad).

An Oriya Brahman boy, handsome, gentle of manner, but fatherless, used to visit the Master at Puri daily, bow to Him and hold converse with Him. The Master was as life unto him, and he enjoyed the Master's favour. Damodar could not bear to see this attachment, and again and again forbade the boy [to come]. But he could not live without seeing the Master ; he came daily and the Master showed him great love ; it is natural for a boy to come where he meets with love.

The sight grieved Damodar, but he could not say anything as the boy heeded not his prohibition. One day the boy visited the Master, who lovingly inquired after his [health]. After a time the boy left. Damodar could not contain himself any longer, but burst out with, "In other connections you are called a *Goswami*. We shall soon know what sort of Goswami you are! All men will soon sing the praise of our Goswami! His reputation will be now established at Puri!"

The Master, hearing it, asked, "What is this that you are talking, Damodar?" The man replied, "You are a free God. You act as you please. Who can forbid you? But who can shut the mouth of the garrulous world? You are a wise man. Why then do you not reflect deeply? Why do you love a widow's son? True, she is chaste and an ascetic; but she has the faults of being beautiful and young. You too are youthful and extremely handsome. This will give an opportunity to scandal-mongers to whisper."

Damodar ceased speaking. The Master, pleased at heart, smiled and reflected, thinking "This is a current of the purest love. I have no well-wisher like Damodar."

Another day, the Master took Damodar aside and said, "Damodar, go to Navadwip, and stay there with my mother. I do not see any other guardian for her than you. You have warned me even! I have no candid friend like you among my followers. Unless a man is candid (*lit.*, impartial), virtue cannot be guarded. You have done something which even I cannot do. You have reprimanded me, what shall we say of others? Go to my mother's house and remain at her feet. In your presence nobody can act freely. Come here occasionally to see me, and then return there quickly. Convey to mother my millions of salutation. Make her happy with the news of my happiness. Say that I have sent you to her to tell her constantly of me. So saying delight her heart......"

(The miracles of the Vaishnav saint Haridas Thakur, *not translated*).

When Rup Goswami, after visiting the Master at Puri, went to Bengal for returning to Brindaban, his brother Sanatan came from Mathura to Nilachal. He travelled by the Jharikhand jungles (Santal parganas), now fasting, now chewing [dry grains]. Scabs broke out on his skin from the bad water of Jharikhand and the irregularity of diet, and exudations ran down his body.

On the way he sadly reflected, "I belong to a low caste. My body is vile. I shall fail to see the Master when I go to Puri. He lives, I hear, near the temple. But I dare not go near it, as the servitors of Jagannath are constantly passing there on business and it will be a sin if I [accidentally] touch them. Therefore, I shall renounce my body by throwing myself under the wheels of Jagannath's car when the god is taken out in the car procession; thus shall I attain at a holy place relief from my pangs and the salvation of my soul."

So resolving, he came to Nilachal and alighted at Haridas's place. He bowed at the feet of Haridas, who learning his name embraced him. His heart yearned for the sight of the Master. Haridas assured him that He would soon come.

The Master, after witnessing the *Upala-bhog* of Jagannath, came there with His disciples to meet Haridas. The two prostrated themselves at His feet. The Master raised Haridas and embraced him. Haridas said, "Here is Sanatan, bowing to you." The Master looked at Sanatan with interest and advanced to embrace him, while Sanatan ran backwards shouting, "Touch me not, Master, I beseech Thee. I am of low caste, and in addition my skin is running with exudations." But the Master embraced him by force, and His fair body was stained with Sanatan's sores. He introduced all His disciples to Sanatan, who bowed at their feet. With them all the Master sat down on the raised terrace, while Haridas and Sanatan sat below. He inquired after Sanatan's health, who replied "My supreme bliss is that I have gazed on Thy feet." The Master then asked about the Vaishnavs of Mathura, and Sanatan reported that they were well.

The Master said, "Rup [your brother] was here for ten months, and he left for Bengal only ten days ago. Your [youngest] brother Anupam has died on the bank of the Ganges. He was a staunch devotee of Ram." Sanatan replied, "I have been born in a low family; all sorts of wickedness and wrongdoing were my hereditary burden. Such a family thou hast accepted, without scorning it! My whole family has been blessed by thy grace. This Anupam was devoted to Ram-worship from his childhood. Day and night he used to meditate on the name of Ram, hear the *Ramayan* read, and chant it. He used to live with Rup and myself constantly and listen with us to Krishna's deeds and the *Bhagabat*. We one day tested him saying, 'Listen, dear, Krishna is very delicious; he abounds in beauty, sweetness, love, and grace. Do you, therefore, adore Krishna in our company. We three brothers shall dwell together in the delights of discourses on Krishna.' So we two urged him again and again. Our influence turned his mind a little and he responded, 'How long can I resist your command? Initiate me in the *mantra* and I shall adore Krishna [in future].' So saying, he paced up and down all the night, waking and crying how he could leave Ram's feet. Next morning he told us, 'I have sold my head to the feet of Ram, and it pains me excessively to draw my head away thence. Have mercy on me and permit me to worship Ram's feet birth after birth.' Then we two embraced him and praised him saying 'Noble is the firmness of thy faith.' Master, when you bless a family, it enjoys every good, and all its troubles disappear."

The Master replied, "Just in the same way did I test Murari Gupta before. That *bhakta* is noble who does not leave his Lord's feet. That Master is blessed who does not abandon his own devotee...... It is well that you have come here. Dwell in the same house with Haridas."

One day the Master came there, as was his daily wont, to meet the two, and began abruptly to speak, "Sanatan! If giving up life could have made one gain Krishna, I could have sacrificed my life a million times over in a moment. It is not by courting death but by adoration that we can gain Krishna. There is no other way of gaining him than *bhakti*. Suicide and the like are a low dark (*támas*) kind of *dharma*. But the *támas* and *rajas* kinds of *dharma* cannot give us the essence of Krishna. Without *bhakti* there cannot be love, and without love Krishna cannot be attained.

"Suicide and the like are a *támas* dharma, and the cause of sin; through them a devotee cannot attain to Krishna's feet. The loving *bhakta* wishes to quit his body when separated from his Lord; but when love has brought Krishna to him, he cannot think of death......

Give up your evil intention and listen to the *kirtan*, and soon will you get the treasure of love for Krishna. Even a low-caste man is not unfit to adore Krishna. Even a well-born Brahman is not, [merely by reason of his birth] worthy to adore him. He who adores is great; the man wanting in devotion is low and despicable. In the worship of Krishna there is no distinction of caste or pedigree. The Lord is more gracious to the lowly, while the high-born, the learned, and the rich are too proud [in His eyes].

"Among the methods of adoration the chief are the nine kinds of *bhakti*, which is most potent in giving us

Krishna's love,—even Krishna himself. The highest of these is *nám-sankirtan,* chanting the Name. Chant the Name with a pure soul and you will win the treasure of divine love!"

Sanatan marvelled when he heard all this, thinking "The Master is omniscient. He has divined my plan of suicide and forbidden it." Then he clasped the Master's feet, crying, "You are omniscient, gracious, free, and God. I move like a wooden machine as you turn my handle. I am lowly, a wretch, and wicked of disposition. What would you gain by keeping *me* alive?"

The Master replied, "Your body is my property. You have given yourself up to me. How dare you think of destroying what is another's property? Cannot you distinguish between a crime and a just deed? Your body is my chief instrument; with it I shall carry out many purposes. The exposition of the nature of devotion, the devotee and Krishna-*prem,* the duties and daily practices of Vaishnavs, the establishing of devotion to Krishna, love for Krishna and service, the restoration of forgotten holy places, the teaching of asceticism, the preaching of this faith at Mathura and Brindaban which are my favourite places,—all these I wish for. But by my mother's command I live at Nilachal, and therefore I cannot preach the religion at Mathura in person. The body by means of which I want to do all these works, you want to give up. How can I allow it?"

At this Sanatan said, "I bow to thee. Who can fathom the depths of thy heart? As the juggler makes the wooden puppet dance, while it knows not what it plays or what it sings, so, too, does the man whom you inspire, dance without knowing why he is dancing or through whom."

Thereafter the Master embraced the two and left for His home to do His noontide devotions.

Haridas mourned to Sanatan, "None can be compared with you in good fortune. The Master has declared your body to be His own property. He will do through you at Mathura the work that He cannot do in His own person. Through you He will compose the exegetics of *bhakti*, and lay down its scriptures and practices. [Alas!] my body has been of no service to the Master. My body, though born in the [holy] land of Bhárat, has become futile."

But Sanatan consoled him saying, "Who else is your equal? Among the Master's followers you are the most fortunate. The work of His incarnation is the preaching of the Name, and that work He does through you. Daily do you chant the Name three hundred thousand times. Before all do you hold forth on the glory of the Name."

The Bengal *bhaktas* came on pilgrimage, as before, on the occasion of the Car festival, and stayed with the Master for the four months of the monsoon. The Master introduced to them Sanatan who bowed at their feet and they favoured him. His excellent character and [deep] scholarship endeared Sanatan to all.

In the month of Jyaishtha the Master went to Yameshwar Tota (garden) to dine at the entreaty of His *bhaktas*. At noon He called for Sanatan, who delighted to hear of it, and went to Him by way of the sea-beach. He reached the Master with his two feet blistered [by the hot sand]. ......The Master asked "By what route have you come, Sanatan?" He replied, "By the sea-side." Then the Master said, "Why did you come over the hot sand? Why did you not take the cool path before the Lion Gate (*singhá-dwár*)? The hot sand has blistered your feet. You cannot walk; how could you bear the journey?"

Sanatan replied, "It was no great hardship. I did not feel that my feet were being blistered. I am not entitled to pass by the *singhá-dwár* road, especially, as the servitors of the god Jagannath frequently pass along it and it would be a disaster if I touch any of them."

The Master's heart was pleased to hear of it, and He began to tell Sanatan, "Though you are the saviour of the world and your touch can purify even the gods and sages, yet it is the sign of a [true] *bhakta* to respect the dignity [of rank or caste]. It is an ornament to a *sadhu's* character to observe distinctions (*maryádá*) of rank. Not to do so is to court public ridicule and to destroy one's own earthly life and spiritual welfare as well."......

Sanatan's body was covered with running eruptions. The Master embraced him in spite of prohibition, and His body was stained with the exudation, at which Sanatan grieved.........

But the Master said, "The body of a Vaishnav is not material. It is supra-physical and full of the *chit* and *ánanda* of *bhakti*. At the time of his initiation the *bhakta* surrenders himself to Krishna, who then renders him equal to his own self, and fills the body with his own *chit* and *ánanda*. The Lord Krishna has visited Sanatan's body with sores only to test *me*. If I had in disgust refused to embrace him, I should have been guilty in the eyes of Krishna......"

So saying, He embraced Sanatan again, and lo! the sores disappeared and his body assumed a golden hue!

After the *dol-yatrá* he was given leave to depart to Brindaban with minute instructions as to what he should do there to propagate the faith. [A long list of the Vaishnav literature produced by Rup, Sanatan, and their nephew Jiv, the son of their youngest brother Vallabh Anupam,—*not translated here*].

CHAPTER XXIV

Meeting with Vallabh Bhatta; the Master stints His food

Thus did the luminous Gaur (Chaitanya) perform many feats in many a playful way with His *bhaktas* at Nilachal. Though His heart was inly pierced with the pang of separation from Krishna, yet He did not express it outwardly lest His disciples should grieve. When, however, His intense love-sickness [for Krishna] did break forth, His agony baffled descrpition. The Krishna-talk of Ramananda and the [sacred] singing of Swarup saved the Master's life amidst the pain of separation from Krishna. In the day-time His mind was diverted by the diverse company that He met, but in [the solitude of] night His love-sickness waxed strong. To please Him these two always kept Him company and consoled Him with verses and songs about Krishna.

[Account of how Raghunath-das, the son of a very rich revenue-farmer, escaped from his home at Saptagram in Bengal, joined the Master at Puri and lived in utter lowliness by begging.]

One year Vallabh Bhatta came and met the Master, bowing at His feet. The Master embraced him as an adorer of Vishnu (*bhágabat*) and with honour made him sit close to Himself.

Meekly did the Bhatta address the Master, "Long have I desired to see you and to-day Jagannath has gratified that wish. Lucky is he who can behold you, for you are as it were God in a visible form. Even to remember you [from a distance] hallows a man. No wonder, then, that the sight of you makes one blessed. (*Bhágabat*, I. xix. 30.) The distinctive religion of the modern age is the *kirtan* of Krishna's name, and this religion cannot be established without Krishna's own power. That you have founded this faith proves that you are inspired with Krishna's divine force. Whosoever beholds you, swims in the stream of the love of Krishna. Only Krishna's spirit can call forth this love, as the scriptures say that Krishna is the sole inspirer of *prem* (love)."

The Master replied, "Listen, great-minded Bhatta! I was a *sannyasi* following the theory of illusion (*máyá-vád*); I knew not *bhakti* for Krishna. The Goswami Adwaita Acharya is God incarnate; *his* society has cleansed my mind. He has no peer in the knowledge of all the Shastras and in devotion to Krishna, and therefore he has been rightly named *A-dwaita* 'without a second'... Nityananda, Sarvabhauma Bhattacharya, Ramananda Ray, Damodar Swarup, Haridas Thákur,...... Acharya Ratna and many other *bhaktas* have all taught me Krishna-love and true *bhakti*, and have preached to the world love for the Krishna-name."

So spoke the Master artfully, as he knew the Bhatta to be very proud of his learning, and to have long cherished the conceit that he knew all the *bhakti*-theology of the Vaishnavs and could expound the *Shrimad Bhágabat* best. The Master's words curbed this pride of the Bhatta, and he longed to know the many disciples whose Vaishnav character the Master had just extolled. He asked, "Where do these Vaishnavs live? How can I meet them?" The Master replied, "Some live here, some on the bank of the

Ganges (*i.e.*, at Navadwip, Panihati etc.). These latter have all come here for the Car festival, and have taken up lodgings in this place. Here will you meet all of them."………

Next day when all the Vaishnavs came to the Master's place, He introduced them to the Bhatta. Their Vaishnav-splendour filled the Bhatta with amazement and he looked like a firefly in their company. Then he feasted the Master and His disciples on huge quantities of *mahá-prasád*. The *sannyasis* sat down with Paramananda Puri on one side. The Master sat down between Adwaita and Nityananda, while His disciples sat before and behind. The *bhaktas* from Bengal were countless; they filled the yard row on row. Vallabh Bhatta marvelled at the sight of them and bowed at the feet of each. He himself served the *mahá-prasád* to the Master and the *sannyasis*. They shouted *Hari! Hari!* on receiving the *prasad*. The roar of Hari's name filled the universe. The Bhatta gave away garlands, sandal-paste, betel-leaf and nuts and delighted all with his reverence.

On the day of the Car procession, the Master began *kirtan*. As before, He formed seven distinct groups of singers, under Adwaita, Nityananda, Haridas, Vakreshwar, Shribas, Raghav Pandit, and Gadadhar, who sang at different places. The Master roamed about shouting *Hari*, while fourteen drums (*mádal*) lifted up the din of the *sankirtan*. The sight filled Vallabh Bhatta with marvel; he flew into a transport of delight and could not control himself. Then the Master stopped the dance of the others and began to dance Himself. As he gazed on the Master's beauty and the exuberance of His *prem*, the Bhatta believed that the Master was Krishna himself!

After the festival the Bhatta begged the Master, saying, "I have written a commentary on the *Bhágabat* and want to read it to you." The Master replied, "I do not understand the meaning of the *Bhágabat* and am not qualified to hear [and judge] any interpretation of it. I only sit down and recite Krishna's name, and even then fail to complete the promised number of recitations in twenty-four hours." The Bhatta rejoined, "I have made an exposition of the meaning of Krishna's name in my commentary. Listen to it." But the Master objected, "I do not pay any regard to the many senses of Krishna's name ; I only know that he is Yashoda's darling son and darkly beautiful [like the *Tamál* leaves]. This only I know for truth, and I have not arrived at any other meaning of the name." At the Master's slight, the Bhatta went back to his quarters, downcast in mind. (He took his commentary to the chief disciples, and even read out parts of his own motion, but they slighted it and he was abashed).

Daily did Vallabh Bhatta go to the Master's place and dispute with [Adwaita] Acharya and other disciples. Whenever he established a proposition, the Acharya used immediately to refute it. Before them Vallabh Bhatta appeared like a crane in the company of majestic swans.

One day the Bhatta asked the Acharya, "Mankind is feminine, and Krishna is their husband, so you hold. No devoted wife utters her husband's name. And yet you repeat Krishna's name. What sort of *dharma* is this?" The Acharya replied, "*Dharma* in the flesh is sitting before you. Ask Him, and He will justify it."

Then the Master broke in, "You do not know the essence of *dharma*. It is the *dharma* of a true wife to obey her husband's commands. Our husband has commanded us to chant his name ceaselessly. No true wife can disobey his command, and so we chant his name and derive from it the fruit of the birth of love for Krishna's feet." This silenced Vallabh Bhatta and he went home sorrowing at his public humiliation.

Another day he came to the Master's assembly and said rather boastfully, "I have refuted [Shridhar] Swāmi's commentary on the *Bhágábat*. I cannot accept his interpretation......Where his view differs from mine, I do not follow the Swami." The Master smiled and remarked, "One who does not follow (her) *swami* (=husband) is ranked among harlots!"

Chaitanya had come to earth as an *avatár* for the good of mankind; by various humiliations He purified the proud heart of the Bhatta...... At night Vallabh Bhatta began to reflect in his own house, "Formerly the Master favoured me greatly at Allahabad, when He accepted my invitation to dinner in the company of His disciples. Why then is His heart turned away from me now? Let my heart be free from the pride of gaining victories in debate. The God-souled does good to all. I am filled with the pride of asserting myself, and He humiliates me in order to cure me of this pride."

So thinking, next morning he came to the Master and meekly praising Him took refuge at His feet, saying, "I am ignorant and have foolishly displayed my learning before you. You are God and out of your natural grace you have removed my pride by means of disgrace......The blindness of pride has been removed from my eyes through the collyrium of your grace now, and true knowledge has dawned on me. I have sinned. Forgive me; I take refuge with thee; lay thy feet on my head."

The Master checked him saying, "You are a scholar and a devotee at the same time. Where these two qualities are present, there pride cannot exist. You have written a commentary on the *Bhágabat* in scorn of Shridhar Swami! ......I understand the *Bhágabat* through the grace of Shridhar Swami; he is the world's *guru*,—my *guru*. What you write contrary to Shridhar is labour lost; no one will accept it. Therefore, write your commentary on the *Bhágabat* in the footsteps of Shridhar. Leave off your pride and adore the Lord Krishna. Give up your failings and join the *kirtan* of Krishna, and you will soon attain to Krishna's feet."

Then the Master agreed to dine at Vallabh Bhatta's house once again...... The Bhatta used to meditate on God as the child Gopál. But the society of Gadadhar Pandit turned his mind, and he longed to adore the youthful Gopal. He begged the Pandit to teach him the *mantra* and ceremonial of this kind of adoration, but Gadadhar declined to act without the Master's permission...Another day Gadadhar Pandit invited the Master, who agreed and at the dinner permitted Vallabh Bhatta to be initiated by Gadadhar.

HOW THE MASTER STINTED HIS FOOD

Ramchandra Puri Goswami came to Nilachal and there met the Master and Paramananda Puri......Jagadananda Pandit invited Ramchandra Puri and fed him on the *prasad* of Jagannath. After the meal the Puri asked Jagadananda to feed on the food left over, and serving the *prasad* repeatedly made him eat much. And thereafter, washing his hands and mouth, Ramchandra Puri began to cavil, "I had heard that Chaitanya's *bhaktas* were great gluttons.

Now I see it with my own eyes to be true. By gorging *sannyasis* with so much food, their piety is destroyed. You are *bairagis* and yet you are such huge eaters! Your *bairagya* is not sincere."

Ramchandra Puri was notorious as the universal fault-finder, having been cursed for it by his own religious preceptor, Madhavendra Puri. He now dwelt at Nilachal, detached by nature, staying at one place for some time, taking his meal at some [other] place without having been bidden, and taking note of what others ate.

The Master was daily fed at different houses, at a cost of four *pan* of *cowries* [*i.e.*, one anna] for the three of them,—the Master, Kashishwar, and Govinda (His body-servant.)...Ramchandra Puri closely inquired into the Master's abode, manners, food, bed and travels. He could not reach the Master's merits, but roaming in search of His defects, could not find any. Then he began to slander the Master to all the people, saying, "He is a *sannyasi* and yet eats sweetmeats. How can such luxury enable him to control the lusts of the flesh?"

He daily came to visit the Master, but only to pry into His shortcomings,—for that was the only work of the Puri,—while the Master did him reverence as His *guru*. He knew of the slanders spoken by the Puri [against Him], but welcomed and honoured him greatly. One day the Puri came to the Master's house in the morning, and noticing some ants on the floor, delivered this covert attack, "Verily sweetmeats were brought here last night, for ants are running about. A wonder! *sannyasis* dead to the world have such gluttonous cravings!" And then he left in a hurry.

The Master now saw with His own eyes what He

had only heard before, [about the slander spread against Him]. He called Govinda and told him, "From to-day my meal will be one packet of rice and curry of the *pinda-bhog* worth 20 *cowries* [*i.e.*, one quarter-anna]. Don't accept any food above this for me. If you bring more, you will not see me here."

Half of this the Master ate and the other half He left for Govinda, and both remained famished. Then He commanded Govinda and Kashishwar to beg their food elsewhere. Thus some days passed in great hardship. Hearing of it, Ramchandra Puri came to the Master...... and smiling told Him, "It is not a sannyasi's *dharma* to gratify his appetite. He eats just enough to fill his stomach anyhow. I find you lean and hear that you eat only half your fill. This drying *bairagya* is not a sannyasi's *dharma*. A sannyasi performs true *jnan-yog* when he fills his stomach as far as is necessary but does not enjoy his food. (*Gitá*, vi. 16-17.)"

The Master replied, "I am an ignorant child and your pupil. It is my good fortune that you are teaching me." Ramchandra Puri then left.

Next day the bhaktas headed by Paramananda Puri complained to the Master against Ramchandra as a universal fault-finder and instigator of gluttony, which he afterwards censured. They urged Him not to listen to Ramchandra and famish Himself, but to return to His old diet and accept invitations. But the Master replied, "Why do you blame Ramchandra Puri? He expounds the natural *dharma*, and has done no wrong. It is very wrong for a sannyasi to have a lustful palate. It is a sannyasi's duty to eat just as little as will keep body and soul together." They all pressed Him hard, and yielding to their entreaty He fixed His rations at one-half of its former cost, *viz.* at two *pan* of *cowries* [*i.e.*, half anna],—which was shared by two, sometimes three persons. If a Brahman whose cooking He could not eat, invited Him, He took only *prasad* worth two *pan* of *cowries*. If it was a Brahman whose cooking He could eat, He took a little of *prasád* [purchased with money] and a little of the meal cooked in His host's house. But at the houses of Pandit Goswami, Adwaita Acharya, and Sarvabhauma, He ate whatever they asked Him, for there He had no independence; He had come down to earth to render His devotees happy.

After a time Ramchandra Puri left Nilachal on a pilgrimage, to the intense delight of the Vaishnavs, who felt that a heavy stone had been lifted from their heads! They now freely invited the Master to kirtan and dance, and all freely partook of the *prasad*.

CHAPTER XXV

The love of the pilgrims from Bengal

The Bengal *bhaktas* came to Nilachal [carrying loving presents,—food and preserves, for the Master]. It was the day of Jagannath's sporting in the water of the Narendra tank. The Master came there with His followers to see the water-sport and there the Bengal pilgrims met Him. The Bengal musical parties were singing the kirtan ; on meeting the Master they began to weep in love. The water-sport, instrumental music, song, dance and kirtan created a tumult on the bank, while the boats plied merrily on the water. The mingled din of the kirtan and weeping of the Bengalis filled the universe. Then the Master entered the water with His disciples and sported gleefully with them all. These water-sports have been described in detail by Brindaban-das in his *Chaitanya-mangal*. I shall not repeat them here.

Another day the Master went with His party to behold Jagannath at his rising from bed. There He began the *berá kirtan*. Seven parties began to sing, and seven chiefs danced in them,—Adwaita Acharya, Nityananda, Vakreshwar, Achyutananda, Shribas Pandit, Satyaraja Khan and Narahari-das. The Master visited all the seven groups, each thinking that He was with it only! The roar of the kirtan filled the earth ; all the citizens came out to see it ; the king came with his Court and gazed from a distance, the queens beheld the scene from the roofs of houses. The earth trembled under the influence of the kirtan. Men shouted *Hari!* thus adding to the din. After a while, the Master was inclined to dance Himself. Around Him the seven parties sang and beat their instruments; in the centre He danced in supreme transport of love. He recollected the Oriya verse, *Jagamohan parimundá jáun!* 'Charmer of the universe! I abase myself before Thee', and bade Swarup sing it. To this air He danced in ecstasy, while all the men around swam in tears of love. With uplifted arms He cried, "Chant! chant!" and they in delight shouted *Hari! Hari!* At times He fell down in a trance and ceased to breathe, then suddenly started up with a roar. Frequent tremour burst over His body, making it look like the *shimul* tree,—now it was quivering and now it stiffened. The sweat burst through every pore in His skin. With faltering speech he muttered *ja ja, ga ga, pari pari,*—every tooth in his mouth shaking as if about to be loosened......Even in the third quarter of the day His dance did not cease. All the people in ecstasy forgot [fatigue of] body and [the distinction of] self and others. Then Nityananda resorted to a device; he silenced the *kirtan*-singers gradually, and only the leaders of the seven groups continued singing with Swarup, but in a low tone. At the cessation of noise, the Master came to Himself somewhat. Then Nityananda told Him how fatigued all were. The Master at this put an end to the *kirtan* and went to bathe in the sea with them all.

Then with all His *bhaktas* He partook of the *prasad*, dismissed them, and retired to sleep at the door of the *gambhira* (room). Govinda came to rub His feet, as was the usual practice, before going to feed on His leavings.

The Master had stretched Himself at full length across the doorway; Govinda could not enter the room and begged Him to move aside a little, but He declined saying that He was too weak to stir His limbs, and told Govinda to do whatever he liked. Then Govinda threw his sheet over the Master's body and entered the room leaping over Him. His shampooing threw the Master into a sweet sleep and relieved Him of His fatigue. After two *dandas* (48 minutes) He woke, and seeing Govinda there, asked in anger, "Why are you here still, *Adi-basyá*? Why did you not go away for your meal when I fell asleep?" Govinda replied, "You lay blocking the doorway, and I found no path for going out of the room." But the Master rejoined, "How, then, could you come in? Why did you not go out in the same way that you entered?"

Govinda returned no answer, but reasoned within himself, "I must do my appointed work, even if I have to commit any fault or go to hell for so doing. For the sake of doing my duty I do not hesitate to commit a million sins, but I fear even the touch of sin for my own personal needs."

This year the Bengal pilgrims came in large numbers, —two to three hundred of them, including many women. Shivananda Sen acted as their guide and caretaker on the way.

They came to Puri and met the Master, the women gazing at Him from a distance. They were all given lodging-houses and invited by the Master to eat the *mahá-prasád*......The entire family of Shivananda enjoyed His grace......... After the meal He told Govinda to give the leavings on His plate to Shivananda's wife and sons so long as they stayed there. A sweetmeat-seller (*modak*) of Nadia, named Parameshwar, had his shop close to the Master's paternal house. In His boyhood He used to visit this man's shop and the man used to treat Him to confects made with milk. He loved the Master from His infancy, and this year came to see Him. He prostrated himself before the Master saying, "I am Parameshwar." In delight at seeing him the Master asked, "Parameshwar! are you well? It is a happy thing that you have come." The man added "Mukunda's mother has come", [meaning his own wife]. The Master was shocked to hear the name of a woman, but out of love for Parameshwar said nothing. The loving simple-minded grocer did not know the ways of the learned; these qualities inly delighted the Master....

Four months passed away in the usual way, and then He permitted the pilgrims to return to Bengal. They invited Him to dinner and He lovingly spoke to them all, "Every year you come here to see me, undergoing many hardships on the two journeys. For this reason I feel inclined to forbid your coming, but the pleasure of your society tempts my heart. I had commanded Nityananda to live in Bengal. He has come here in defiance of my order; what can I say to him? The [old] Adwaita Acharya, leaving his wife, children and home behind, performs a long and difficult journey to meet me. How can I repay the debt of his love? I merely sit here at Nilachal without having to do any exertion for your sake. I am a *sannyasi*, without wealth. With what shall I repay my debt to you? My only property is my body, and this I give up to you. Sell it, if you list."

The Master's speech melted their hearts; tears ran down their cheeks without ceasing. He, too, wept clasping their necks, and weeping embraced them. So, they could not set out on their journey home that day, but passed five or seven days more at Puri in the same way. ....At last the Master consoled them and gave them leave to depart with composure of mind.

The *bhaktas* left the city weeping. The Master remained there in sadness of heart.

Last year Jagadananda, the Master's companion, had by His leave gone to Nadia to see mother Shachi......... She in delight listened day and night to his discourse on the Master and His doings......... All the *bhaktas* of Nadia met him and entertained him in their houses, listening in rapture to his talk about the Master's inmost things. At the house of Shivananda he prepared a pot of medicated oil, scented with sandal-wood, and taking it to Nilachal asked Govinda to rub it on the Master's head, to cure Him of bile, wind and other sickly humours......... Govinda reported it, but the Master replied, "A *sannyasi* is forbidden to rub oil, especially scented oil. Present it to the temple of Jagannath, where it will be used in lighting lamps, and his labour will be supremely rewarded."

Some ten days afterwards, Govinda repeated Jagadananda's request that He should accept the oil. The Master burst forth in anger, "Very well, engage a servant to rub me with the oil! Is it for such pleasures that I have turned *sannyasi*? What is ruin to me is a sport to you! Every one who will smell the fragrant oil on my person in the streets, will call me a carnal *sannyasi*!" Govinda remained silent on hearing this.

Next morning, when Jagadananda came to the Master, He said, "Pandit! you have brought for me oil from Bengal. But I am a *sannyasi* and cannot accept it.

Present it to Jagannath to light the lamps of the temple. That will be the reward of your labour." The Pandit replied, "Who has told you this piece of falsehood? I never brought any oil from Bengal." So saying, he brought out of the room the pot of oil and broke it on the floor of the yard in the Master's sight. Then he ran back to his own house, bolted the door of his bed-room from within, and shut himself up there [without taking any food]. On the third day the Master went to his door and cried out, "Rise, Pandit! you must feed me to-day on your own cooking. I shall come back at noon. I am now off to see Jagannath." So saying, He left the house. The Pandit rose from his bed, bathed, cooked, and at noon, when the Master returned, placed the dishes before Him on the leaves and bark of the plantain-tree. The Master said, "You must dine with me. Serve your meal on another leaf." But the Pandit entreated Him to eat first and let him sit down to his meal after his guest......... The vegetable soup was delicious and the Master cried out, "When one cooks in anger, it tastes so sweet! This is a proof of Krishna's grace on you.".........

The Pandit served and the Master ate, willing but unable to rise from the feast, and eating ten times His usual food, in fear lest the Pandit should fly into a rage again and fast himself! After the dinner, the Master went back to His lodgings, leaving Govinda there to see that the Pandit broke his fast. Jagadananda sent Govinda back to rub the Master's feet, and put Him to sleep. But He again bade Govinda go and see that the Pandit was really eating! When Govinda reported the fact, then the Master lay down in bed in peace of mind.

CHAPTER XXVI

The Master's love-sickness for Krishna ; His visions and transports of bhakti

The Master felt his separation from Krishna just as the milk-maids did after Krishna had left Brindaban for Mathura. Gradually He began to break out in wild lamentations, even as Rádhá had talked in delirium on meeting with Uddhav. Ever did the Master consider Himself as Radha, and felt [and acted] like her. No wonder, for such is the course of *divya-unmád* (spiritual ecstasy).

One night when He was sleeping, He dreamt of Krishna in the *rása* dance ; the god was bending his body gracefully and playing on the flute, wearing a yellow garment and garlands of flowers, and looking like the picture of Love ; the milkmaids were dancing in a circle, joining their hands together, while in the centre Krishna frolicked with Radha. The sight inspired the Master with the same mood ; He felt that He was at Brindaban and had gained Krishna's company.

As He was late in rising, Govinda wakened Him ; but He saddened when He became conscious of the real world. After performing the necessary acts of the morning He went to behold Jagannath. He stood close to the image of Garuda, while hundreds of thousands of worshippers thronged in front of Him. An Oriya woman, unable to see the god on account of the crowd, climbed upon the Garuda and rested one foot on the Master's shoulder.

Govinda saw it and hurriedly pushed her away, but the Master forbade him to make her dismount from His shoulder, saying, "Don't remove her. Let her gaze at Jagannath to her heart's content". The woman, however, quickly got down on seeing the Master and fell at His feet. The Master remarked, "Jagannath has not inspired *me* with this woman's passionate longing for him. Her body mind and soul are so absorbed in the God that she did not notice that she was treading on my shoulder! She is blessed. Let me worship her feet that I too may have her intensity of devotion."………

Sadly did the Master return home, and sitting down on the ground began to draw lines on the floor with His finger-nails. Tears streamed from His eyes and blinded His vision. "Alas!" He cried, "after gaining Krishna, I have lost him. Who has taken away my Krishna? Where have I come?" In His trances He quivered with delight; but when He regained consciousness, He felt that He had lost His treasure, and sang and danced like mad, though He went through His bath, dinner etc. by mechanical habit.

The ten forms of love-sickness possessed Him day and night, never giving Him rest. Ramananda Ray by reciting verses [from Vidyápati, Chandidás and *Git-Govinda*] and Swarup by singing songs on Krishna's acts, brought the Master somewhat back to His senses. At midnight they laid Him to bed in the inner room, and Ramananda returned to his own house, while Swarup and Govinda slept at the door. It was the Master's wont to wake all night, loudly chanting Krishna's name. [To-night] noticing the silence within, Swarup pushed the door open. He found the other three doors [also] closed from within, but the Master was not in the room. They became alarmed at His absence, lighted their lanterns, and went out in search of Him.

They found the Master lying on an open space a little north of the Lion-gate of the temple. His body was 5 or 6 cubits long; He was unconscious and His breathing had ceased! Each arm and leg was three cubits long and consisted only of bones and skin. His hands feet neck and waist were disjointed from the trunk by half a cubit and the places of junction were covered with the bare skin. He was foaming at the mouth and His eyes were fixed in a deadly stare.

This sight of Him made the *bhaktas'* very life go out of their bodies. Then Swarup with all the disciples loudly dinned the name of Krishna into the Master's ears. After a long while the name entered His heart, and He shouted *Hari-bol!* He became conscious and His limbs were joined to His trunk again, as before. This miracle of the Master has been reported by Raghunath-das in his *Chaitanya-staba-kalpa-briksha.........* As Raghunath-das always lived with the Master, I accept as true and write here what I have heard from him.

One day the Master, on the way to the sea, suddenly looked at the Chatak hillock, and taking it to be the Govardhan hill, He ran towards it in rapture with the speed of the wind...... Govinda could not overtake Him. A hue and cry was raised and there was a great bustle. Everyone ran up from where he was,—Swarup, Jagadananda, Gadadhar, Rámái, Nandái, Nilái Pandit, Shankar Puri, Bharati Goswami, all went to the sea-shore. The lame Bhagabán Achárya hobbled slowly behind.

After running at first like the wind, the Master

suddenly became stiff on the way, unable to move further. Every pore of His skin swelled like a boil, the hair stood on end on them like the *kadamba* flower. Blood ran out of His pores like sweat. His throat gurgled, not a syllable could He utter. Ceaseless tears ran down both His cheeks .... He lost colour and became death-pale like a conch-shell. Then a quivering burst over His frame like a tempest on the bosom of the sea. Trembling, He fell down on the ground, and then Govinda came up with Him, sprinkled Him with water from the flask, and fanned Him with his sheet. Swarup and the rest now arrived and all began to weep at the Master's plight. They loudly sang the *kirtan* in His hearing and sprinkled Him with cold water. After they had done so many times, He rose up with the cry of *Hari-bol!* The Vaishnavs in delight shouted *Hari! Hari!* The sound of joy rose up from all sides......... Half-conscious again, the Master addressed Swarup, "You have brought me back from Govardhan to here. You have snatched me away from viewing Krishna's *lila,*......... among the herds of cows and calves, Radha and her handmaids, on Govardhan hill......... Why have you brought me away thence, only to cause me grief?" So saying, He wept, and the Vaishnavs wept at His plight.

Thus did the Master live at Nilachal, plunging day and night in the ocean of grief at separation from Krishna. In the early autumn nights—radiant with the moon in a cloudless sky, He roamed up and down with His disciples, visiting garden after garden in delight and reciting or listening to the songs of *rása lila.* At times, overcome with love, He danced and sang ; at other times He imitated the *rása lila* in that mood : at times in a transport of passion He ran hither and thither, at others He rolled on the ground in a faint. As soon as He recollected a verse of the *rása lila* He expounded it.

I cannot describe all the acts He performed from day to day in these twelve years [of residence at Puri], lest it should make my poem too long.

While rambling thus, the Master one night suddenly caught a sight of the sea from *Ai-tota.* The moonlight silvered the heaving billows—they sparkled like the water of the Jamuna. Unseen by others, the Master went to the sea and leaped into it. He fainted and knew not what He was doing ;—the waves now sank Him, now floated Him ; on the waves He was carried about like a dry tree-trunk. On the waves He drifted towards Konárak, now under water, now above it,—and he dreamt all the time of Krishna sporting in the Jamuna with the milkmaids.

In the meantime, Swarup and other followers were startled when they missed Him. Uncertain whither He had gone, to the Jagannath or any other temple, to some other garden, the *Gundicha* house or the Narendra tank, to the Chatak hill or to Konarak,—they searched for Him everywhere. A party of them came to the beach and there walked, looking out for Him, till near daybreak, when they concluded that He had disappeared from the earth. They all thought that the worst had happened.

They took counsel on the beach, and some of them went towards the Chiráyu hill, while Swarup moved eastwards with a party searching for the Master in the sea-water. Overwhelmed with sorrow, almost out of their senses, they still walked on searching for Him in their love.

They met a fisherman coming towards them with his net on his shoulders, laughing weeping dancing and singing "Hari! Hari!" Swarup questioned him in surprise, "Tell us, fisherman, have you met a man on this side? Why are you in this mood?" The fisherman answered, "I have not seen any man here. But a dead body was caught in my net, and I carefully dragged it ashore, thinking it to be a big fish. The sight of a corpse frightened me, and when I was clearing my net I happened to touch it. At once the spirit of the dead entered my body, striking me with tremor, weeping, choking of voice, and bristling up of hair......... It lay stiff as a corpse, with a fixed stare in the eyes,—but at times it groaned, at others remained inert......... If I die of the possession of this ghost, how will my wife and children live?...... If I can find an exorcist, he will expel the evil spirit from me. I work at my trade of catching fish alone at night, but no ghost can seize me as I remember the god Nrisingha. This ghost, however, holds me with a double grip when I repeat Nrisingha's name. Don't go there, I advise you, lest this ghost should possess you, too."

From these words, Swarup understood it all, and told the fisherman gently, "I am a great ghost-doctor, and I know how to lay spirits." He uttered some verses, laid his hand on the fisherman's head, gave him three slaps, and cried out "The evil spirit has left you. Fear no more." The man now became a little composed. Swarup reassured him, "He whom you have taken for an evil spirit, is no ghost, but the Lord Sri Krishna-Chaitanya. In a transport of love He had jumped into the sea. Him have you raised in your net. His touch has thrilled you with Krishna's love,—which you have mistaken for the possession of a ghost. Now that your fear is gone and your mind has been calmed, show me where you have landed Him."

The fisherman said, "I have often beheld the Master. It cannot be He; it is of more than man's size."........

The fisherman led them all to the place. They beheld Him lying on the ground, huge-bodied, pale-skinned from immersion in water, coated with sea-sand. His limbs were abnormally long, loose and with the skin flapping. Over such a long path they could not carry Him home; so they removed His wet loin-cloth and put a dry one on Him, and laid Him down on a sheet of cloth after brushing away the sand. Then they lifted up the chant of Krishna's *kirtan* and poured it into His ears. After a time the word entered His brain and He leaped up with a roar; His limbs were rejoined and returned to their proper places. Half-unconscious still, He looked hither and thither [in perplexity]...... He spoke, as if from the sky, "Beholding the Jamuna [in the ocean] I went to Brindaban, and there found Braja's darling sporting in the water with Radha and the other milkmaids. I stood on the bank gazing on the scene, while one of the *sakhis* (female comrades of Radha) pointed out the mysteries to me." [A long but highly poetical description, *not translated*.]......... Krishna, Radha, and their companions rose from the water, dressed themselves, partook of a rich picnic, and all retired to sleep. My heart was filled with bliss at the sight. Just then you caught hold of me, and with a great noise brought me here. Ah! where is the Jamuna, where Brindaban, where Krishna, and where the milkmaids? You have destroyed that bliss!"......

Then Swarup made Him bathe [in the sea] and brought Him home, to the delight of all.

CHAPTER XXVII

The Master's last year on earth

Thus did the Master in love-madness for Krishna lament night and day. Jagadananda Pandit was very dear unto Him, and was every year sent by Him to Nadia to console his forlorn mother Shachi. "Go to Nadia", so the Master charged Jagadananda, "convey my salutation to mother, touch her feet on my behalf. Tell her to remember that I go there daily (in the spirit) to bow to her ...... That I have taken the sannyasi's vow leaving her service only shows that I am mad and have really undone all *dharma*. Mother! pardon this fault of mine. I am obedient to thee, I am thy son. It is at thy bidding that I am living at Nilachal. I cannot leave thee while life remains to me." The Master presented to His mother (at the Puri's suggestion) the consecrated cloth that He had received at the *Gopa-lila* with choice *prasad* of Jagannath. He was the crowning example of filial piety, for even though a *sannyasi* He served His mother.......

After receiving an enigmatic message in verse from the Acharya Goswami (of Shantipur) through Jagadananda when he returned to Puri, the Master plunged into a deeper trance. His ecstasy at Krishna-separation was doubled. He raved frantically day and night, identifying Himself with Radha. Suddenly imagining that Krishna was leaving Brindaban for Mathura, He (in the character of Radha) was seized with dizziness and developed madness, mourning deliriously while clasping the neck of

Ramananda and addressing Swarup as one of the *sakhis* (*i.e.*, Radha's companions). He repeated the verse which Radha had spoken to Vishákhá (her handmaid) and held forth on it.........

Thus did Gauranga weep, saying, "Alas! alas for Krishna! where hast thou gone?" Swarup and Ramananda consoled Him in many ways, singing joyous songs, which calmed Him a little.

These lamentations were carried on to midnight. Then Swarup laid the Master to bed in His room. Ramananda left for his home, and Govinda lay down at the door of the room. Love for Krishna was thrilling the Master's heart; He awoke and began to sing the Name; the pang of separation convulsed His heart, and He began to rub His face against the wall; His face, cheeks, nose were all lacerated, but in the vehemence of ecstasy He knew not of the blood streaming down.

All night He battered His face thus. Swarup, noticing the groaning sound, lighted a lamp, entered the room and saw His face. In intense grief the two brought Him back to His bed and soothed Him. Swarup asked, "Why didst thou do this?" The Master answered, "I could not contain myself in the room in my [love] anxiety. I rushed in search of the door in order to go out very soon. I could not find the door and only knocked my face against the four walls. It was torn, it bled, but still I could not go out."

Then, Swarup in anxiety took counsel of the other *bhaktas* next day and made Shankar Pandit sleep in the Master's room, nursing His feet. In fear of Shankar He could not leave the room nor knock His face against the walls. These feats Raghunath-das has described in his *Chaitanya-staba-kalpa-briksha.*

One *Baishakh* night, when it was full moon, the Master went with His *bhaktas* to visit the great Jagannath-vallabh park. The trees and creepers were in full bloom as at Brindaban, the green parrots, bees and cuckoos were discoursing [love]. The Zephyr was blowing laden with the scent of flowers, and freshening made the tree-tops dance. Under the bright moonlight the plants and creepers blazed in a silvery sheen. Spring pervaded the atmosphere. The sight threw the Master into a rapture. He bade the stanza *Lalita labanga latá* [of the *Git-Govinda,* canto ix. verse 6] be sung, and moved up and down dancing with His followers. Passing thus from tree to tree, He came under an *Ashoka* tree and lo! he beheld Krishna standing there. He rushed to meet Krishna, who disappeared laughing...... The Master, losing Krishna after having caught sight of him, fell down in a faint. The odour of Krishna's person filled the garden; it took away the Master's senses, it maddened Him, and He began to sing and hold forth on the verses that Radha, enamoured of the scent of Krishna's body, had addressed to her *sakhi*.........

Swarup and Ramananda sang, the Master danced in rapture, and thus the night wore on to dawn.

THE LAST CHARGE TO THE APOSTLES

Thrilled with delight, the Master spoke, "Listen, Swarup and Ramananda Ray! the supreme healer in this iron age is *sankirtan of the Name.* It is [equivalent to] the Vedic sacrifice, and the true sacrificer in it is rewarded with Krishna's feet. Sankirtan enables us to conquer sin and the world; it creates purity of soul, all kinds of *bhakti* and devotional practice...... Chant the Name at meals, in bed, here there and everywhere. It is not restricted to a particular place or time,—it works everywhere. It bears the name of *sarva-shakti* (omnipotent).

"Listen, Ramananda, to the way in which the Name should be recited in order to conceive a passion for it. The devotee, if high of rank, should regard himself as lowly like the grass. He should learn patience from the tree, which does not cry out even when it is cut down and which does not beg for water even when it is perishing of drought, but on the other hand gives away its possessions to all who ask of it, bears sun and rain itself but protects others from them. The Vaishnav, however high, should be free from pride; he should venerate all forms of life as animated by Krishna. Take Krishna's Name thus, and you will be inspired with *prem.*"

As He spoke He was filled with growing meekness of spirit and began to beg for pure *bhakti* at Krishna's hands. The true devotee, as is the law of love, holds that he has not even a particle of faith in Krishna! *"Lord! I ask not for wealth or followers or the gift of poesy. Give me in birth after birth only unreasoning instinctive devotion to God."*

In utter lowliness of spirit He proclaimed Himself a worldly-minded creature and prayed to be inspired with a slave's devotion (*dásya bhakti*). *"O Nanda's son! Have pity on this thy servant sunk in the dread ocean of the World! Look on me as a particle of dust on thy lotus-feet!"* Next, He was seized with the anxiety of humility and begged of Krishna, "Without the wealth of thy love my life is poor and futile. Make me thy slave and give me the treasure of thy love as my wages."

Then came the mood of melancholy-humility: *"My eyes are running with tears like the rainy sky. A moment is as long to me as an aeon. The absence of Govinda (Krishna) has made the universe empty to me!"*

In this way He recited His own eight Sanskrit verses on the different moods of *bhakti* and expounded them all. For twelve years He thus tasted the sweets of Krishna-love day and night with His two friends. These acts of His are endless, even a thousand narratives cannot arrive at their end......... Therefore, I bow my head and conclude His *lilás* here...... I bow at the feet of all my Vaishnav hearers and end my history of Chaitanya's acts.

The last scene (translated from the *Chaitanya-mangal* of Jayananda, p. 150) :—

When dancing at the Bijayá of the Car festival in the month of Ashárh, His left toe was suddenly pierced by a brick [lying on the road]. When Adwaita left for Bengal, the Master secretly told him [of His coming disappearance]. With all His followers He sported in the water of the Narendra tank [for the last time]. On the sixth day of the moon, the pain in His toe grew severer, and He was forced to take to His bed in the garden. Here He told the Pandit Goswami that He would leave the earth next night at 10 o'clock. Celestial garlands of many-coloured flowers were thrown on Him from the unseen. Celestial singers (*vidyádhar*) began to dance on the highway. The gods began to cry out, "Bring the heavenly chariot!" The Master mounted into Vishnu's car with the figure of Garuda on its spire. His material body lay behind on the earth, while He went to Vaikuntha (Vishnu's heaven). Many of His servants killed themselves by serpent-bite. Meteors and thunderbolts fell on the earth. At the news Nityananda and Adwaita Acharya, Vishnupriya and Shachi swooned away...... Purushottam and other servitors of the Master grew speechless at His departure......

Nityananda consoled the disciples and vowed before them, "We will keep the Name alive. We will make all men, down to the Chandáls, Vaishnavs. We will not differentiate [low] castes like the Chandals or Muslims, but will give them all love and *bhakti* and make them all dance [with us] at *kirtan*...... We will make the realms of Bengal and Orissa blessed." The Vaishnavs shouted applause at his words.

Works of JADUNATH SARKAR, M.A.

History of Aurangzib

4 vols., Rs. 3-8 each.

Vol. I. Reign of Shah Jahan

Vol. II. War of Succession

Vol. III. Northern India during 1658-1681, *(2nd Ed.)*

Vol. IV. Southern India. 1644-1689

Vincent A. Smith.—"You are doing first class work......I repeat with all sincerity that I have the highest opinion of your learning, impartiality and critical ability. I trust that you may be long spared to continue your good work of giving honest history." (29 Dec. 1919.)

W. Crooke.—"There is no student of the present day who has done more valuable service than yourself." (20 May, 1921.)

G. Ferrand.—"Thrice certainly, among the modern historians of India, Jadunath Sarkar occupies one of the first, if not the first place." (*Journal Asiatique*, April-June, 1921.)

Sir R. C. Temple.—"The first connected authentic account of these two reigns......The footnotes are of special value......as they provide an exhaustive bibliography which cannot but be of the greatest assistance to the students of this period of Indian history." (*Ind. Antiquary*, July, 1913.)

Sir E. D. Ross.—"The author seems to me to have *used all the* available *Persian materials* and to have used them *with discrimination* and care. *His manner of treating* the subject might well serve as *a model* to writers dealing with other periods of Indo-Musalman history." (29 Oct., 1908.)

English Historical Review.—"The author has been indefatigable in consulting all accessible authorities, many of which are still in manuscript ; while his zeal has led him to visit the sites of the more important of Aurangzib's battles. He *writes graphically* in an easy, *flowing style.*" (April, 1913.)

W. Foster, C.I.E.—"It is easily the best authority on the period with which it deals." (*J. R. A. S.*)

Journal, Royal Asiatic Society.—"Gives an excellent account of the great emperor.........Written in an easy style.........a very readable book." (October, 1913.)

W. Irvine, Esq., I.C.S.—".........I like the style—from this first impression—. it being a judicious compromise between the over-crowded stiffness of my *Later Mughals* and mere popular, journalese writing,—yet without any sacrifice of exactness......

Studies in Mughal India

Contains 22 Essays **320 Pages, Rs. 2.**

Zebunnissa vindicated.
History of Orissa in the 17th century.
Revenue Regulations of Aurangzib.
Art in Muslim India.
Education in Muhammadan India.
Daily Life of Shah Jahan and Aurangzib.
Biography of Aurangzib, 31 pages.
Khuda Bakhsh, the Indian Bodley.
Who built the Taj?
The Companion of an Empress.
The Wealth of Ind. 1650.
A Muslim Heroine.
Feringi Pirates of Chatgaon.
The Mughal Conquest of Chatgaon.
Education of a Mughal Prince.
Shaista Khan in Bengal.
Nemesis of Aurangzib.
A Hindu Historian of Aurangzib.
An Indian Memoir-writer of the 17th century.
Oriental Monarchies.
William Irvine.

Asiatic Quarterly Review.—"A series of essays on Aurangzib and his times of the *most entertaining* description." (April, 1913.)

Indian Antiquary.—"All the essays are *brightly written* and several *contain information* not hitherto available in English." (June, 1913.)

Athenæum.—"This should prove a useful handbook to students of Indian History." (18 Jan., 1913.)

V. A. Smith.—"The *essays are charming,* and with constant practice your style has attained ease and flexibility."

Shivaji and His Times

2nd Ed., revised and enlarged, with a fine portrait, Rs. 4.

A new and fully detailed critical study of Shivaji's life and character based on an exhaustive use of all the available original materials—Persian, Marathi, Hindi, Dutch and English—most of which were unknown to Grant Duff. It is the most comprehensive and correct narrative of the rise of the Marathas with minute details and exact dates, the complex interaction of Deccan politics has been clearly shown by references to the history of the Muslim Powers there in the 17th Century.

Shivaji's character and achievements, and the Maratha institutions and system of government are discussed in two long chapters (45 pages), and the lessons taught by the rise and fall of the Marathas are clearly unfolded. Critical bibliography (15 pages).

V. A. Smith.—"A conscientious presentation of recorded facts ......Bold and deliberately provocative book, merits the closest study ...... A sound critical historian." (*J. R. A. S.*, Jan., 1920.)

G. Ferrand.—"All the works [of this author] have received a most flattering welcome ; *Shivaji and His Times* merits the same praises that have been bestowed on the preceding works. It......constitutes a thrice important contribution to the history of India in the 17th century." (*Journal Asiatique*, 1921.)

Sir R. C. Temple.—"The book is indeed History treated in the right way and in the right spirit... He has access *to the best information* and the linguistic knowledge and capacity to use them."

Anecdotes of Aurangzib

(Persian text, with an English translation notes and a long life of Aurangzib)

The anecdotes, 72 in number, have been translated from a Persian work (the *Ahkam-i-Alamgiri*, ascribed to Aurangzib's favourite officer Hamiduddin Khan Nimcha), which no other historian has yet used and whose very existence was hardly known before. Two fragmentary MSS. of it were discovered by Prof. Sarkar ; and with the help of these and of two others, he has edited the text, and written an English translation, enriched with full historical and textual notes.

The work is exceedingly interesting and valuable, as it throws much new light on Aurangzib and exhibits many unknown traits of his character, his pithy sayings, and his principles of government.

The anecdotes illustrate the following topics among others : His last will and testament. Advice to his sons on the art of government, His strictness in maintaining the royal prerogatives, His suspicious watching of his sons, His strict justice, His treatment of his officers, advice to them, His treatment of Shias and Hindus, and orders concerning them.

Indian Antiquary.—"The *Anecdotes* is of real value to English students desirous of closer acquaintance with the individuality of the last of the great Mughals......The anecdotes have lost little of their vigour by translation and the editor has elucidated the text by valuable notes."

Economics of British India

Fourth ed., revised enlarged and brought up-to-date. Rs. 3.

This book gives, in one volume of manageable size, a complete account of India's physical features, economic products and resources, industries, transport facilities, currency, public finance, labour laws, land tenure system and legislation, foreign trade, &c. A vast number of blue-books and other authoritative works have been consulted and the statistics brought up-to-date (1917). The economic transformation caused in India by British rule, the gold standard, high prices, protection and *Swadeshi*, technical education, village industries, land revenue policy, factory legislation, and other current topics have been dealt with in a *lucid and accurate* manner, and helps to a study of them afforded in the form of the latest statistics, a statement of the present position of these questions, the arguments on both sides, and exact references to sources of information. The modern Indian citizen cannot do without this book, if he wishes to follow the economic discussions in our press and legislature with intelligence and interest. Foreigners, especially tourists, will find in it the handiest and most complete description of India's economic condition and problems in the English language, and an indispensable guide to a right understanding of the country and its people as they are to-day.

Jules Sion.—"This little book is the best work that we possess on the economic condition of India. For all essential questions one finds here a very concise but very substantial exposition, nourished with facts and figures and of great personal charm." (*Annales de Geogr.*, Paris.)

J. R. A. S.—"A good little book on a big topic."
Modern Review.—"An indispensable *vade mecum.*"

Sir Theodore Morison.—"An authoritative work on Indian economics can only be written by an Indian. *The author* of the present book *appears to possess* the further essential qualifications of *courage and independence.*"

The conscientious investigation of detail which was characteristic of *that work* [*The India of Aurangzib*] *is no less evident in the present economic treatise.* Much information which is only accessible in Blue-books and official publications is here presented in a convenient form ......Mr. Sarkar's reflections upon the rise in the standard of comfort (Ch. IV.) are *shrewd and convincing*, and are fortified by some interesting personal observations." (*Economic Journal*).